# Wisdom's Way

# The Christian I Ching

# Wisdom's Way
## The Christian I Ching

Roger Sessions

The Christian I Ching Society

For everything there is a season,
and a time for every matter under heaven:

a time to be born, and a time to die;
a time to plant, and a time to pluck up what is planted;
a time to kill, and a time to heal;
a time to break down, and a time to build up;
a time to weep, and a time to laugh;
a time to mourn, and a time to dance;
a time to throw away stones, and a time to gather stones together;
a time to embrace, and a time to refrain from embracing;
a time to seek, and a time to lose;
a time to keep, and a time to throw away;
a time to tear, and a time to sew;
a time to keep silence, and a time to speak;
a time to love, and a time to hate;
a time for war, and a time for peace.

—Ecclesiastes 3:1–8

# Table of Contents

## Part I: Introduction

## Part II: The Christian I Ching

**Appendices**

# Part I: Introduction

# Acknowledgments

I am very grateful to the many who offered suggestions and encouragement based on early drafts of this book. These include Barbara Joy Ayala, Hilary Barrett, Anne Beversdorf, Aneya Elbert, James Hamilton, Jeremy Helm, Maria J. Mateus, Mary McIntosh, Michael and Sabrina of PostNet Lake Mill Printing, Cindy Robertson, Emily Sessions, Hilary Siemer, Jean Springer, and Judy Webster.

The back cover bio photo was taken by Maria J. Mateus. All other photos are the work of the author.

The I Ching stalks pictured on the front cover are crafted by Jane English, www.eheart.com.

*I Ching is a discernment tool not an oracle or divining*

*Carl Jung predating male / adultn.*

# Preface

The I Ching is an ancient book of Chinese wisdom. It is considered one of the hundred most influential books of all time. The I Ching shows us how every situation we might face can be understood in terms of situational archetypes that have been known and studied for thousands of years.

As understood by contemporary Christianity, the I Ching is a discernment tool that allows us to better understand (discern) God's will within the context of specific situations. We ask the questions. We receive God's Wisdom through the I Ching.

There is a strong relationship between the universal metaphors that are expressed in dreams and the sixty-four situational archetypes that are expressed in the I Ching. It is no wonder then that Carl Jung, who wrote so powerfully about the metaphors and meaning of dreams, was so fascinated by the I Ching.

Jung discovered the I Ching in his midthirties and studied it for the next forty years. In his autobiography, he describes his introduction to the I Ching and his subsequent incorporation of it into his practice.

> During the whole of those summer holidays I was preoccupied with the question: Are the I Ching's answers meaningful or not? If they are, how does the connection between the psychic and the physical sequence of events come about? Time and again I encountered amazing coincidences which seemed to suggest the idea of an acausal parallelism (a synchronicity, as I later called it). So fascinated was I by these experiments that I altogether forgot to take notes, which I afterward greatly regretted. Later, however, when I often used to carry out the experiment with my patients, it became quite clear that a significant number of answers did indeed hit the mark.

- Carl Jung, *Memories, Dreams and Reflections*

This book is an introduction to the I Ching for Christians. The book is in two parts. The first part lays the Christian theological foundation for discernment tools in general and the I Ching in particular. It also describes the process of dialoging with God through the I Ching. The second part is a Christian reinterpretation of the sixty-four situational archetypes that make up the I Ching.

Why do we need a "Christian reinterpretation" of the I Ching? The I Ching is not easily approachable by modern Christians. The images are difficult to understand. The language is archaic. There are frequent references to historic Chinese events that are not part of our cultural awareness. The discussion is often sexist. Layered on all of this is a Christian distrust of anything that promises a mystical connection with the divine.

*ACausal Parallelism*
*Synchronicity*

As I started thinking about this book, I knew I wanted to present the I Ching in a way that would make its profound wisdom accessible to Christians. How could I do this? Should I explain each of the archaic images? Describe what the ancient language means? Rationalize the sexism? One night, I had a dream.

I am in my church. It is the time in the service for Eucharist, the ritualistic receiving of Christ as spiritual nourishment in the form of bread and wine. I approach the altar with others, and we kneel to receive the Eucharist. But instead of being served bread, we are each served a hexagram (a pictographic representation of one of the archetypes of the I Ching). We eat the hexagrams just as we would have eaten the bread. My hexagram has a taste that is beyond description. It seems to melt in my mouth and has the sweetness of honey. It leaves me feeling completely satisfied. The others around me are having similar experiences.

I believe this dream has two meanings: First, that Christ is present in the hexagrams as Christ is present in the Eucharist. And second, that while the I Ching has tremendous nourishment to offer Christianity, that nourishment will be accepted only if it is presented within the context of Christianity. Of course, I wanted to hold on to the inspiring wisdom of the I Ching. But rather than use images and metaphors that spoke to Chinese literati three thousand years ago, I would use analogous images and metaphors taken from the Bible today. I would replace the archaic and sexist language of ancient China with modern and inclusive language from contemporary Christianity.

None of this is changing the core of the I Ching. The core of the I Ching is the sixty-four situational archetypes that lie beneath the words. The challenge is to modernize the words and still reflect the essence of the archetypes. These archetypes are as alive and rich today as they were ninety years ago when Jung sat marveling over the dialogue unfolding before him, or two thousand years before that when Confucius sat huddled by his lantern studying that same rich store of wisdom that even then was ancient and venerable.

Have I chosen the right approach to introducing Christians to the I Ching? Soon after beginning this book, I had a validating experience in the form of what Jung would call a "synchronicity."

I am at a restaurant with my friend Judy. I am describing my idea for *The Christian I Ching*. I have told her about my dream. I am excited about how the work is progressing. I am giving her an overview of the situational archetypes and how they can be understood within contemporary Christian theology. When I finish, Judy has something she wants to show me. She has the book *Natural Spirituality: Recovering the Wisdom Tradition in Christianity* by Joyce Rockwood Hudson. It is a

book that will be used in a class Judy and I will soon be taking together. We have just received the book, and we thought we would take a look at it over dinner. As Judy hands me the book, it drops to the table in an open position. I look at the page the book has opened itself to. It is Appendix B, a single-page overview of *The I Ching*.

My dream and my synchronicity event were validated by yet another event: a reading from the I Ching itself. When I asked God through the I Ching to offer advice on this project, the response was strongly positive. I can't describe the response until I explain more about the I Ching, but I will come back to this response in Chapter Four. My point here is that dream analysis, synchronicity awareness, and I Ching dialoguing are strongly synergistic. This is because, in the language of Jung, they are all windows into the same collective unconscious, that mystical zone in which our individual identities dissolve and "there is neither Jew nor Greek, there is neither slave nor free, there is no male and female" and in which we are all one in Christ (Gal. 3:28)

This makes *The Christian I Ching* a natural companion to spiritual dream analysis. You are likely to find your I Ching dialogues shedding light on your dreams, and your dreams helping to clarify your I Ching dialogues. And as you start paying closer attention, you are likely to find both echoed in the "random" events that perhaps aren't so random after all.

Reclaiming God's Wisdom is important for more than just the individual; it may be critical for our collective survival. Virtually all the problems of the world can be traced back to the idolization of Ego at the expense of God. This is the underlying message of the Garden of Eden story in the Hebrew Bible. We no longer look to God to define right from wrong; we look to ourselves. We *think* we know good from evil. But our judgments are distorted by the lens of Ego.

Ego is a poor substitute for God. God tells us to feed the hungry; Ego tells us to feed ourselves. God tells us to care for the Earth; Ego tells us to plunder the Earth. God tells us that all people are God's beloved children; Ego tells us our own tribe (or race or sex or religion or country) is exalted beyond all others.

The world desperately needs a path back to God's Wisdom. Our own journey to wholeness depends on finding this path. And yet, this path is not hidden—it is right there, waiting for us. God's Wisdom is incarnate in the nature, dreams, and events around us. We just need to open our hearts to receive this Wisdom. *The Christian I Ching* is one tool that can nurture this process.

*The Christian I Ching* will be most effective if used within a holistic program for spiritual wholeness. For this reason, I suggest it be used in the context of spiritual direction. Spiritual directors are specifically trained to guide seekers into a closer relationship with God. A good spiritual director will use many tools to help a seeker clarify God's call. These tools will include prayer, meditation, spiritual exercises, dream analysis, and, now, I Ching dialogues. Be sure to choose a spiritual director who is open to this source of wisdom. Most spiritual directors are members of Spiritual Directors International, so the SDI web site (www.sdiworld.org) is a good starting place for finding a spiritual director.

*The Christian I Ching* opens up a rich and ancient source of wisdom to the contemporary Christian. It presents an opportunity to discern God's will with respect to specific issues. It opens the possibility of a new kind of relationship with God, one in which God's call is not just a theoretical hypothesis but an everyday reality. This book is your invitation to hear and to follow that call.

# Chapter 1: God's Call

God is constantly inviting us into relationship, enticing us with natural beauty, and urging us to participate in the miracle of being alive. Yet we spend most of our lives oblivious to God. We are like the prodigal son; we have been given riches beyond imagination, and we squander them pursuing empty dreams that leave us hungry and hollow. But despite our frivolous behavior, God never gives up on us. God keeps waiting, reaching out, hoping we will return.

We have all had the experience of driving on a familiar road and zoning out. Suddenly we return to awareness and realize we have no memory of driving for the last five minutes. It is as if we were plucked out of the time/space continuum and moved from there to here.

We live our lives like this, on autopilot, in a zone of semiconsciousness. But instead of losing minutes, we lose months, years, decades—and, all too often, entire lifetimes. Jesus tells us this is not life but death. He offers to raise us from this death and embrace life in its fullness. "Follow me," Jesus tells us, "and leave the dead to bury the dead" (Luke 9:60).

God constantly tries to shake us out of our complacency, nudging us and whispering in our ears, "Hey! Remember me?"

## THE STORY OF THE BUTTERFLY

Fifteen years ago, I vividly experienced one of these nudges. I was paddling down Lake Austin in my kayak. I wasn't paying the slightest attention to my surroundings. I was on a beautiful lake on a perfect fall morning, and instead of being present, I was lost in some cacophony of fantasies, worries, hurt feelings, and/or schemes. What it was that so preoccupied me, I have long since forgotten. But what happened next I will never forget.

I had been on the lake for an hour. Out of the corner of my eye, I noticed a single monarch butterfly. It was tracking my kayak. I let my kayak glide to a rest. The butterfly landed on the bow of my kayak. It sat there and watched me for a full minute. I could see it trembling. Then the butterfly fluttered away, tentatively at first, as if to make sure I was still watching.

When the butterfly had reached perhaps fifty feet in height above the lake, I realized where she was heading. Just above my head was a cloud of monarch butterflies stretching as far as I could see in either direction. There were hundreds of thousands of monarchs—perhaps millions. It was one of the most beautiful sights I had ever seen.

They must have been above me the entire time. Yet I never would have noticed them had not that single butterfly left the swarm and decided to pay me a visit.

There are a number of ways you could explain this. You could appeal to statistics. You could say that with so many monarchs, the landing of one of them on my kayak was just random chance. You could appeal to biology. You could point out that my kayak was the same color as the flowers on which monarchs feed. The monarch just thought I was a giant flower!

But neither of these explanations can account for a simple fact. It was just one butterfly. It wasn't dozens of butterflies or no butterflies. It was exactly *one* butterfly! What are the chances that just a single butterfly out of hundreds of thousands would choose just that moment to visit just that kayak?

I have another explanation. Imagine you are a painter and that you have created a beautiful painting. It is stunning, breathtaking, a truly once-in-a-lifetime masterpiece. Now somebody is walking past your work of art. He isn't paying any attention. He is looking at his feet and grumbling about something. What would you do? Wouldn't you go up to him and shake him? Wouldn't you say, "Hey you! Stop being so self-centered! Open your eyes and look at this amazing work that is right in front of you! I did this just for you! Now pay attention!"

That's what I think happened. Although in this case, the artist sent an emissary, a messenger, an angel. A butterfly.

But even butterflies can only do so much. They can bring us the messages. We need to open our hearts to receive those messages. I was fortunate that day. Somehow that butterfly found a chink in the armor of my heart. I wonder how many butterflies I have ignored in my life. I'm sure they are used to being ignored. In the Western world, we do it so well.

Once, people were open to experiencing God through nature. The Bible tells of a prophet seeing the Holy Spirit descending in a white dove. It tells of a tired and lonely man hearing God's voice in a burning bush. It tells of sky gazers seeing the birth of a messiah in a star. It tells of ordinary men and women hearing God's call to greatness in dreams. It tells of people discerning God's Wisdom through every-day "random" events such as those that drive the I Ching.

Why have we lost this closeness to God? Why do we assume that the world of God and the world of humans are separate? Why do we assume that God no longer speaks to us in the daily events of our lives? Why are we so deaf that we can no longer hear God's word?

## THE PROBLEM OF EGO

The problem, I believe, is Ego. Not the healthy ego of knowing that we are God's beloved (which I will write with a little *e*), but the unhealthy Ego of believing that we ourselves are God (which I will write with a capital *E*). Ego tells us we don't need God. *We* are what is important. *We* know right from wrong. If there are any worthwhile messages, *we* will be sending them.

There is no room for God in this Ego-centric view of the world—except, perhaps, for a God that will do *our* will, punish *our* enemies, bolster *our* sense of worth; a God that will serve as our messenger boy. There is always room for that kind of God.

The Christian with a mystical bent will object to my description of God as outside of ourselves. What do you mean, this Christian asks, by saying *Ego* tells us that we are God? We are God! For this Christian, I might explain Ego slightly differently. The *ego* tells me I am God because we all are God. The *Ego* tells me I am God because you are not.

Regardless of the words we use to describe self, God, Ego, ego, and Wisdom, we can say one thing for certain: Ego blocks Wisdom. Ego tells us that the world revolves around our needs and that others are there only to serve our needs. We need not worry about their feelings; they have no feelings. In fact, they have no existence, not really. We are real. They are nothing. Ego tells us this, and we believe. And as Ego tightens its grip on our souls, we lose our connections to God. We become empty and hollow. We become unable to love and unable to be loved. Love itself has no point. Love requires relationships with others, and Ego tells us there are no others.

## THE STORY OF ANGRY MAN

The person who personifies for me the problem of Ego is one whose name I don't know. I call him Angry Man. I met Angry Man twenty years ago. I was having a quiet morning coffee in a hotel lobby. It was a small lobby. The front desk was only a few dozen feet from the breakfast area.

The lobby door burst open. I looked up, startled. A middle-aged, somewhat overweight man barged in. His face was red. He was sweating profusely. His tie was loose and crooked. He stomped to the front desk, placed two moist hands firmly in front of the clerk, leaned forward, and demanded, "I need a phone. NOW!"

The clerk looked at him meekly. "Can I help you, sir?"

"I need to call Avis. Right now. Get me their number and give me the phone!"

The clerk hurriedly looked up the number for Avis, dialed it, and handed Angry Man the phone.

Angry Man wasted no time. "You have a lot of nerve. I am about to be late for a very important meeting. My car key doesn't work. Your lousy security system has locked me out of the car. Tell me how to disable the anti-theft system, NOW!"

Oddly enough, I knew what he was talking about. I too had rented an Avis car, and I had noticed a sticker on the side window that said, "Warning! Anti-Theft System in Effect." At the time I too had wondered if I could get locked out of the car. I felt a little pity tinged with anxiety that I might soon face a similar problem.

The Avis clerk must have asked Angry Man some questions about the car, because he shouted, "What the hell difference does it make? It's a white Chevrolet Impala. Just tell me how to open the damn door!"

Another coincidence, I thought to myself. I also rented a Chevrolet Impala. And it's also white. What are the chances of that?

Suddenly I realized what was going on. I went to Angry Man. "Excuse me," I said, "I think you may be trying to get into my car."

Angry Man turned and stared at me in disbelief. He said nothing for several seconds as he tried to process this latest indignity. Then he slammed the phone down and stomped out of the hotel. Not thirty seconds later, I watched a white Chevrolet Impala squeal out of the parking lot, narrowly missing an oncoming car.

I would like to say that was the last time I encountered Angry Man. Unfortunately that would not be true. More times that I care to admit, I have looked in the mirror and seen the face of Angry Man staring back at me. I don't want to see that face again.

Angry Man is a warning. He is the result of seeing yourself as the center of the universe, of seeing no difference between what you believe is true and reality itself, of being arrogant to Wisdom. No butterflies will visit Angry Man. If they do, he will smash them. Angry Man destroys not only himself but also those around him. Earth itself is not safe from Angry Man.

God has not left us defenseless when it comes to Ego. We have been given prophets, Wisdom writings, dreams, and tools for discernment. The discernment tool that has been used by more people than any other is the one we call the I Ching. As the Bible shows us and I will discuss in the next chapter, discernment tools are particularly effective antidotes to Ego. They work by creating an environment in which Ego is stripped of power. When Ego is faced with its own powerlessness, it flees. With Ego out of the way, ego is able to find the space it needs to grow. And we are once again able to hear God's Wisdom.

## DAN'S STORY

My friend Dan gave me a lesson in letting go of Ego and being open to God's presence. I knew Dan for three years. I first met him in the Episcopal Diocese of Texas's school for Spiritual Directors, FinD. He was in the class below me. We had been assigned to the same "small group."

The first day we met, I led our group to a second-floor classroom. I noticed Dan was having a little trouble walking. I made a mental note to choose a first-floor classroom for our next meeting.

Dan's walking got progressively worse as the year progressed. Toward the end of the year, he was diagnosed as having multiple system atrophy. The prognosis for this disease is a slow and sure death as, one by one, nerves lose the ability to support muscular functions. Dan was able to finish up his first year at FinD but then could no longer make the monthly two-hour trek from his house.

For the next few years, I would visit Dan at his home. At first, he could move on a walker. Soon, he could only move in his electric wheel-chair. Toward the end, he was barely able to speak, chew, swallow, or cough.

Dan said that what he appreciated about his illness was that it freed him from Ego. Bit by bit, all his self-pride was taken away. He lost his ability to work, then his ability to be a husband, then his ability to cook, then his ability to take care of himself. He joked with me that now that he could no longer wipe his own butt, what could possibly be left of Ego? He had finally attained enlightenment!

I worried about Dan. I was afraid that he would die a painful death, perhaps suffocating once his nerves no longer passed messages to his diaphragm. I learned of an organization that helped people in terminal situations take control of their own deaths.

On my last visit to Dan, I told him that should he ever desire, I would help him make contact with this organization. Dan had almost no strength at that point. He smiled at me and beckoned me to come closer. He could barely speak. He could barely breathe. He struggled to whisper these words: "Roger, every second I am alive is another gift from God."

Those were the last words I heard from Dan. He died before I had another chance to visit him.

Dan was always surrounded by God. When he was healthy, he communed with God on his nature walks. When he could no longer walk, he communed with God on his back porch while watching the wild birds at his feeders. When he could no longer move, he communed with God in the love of his caregivers and friends.

## GOD'S MESSAGES

Dan had something in common with the butterfly that had visited me so many years before—and, for that matter, with Angry Man. Each one of them was bringing me a life-changing message from God. From the butterfly, "Pay attention to my works!" From Angry Man, "This is how Ego will destroy you!" From Dan, "Every second of your life is another gift from me."

When God needs to speak with us, God will find a way. If it takes a butterfly, then that's what God will use. If it takes an angry man barging into a hotel lobby, then fine, no problem. And if a man is dying and God can find a way to give his death meaning, God will do so. God wastes no opportunity to reach out to us.

But just because God is speaking to us doesn't mean we are receptive. It takes two to tango. We check our e-mail ten times a day, but we will not take ten seconds to listen for God's call. No wonder we think God no longer speaks to us.

When we ignore dreams because we think they are irrelevant, God's word is lost. When we dismiss events that are pregnant with meaning as mere chance, divine messages are missed. When we turn away from discernment tools such as the I Ching because they are not scientific or logical or "Christian" enough, Wisdom is ignored. But God is not scientific. God is about relationships and relationships start with communication, not logic.

Our relationships with God have become structured and hierarchical. We pigeonhole God into a single hour each week. We relegate our relationships with God to professional middlemen: priests, ministers, and preachers. These highly trained professionals lead us in structured prayers, and we'd better do it right. Don't cross your thees and thous. Don't stand when you should kneel. Don't sit in the wrong pew. Dress nicely. Look respectable. Be normal.

As soon as we are two feet out of the church doors, God might as well be a million miles away. God is no more relevant that yesterday's toast.

## EGO AND PRISON

Where I feel God's presence the strongest is in prison. I volunteer for prison ministry. When you watch the power of God's love reach out and transform a soul, one who feels completely lost and unlovable, you understand what Jesus meant when he said, "For truly, I say to you, if you have faith like a grain of mustard seed, you will say to this mountain, 'Move from here to there,' and it will move, and nothing will be impossible for you" (Matt. 17:20).

Prison ministry is a laboratory for the study of Ego. There is a strong correlation between the level of a prisoner's egocentricity and that prisoner's separation from God. The greater the Ego, the greater the separation. At one extreme are prisoners who see themselves as hapless victims and deny any accountability whatsoever for what they have done. They have no concerns or even awareness that others have been hurt by their crimes. These prisoners are trapped in Ego even more than by prison, and they invariably have poor relationships with God. At the other extreme are prisoners who take responsibility for their crimes, empathize with their victims, and see that their crimes have hurt others, sometimes terribly. These prisoners see themselves as sinners in need of redemption. These prisoners have little left of Ego, and consequently God's presence and love infuses their lives. When you are with such people, you cannot help but feel God's presence.

## WISDOM AND GOD

How can we better hear God's word and be receptive to God's presence? The Hebrew Bible gives us an answer.

Say to Wisdom, "You are my sister," and call insight your intimate friend.
—Proverbs 7:4

Who is this Wisdom? Where do we find her? Do we need to read more books? Get more degrees? Attend more church? Attend better churches?

The wisdom that we are told to embrace is timeless. It is the wisdom that has existed since the beginning. It is the wisdom in the world around us, in the trees, in the dreams, in the flowers, in the odd coincidences, in the monarch butterflies, in the prayers of the prisoners, in the voice of a dying man. Even, sometimes, in our churches.

Listen, as Wisdom sings her song:

The Lord created me at the beginning of his work,
the first of his acts of long ago.
Ages ago I was set up,
at the first, before the beginning of the earth.
When there were no depths I was brought forth,
when there were no springs abounding with water.
Before the mountains had been shaped,
before the hills, I was brought forth—
when he had not yet made earth and fields,
or the world's first bits of soil.
When he established the heavens, I was there,
when he drew a circle on the face of the deep,
when he made firm the skies above,
when he established the fountains of the deep,
when he assigned to the sea its limit,
so that the waters might not transgress his command,
when he marked out the foundations of the earth,
then I was beside him, like a master worker;
and I was daily his delight,
rejoicing before him always,
rejoicing in his inhabited world
and delighting in the human race.
—Proverbs 8:22–31

Wisdom is available to us always. We just need to listen to her:

And now, my children, listen to me:
happy are those who keep my ways.
Hear instruction and be wise,
and do not neglect it.
Happy is the one who listens to me,

watching daily at my gates,
waiting beside my doors.
For whoever finds me finds life
and obtains favor from the Lord.

—Proverbs 8:32–36

This brings us to the topic of the next chapter: discernment. Discernment is about listening to Wisdom, hearing her instructions, and, through her, finding life in God.

The main impediment to discernment is Ego. The problem of Ego has a long history. Many discernment stories in the Bible show us how to deal with Ego. While the term *Ego* did not exist until the twentieth century, the problems for which Ego is responsible date to the earliest stories in Genesis. So while our spiritual forbearers may not have known what to call Ego, they still struggled with controlling it. We can learn much from their struggles.

I am laying the groundwork for a particular discernment tool, one that uses a biblical approach to minimizing the damage Ego can do. This tool is rooted far back in antiquity and saw much of its development occurring in parallel with the work that resulted in the Bible. It should be no surprise, therefore, to see so much synergy between the spiritual practice we call Christianity and the discernment tool known as the I Ching.

# Chapter 2: Discernment Tools and the Bible

In the last chapter, I discussed the problem of Ego—that is, the belief that we are God, the idolatry of self. As you might expect, such a belief is not very conducive to hearing God's wisdom. If we want to become receptive to God's Wisdom, we need to do something about Ego. In this Chapter, I am going to explore different approaches the Bible has recommended for dealing with Ego.

## THE STORY OF DOG

My first lesson on the relationship between Ego and wisdom occurred when I was a young child, perhaps six. My family had left the city for a visit to friends in the suburbs. When we arrived, I met Dog. I don't remember Dog's name, just that it was a large friendly dog that loved six-year-old boys. We immediately hit it off. My parents' friends asked if I would like to take Dog out for a walk. I was delighted.

They put Dog on a leash and took me outside. They explained that their house was on a large circle. I couldn't get lost, they said, if I stayed on the circle. Eventually I would return to the house. I wasn't paying attention. I was looking at Dog.

Dog and I started on the walk. After ten minutes, I decided it was time to go back. Then I had a frightening thought. I had no idea what their house looked like. There were at least fifty houses on the circle. Which was the one we had come from? I didn't even know the names of the people we were visiting. How would I find the right house? I was lost!

I needed to remember every detail about the house. It was green. Yes, I was sure it was green. And it was two stories. It was a green two-story house. I could do this.

Dog and I walked around the circle. I didn't see any green two-story houses. The only green houses were one story. And the only two-story houses were white. But it was definitely a green two-story house. Could I have wandered off the circle?

After a half hour, I was starting to feel desperate. I had walked around and around the circle. Dog was getting tired. I was tired too, and scared. What was I going to do?

I decided to let Dog lead us to the right house. I would walk around the whole circle once again, letting Dog go wherever Dog wanted. I would trust Dog to find the house. I would have to trust Dog. I had no choice.

We went halfway around the circle, and Dog showed no obvious interest in any of the houses. Suddenly Dog started veering toward a house. But Dog was wrong. The house Dog was going to was a white single-story house, not a green two-story house. I tried to pull Dog. I was almost crying. Dog was my last hope, and Dog was failing me.

Maybe Dog was heading to one of Dog's friends. Maybe somebody at this house would recognize Dog and could direct me to the right house. It was a long shot, but I had nothing to lose. I nervously followed Dog's lead.

As we got closer, Dog got more excited. Dog barked, and the front door opened. There on the other side of the door were my parents and their friends. "Did you have a nice walk?" they asked. "You must have been having fun, because we watched you walk past the house at least five times."

The more we think we know, the less we are open to God's wisdom, whether that wisdom is expressed through a dream, through the I Ching, or through a dog's gentle tug. It is the meek that shall inherit the earth, not the brilliant.

## DISCERNMENT AND EGO

In the last chapter, I discussed how God calls out to us in the events of our lives. In this chapter, I am going to discuss what we must do to hear God's call. Hearing God's call is one way to describe *discernment*. In the Christian tradition, we understand discernment as the ability to understand which path God means for us to follow. We might think of God as a river of love and ourselves as floating down that river. Discernment then is our ability to see the currents, understand how they flow, and choose a direction that is in accord with the river's rhythms and our unique boat.

We need God. We need God because God is our most fundamental essence. Genesis tells us:

> So God created humankind in his image,
> in the image of God he created them;
> male and female he created them.

—Genesis 1:27

We are the reflection of God. A reflection without that which it reflects is empty. We don't need a new car or a larger house or the latest technological toy to be complete, not really. What we need is to feel grounded in God, the God that is our core being.

God loves us. All the great religions teach this simple truth. Because God loves us, God needs us. God needs us because a love without a beloved is a hollow existence. The Bible is the continuous story of God reaching out to us, beseeching us to open our hearts to God's love, pleading with us to simply accept that we are the beloveds.

We need God, and God needs us. Together, the human and the divine are complete. Separated, they are incomplete.

When we live in accord with the divine image, we are fulfilled. When we can discern what it means to be God's beloved, we are exalted. What makes discernment difficult is Ego. In the last chapter I described Ego (with a capital *E*) as that destructive belief that we are God. I contrasted this to ego (written with a small *e*), which is the healthy knowledge that we are beloved by God. Ego doesn't want us to be in accord with God's image. Ego wants God to be in accord with its own distorted and twisted self-image.

Wisdom is ego's friend and Ego's enemy. The ego knows we can be complete only when we are in relationship with God. The Ego tells us God is irrelevant; our completeness depends only on our own accomplishments and acquisitions. The ego tells us to turn to God to discern which path we should take. The Ego knows which path it wants and doesn't give a hoot for God's opinion on the subject. We all have both Ego and ego giving us advice. We must choose which we will listen to.

Ego will do anything to get its way. It will cheat, steal, and lie. Ego convinced Eve that knowing good from evil would make her as good as God (even worse, that she was *capable* of knowing good from evil). Ego convinced Cain that his brother deserved to be murdered for winning God's favor. Ego convinced Joseph's brothers to sell him into slavery. Ego whispers in each of our ears and tells us about the nice things we should have, the respect we have earned, the social status that is our birthright. The *last* thing Ego wants is discernment. Would you?

My walk with Dog was my first experience with the battle between Ego and discernment. I was sure I was on the right path; I knew where I was going. Ego told me so! Only when I let go of all confidence in self (and therefore of Ego) was I able to trust and follow Dog to show me the right path. And Dog did! Just as God will show us the correct path if we can get Ego to shut up long enough to let God get in a word edgewise.

## WISDOM VERSUS EGO

How do we get rid of Ego? Well, to start with, we don't want to "get rid" of Ego. We just want it to learn to behave, to show a little humility (if that isn't too much to ask of Ego). Ego is like a spoiled child. It has had its way for so long it thinks it can do whatever it wants. Ego needs to grow up and learn some manners. Ego needs to become ego.

Wisdom uses every tool at her disposal to work around Ego's subversive influence.

Wisdom uses our dreams. When we are sleeping, the Ego is at rest and is unable to block Wisdom's voice. The Bible contains many stories of Wisdom speaking in dreams. Wisdom promised Jacob a land of plenty in a dream. Wisdom bestowed upon Solomon "an understanding mind" in a dream. Wisdom told Joseph to accept the baby Jesus as his son in a dream.

There is one problem with dreams. We eventually awake. When we do, we once again fall under the spell of Ego. Ego tells us we can't remember our dreams or the dreams don't make sense or that they are the result of indigestion. And Wisdom's voice is lost.

Another tool Wisdom uses to deal with Ego is humiliation. This may sound cruel, but often that is the only way to deal with Ego. That's what happened to me with Dog. I gave Ego every chance to get us home. Eventually, even Ego had to admit it was lost and scared. Only in the face of Ego's humiliation could I turn myself over to Dog.

## EGO AND MOSES

The Bible includes many stories of Ego being brought to its knees so that discernment can occur. One such story is that of Moses. Exodus 3 tells the story of Moses's discernment to lead the Israelites out of bondage. It starts with the familiar story of the burning bush.

> Moses was keeping the flock of his father-in-law Jethro, the priest of Midian; he led his flock beyond the wilderness, and came to Horeb, the mountain of God. There the angel of the Lord appeared to him in a flame of fire out of a bush; he looked, and the bush was blazing, yet it was not consumed. Then Moses said, "I must turn aside and look at this great sight, and see why the bush is not burned up."

—Exodus 3:1–3

The story continues with God telling Moses of his new calling, Moses telling God all the reasons why he is the wrong person for this calling, and God responding to each of his objections in turn. Anybody who has gone through a true discernment will find this a painfully familiar dialogue.

But while Exodus chapter 3 tells the story of Moses's discernment, Exodus chapter 2 tells the less familiar story of Moses's Ego preparation.

Moses is born in enslavement. The Israelites are captive and brutalized by the Egyptian pharaoh. In a particularly cruel decree, the pharaoh orders all the newborn Israelite boys to be murdered (a story that we will hear echoed in the Jesus birth story). But Moses's mother devises a plan to save him. She places him in a basket and hides it in the river reeds. The baby is found by the pharaoh's daughter, who brings up the child as her son, the grandson of the pharaoh.

We can assume that being the pharaoh's grandchild is a pretty cushy gig. You have the best of everything in a world in which most people have very little. You are powerful in a world where most are powerless. You are respected in a world where most are treated as property. The Ego is in hog heaven. No burning bushes are going to disturb this frame of mind.

Then something happens. The grown Moses sees an Egyptian striking one of the Israelites. Moses kills the tormentor. Moses is seen, and, fearing for his life, he flees his privileged world.

He ends up in a foreign land, where he marries a priest's daughter. This is not a Jewish priest; this is a priest of pagan gods. Soon Moses is tending the priest's sheep. Moses has gone from a life of plenty and comfort to a life of austerity and hardship. Moses has lost his roots. He is in a land of strange people, strange customs, and strange gods. He is cut off from everything he knows and loves. What few possessions he now has he carries in a sack. Moses is at the lowest point in his life. He is miserable, decrepit, and powerless. And in this state of shattered Ego, Moses is able to see the burning bush and hear the voice of God. With Ego out of the way, discernment can begin.

## EGO AND JONAH

The Bible story that wins the Oscar for Ego Annihilation is the story of Jonah. This story starts in Jonah 1 innocuously enough:

> Now the word of the Lord came to Jonah son of Amittai, saying, "Go at once to Nineveh, that great city, and cry out against it; for their wickedness has come up before me."
>
> —Jonah 1:1–2

Jonah's Ego is not exactly thrilled with this assignment. His Ego convinces him he doesn't need to listen to God, so he catches the next boat going anyplace but Nineveh. God is not amused and sends a storm that threatens to sink the boat. The crew senses a rat is on board, so they cast lots to see who is to blame. Jonah's name comes up in bright neon lights.

Jonah has his first inkling that maybe this wasn't his best idea. He agrees to be thrown overboard in an attempt to appease God and end the storm. The crew happily obliges, and the storm ends.

Now Jonah is swimming around in the depths of the ocean, close to drowning. I suspect he is having a few words with Ego. Just when he thinks things can't get any worse, a giant fish comes up and sucks Jonah in. Now Jonah is in total despair, sitting in the stinking belly of the fish in total darkness. In desperation, he repents to God. God hears Jonah and causes the fish to vomit Jonah onto dry land.

> The word of the Lord came to Jonah a second time, saying, "Get up, go to Nineveh, that great city, and proclaim to it the message that I tell you." So Jonah set out and went to Nineveh, according to the word of the Lord.
>
> —Jonah 3:1–3

This time, Ego has learned its lesson and is keeping its mouth shut. And Jonah's career as a prophet to Nineveh begins. Which, it turns out, is a good thing for Nineveh. Jonah is able to turn Nineveh away from its evil ways, and God saves the city.

These are some of the tools Wisdom uses to speak to us: dreams, chance events, and humiliation.

But what if we want to ask her advice? The traditional answer is prayer. But discernment through prayer is hampered by Ego, which has its own agenda. We need look no further than the political arena to see how easily Ego can twist prayer to its own self-serving ends.

## BIBLICAL DISCERNMENT TOOLS

The Bible has a suggestion here. The Bible points to the use of what I call *Egoless discernment tools*. They are *Egoless* because they are designed to eliminate, or at least minimize, the corrosive influence of Ego. They are *discernment tools* because they are tools through which one can discern God's Wisdom. For the sake of brevity, I will call these *discernment tools*.

Discernment tools work by interpreting Wisdom's answers through events over which Ego has no control. Ego tells us these events are "random" and not to be trusted. The Bible tells us these events are not random, but directed by God.

The first example of a discernment tool in the Bible is described in Exodus, in the elaborate plans for creating a "breastpiece of judgment."

> In the breastpiece of judgment you shall put the Urim and the Thummim, and they shall be on Aaron's heart when he goes in before the Lord; thus Aaron shall bear the judgment of the Israelites on his heart before the Lord continually.
>
> —Exodus 28:30

We don't know exactly what kind of agents Urim and Thummim were or how they were used, but they were clearly used as agents to discern God's will. For example, in Samuel we read:

> When Saul inquired of the Lord, the Lord did not answer him, not by dreams, nor by Urim, nor by prophets.
> —1 Samuel 28:6

And in Ezra, we read:

> The governor told them that they were not to partake of the most holy food, until there should be a priest to consult Urim and Thummim.
>
> —Ezra 2:63

Another common discernment tool used in the Bible is the drawing of lots. We have already seen one such example, in the story of Jonah. Remember Jonah, and how he tried to escape God's call in a boat?

> But the Lord hurled a great wind upon the sea, and such a mighty storm came upon the sea that the ship threatened to break up. Then the mariners were afraid, and each cried to his god...The sailors said to one another, "Come, let us cast lots, so that we may know on whose account this calamity has come upon us." So they cast lots, and the lot fell on Jonah.

—Jonah 1:4–7

Lots must have been used frequently. Proverb 16 specifically tells us that God speaks through lots: "The lot is cast into the lap, but its every decision is from Yahweh."

The use of lots to hear Wisdom was not limited to the Hebrew Bible. In Acts 1, we read how an apostle replacement was found for Judas, the traitor.

> "So one of the men who have accompanied us throughout the time that the Lord Jesus went in and out among us, beginning from the baptism of John until the day when he was taken up from us—one of these must become a witness with us to his resurrection." So they proposed two, Joseph called Barsabbas, who was also known as Justus, and Matthias. Then they prayed and said, "Lord, you know everyone's heart. Show us which one of these two you have chosen to take the place in this ministry and apostleship from which Judas turned aside to go to his own place." And they cast lots for them, and the lot fell on Matthias; and he was added to the eleven apostles.

—Acts 1:21–26

Both Urim/Thummim and lots are examples of physical apparatuses being used as discernment tools. But other types of discernment tools are also described in the Bible. For example, human actions, as long as they are removed from the influence of the observer's Ego, can serve as discernment tools. We see an example in the story of how a wife was found for Abraham's son, Isaac.

Abraham wanted Isaac to marry a woman from Abraham's birth land, so he sent one of his servants to find a suitable wife. When the servant arrived in the city of Nahor, he camped out by a well at the time of day when young women would come to water the camels. He then set up his plan to find a suitable wife.

> And he said, "O Lord, God of my master Abraham, please grant me success today and show steadfast love to my master Abraham. I am standing here by the spring of water, and the daughters of the townspeople are coming out to draw water. Let the girl to whom I shall say, 'Please offer your jar that I may drink,' and who shall say, 'Drink, and I will water your camels'—let her be the one whom you

have appointed for your servant Isaac. By this I shall know that you have shown steadfast love to my master."

Before he had finished speaking, there was Rebekah, who was born to Bethuel son of Milcah, the wife of Nahor, Abraham's brother, coming out with her water-jar on her shoulder. The girl was very fair to look upon, a virgin whom no man had known. She went down to the spring, filled her jar, and came up. Then the servant ran to meet her and said, "Please let me sip a little water from your jar." "Drink, my lord," she said, and quickly lowered her jar upon her hand and gave him a drink. When she had finished giving him a drink, she said, "I will draw for your camels also, until they have finished drinking." So she quickly emptied her jar into the trough and ran again to the well to draw, and she drew for all his camels. The man gazed at her in silence to learn whether or not the Lord had made his journey successful.

—Genesis 24: 12–21

The events of nature are used as discernment tools. Gideon used such a discernment tool to ask God if he was truly chosen to save Israel:

Then Gideon said to God, "In order to see whether you will deliver Israel by my hand, as you have said, I am going to lay a fleece of wool on the threshing-floor; if there is dew on the fleece alone, and it is dry on all the ground, then I shall know that you will deliver Israel by my hand, as you have said." And it was so. When he rose early next morning and squeezed the fleece, he wrung enough dew from the fleece to fill a bowl with water.

—Judges 6:36–38

When we need to ask God specific questions, the Bible repeatedly suggests the use of discernment tools. The main advantage of these tools is that they are resistant to the manipulations of Ego.

But Ego is a crafty little devil. Since Ego is unable to influence the outcome of these tools, Ego resorts to the next best option: attacking the tools themselves. They are unreliable, not scientific, the result of random chance, un-Christian. If all other arguments fail, these discernment tools are the work of Satan. Ego loves Satan, whom it frequently calls upon to deflect attention from itself. But the Bible tells us a very different story.

## DISCERNMENT VERSUS FORTUNE TELLING

It is important to understand the difference between a discernment tool and a fortune-telling device. Fortune telling (that is, predicting the future) is specifically prohibited by The Bible. For example, in Deuteronomy we read:

No one shall be found among you who makes a son or daughter pass through fire, or who practices divination, or is a soothsayer, or an augur, or a sorcerer, or one who casts spells, or who consults ghosts or spirits, or who seeks oracles from the dead. For whoever does these things is abhorrent to the Lord.

—Deuteronomy 18:10–12

There is a good reason fortune telling, or divination, is prohibited by the Bible. Even God does not "know" the future. God guides the future, but even God can only go so far. We have free choice, and the choices we and others make in part determine the future.

Discernment tools are not used for predicting the future; they are used for asking Wisdom's help in laying the groundwork for the future God wants. Whereas fortune telling is prohibited by the Bible, discernment tools are encouraged and used throughout both the Hebrew and Christian Bibles.

A discernment tool by itself has no power. Only God can breathe life into a discernment tool. But it seems God wants to communicate with us. The Bible tells us that as long as we approach God from an ego-centric perspective (as God's beloved) God will use these discernment tools. It is when we approach God from an Egocentric perspective (as God's superior) that these tools become barren, as Saul discovered when Yahweh would not answer him "either by dreams, or by Urim, or by prophets" (1 Sam. 28:6).

We see, then, a three-way relationship between the discernment tool, the discerner, and God. The discernment tool must be one that is truly Ego free. The discerner must be one who is truly receptive to God's wisdom. And God must be willing to speak. But God is always reaching out to us. If we aren't hearing God, the problem is on our side.

How can we be sure that the discernment tool is truly Ego free? This is more difficult than it sounds. The Ego has a way of creating "heads, I win/tails, you lose" outcomes. The best way to be sure the discernment tool is "fair" to God's Wisdom is to use one that is well understood and has withstood the test of time. This makes the I Ching an attractive candidate, since it has been studied by some of the greatest scholars in history and has been in continuous use for thousands of years.

But the I Ching is much more than a discernment tool; it is a complete framework for understanding God's wisdom. It is your guide to the mystical space in each of us that Genesis calls *the image of God*. In this space, God calls you to wholeness. The I Ching can help you hear this call.

Predicting the future is specifically prohibited by the Bible

# Chapter 3: Validating the I Ching

I am an INTP. I suspect that at least 50 percent of people reading this know what this means. Among those who are trained spiritual directors, the number is probably 90 percent.

This is my personality type based on the widely popular Myers-Briggs Type Indicator. For brevity's sake, I will just call this Myers-Briggs. Myers-Briggs is taught in almost all training programs for spiritual direction, and at least half of all spiritual directors could tell you their type as easily as they could tell you their name: "Hi! I'm Carol. I'm an INFP."

The use of Myers-Briggs extends far beyond spiritual direction. It is used in almost any situation in which knowing something about a person's psychological makeup is considered helpful. I have seen it used in leadership schools, church training groups, career counseling, and teacher education.

My purpose here is not to explain Myers-Briggs in detail. I have two goals in this chapter. First, I hope to use Myers-Briggs as an example of a categorization framework such as the I Ching. Second, I hope to formalize the approach used to validate Myers-Briggs and see if that same approach can be used to validate the I Ching.

## CATEGORIZATION FRAMEWORKS AND DISCERNMENT TOOLS

Let's start by defining a categorization framework. A categorization framework is any framework that allows you to sort items into categories. Once an item has been categorized, we know something about the item that we didn't know before, namely that it shares common characteristics of that category.

All categorization frameworks have three features. They have some number of *categories*. They have *characteristics* associated with each of those categories. And they have a *sorting mechanism* that looks at a new item and figures out which category it lives in.

The discernment tools I discussed in the last chapter are also categorization frameworks. They are used to sort out choices into those God wishes for us and those God does not wish for us. Any discernment tool is also a categorization framework.

The discernment tools I discussed had a limited number of categories, such as "Who should we throw overboard?" (Jonah) or "Who should Isaac marry?" (Rebekah). But discernment agents need not be so simplistic. When we look at the I Ching, we will see how it can be used to make highly nuanced choices.

## COMMON CATEGORIZATION FRAMEWORKS

We use categorization frameworks all the time. A very simple example of a categorization framework we use on a daily basis is the US postal zip code system. The US postal service processes over 560 million pieces of mail per day. Some are postcards from vacations, some are catalogs, some are bills, some are junk mail. In order to process this mountain of mail efficiently, the post office needs to sort the mail into categories that support the post office in fulfilling its mission of delivering mail.

So the postal service uses a categorization framework based on geography. It has a relatively small number of zip codes, about forty-three thousand. While forty-three thousand may not seem that small, it is tiny compared to the 560 million pieces of mail that are sent every day. On average, each zip code gets thirteen thousand pieces of mail per day.

The zip code system has been designed to quickly tell the postal service the most important information it needs about a piece of mail: where it is going. In many cases, the zip code even identifies the person who will deliver the mail.

So for the categorization framework known as the zip code, the categories are the forty-three thousand zip codes. The characteristics associated with those categories are geographic information such as city and neighborhood. And the sorting mechanism is simply the zip code on a piece of mail.

Some categorization frameworks are so common we don't even think about them. If you go to the store to buy butter, you place butter in the dairy category and then go to the section of the store that sells dairy products. Your understanding of the grocery categorization framework allows you to find butter quickly even if this is your first visit to a particular store. If you are at a restaurant and you want cake, you look at the dessert section of the menu. You separate good foods from bad foods, friends from foes, safe situations from dangerous situations. You do this so automatically that you aren't even aware of the process you are using. Yet the categorization frameworks you are using are no less sophisticated than the zip code system used by the post office.

## MYERS-BRIGGS AS A CATEGORIZATION FRAMEWORK

Myers-Briggs is another categorization framework. It has sixteen categories. It has items it can sort into categories, namely human personalities. And it claims that once you know a person's personality category, you can accurately predict that all or most of the characteristics common to that category will apply to that person.

For example, once you know I am an INTP, you can predict that I will be critical and precise and driven to understand situations using logical analysis. This probably explains why I am fascinated by categorization frameworks.

Myers-Briggs uses a much more complicated sorting mechanism than does the post office's zip code sorting system. Myers-Briggs uses a questionnaire consisting of between four and one hundred either/or questions. Your answers determine your personality category.

Myers-Briggs says that a personality can be either Extraverted or Introverted; Sensing or Intuitive; Thinking or Feeling; and inclined toward Judgment or Perception. Since either of these choices (say, Sensing or Intuitive) can be mixed with any other of these choices (say, Thinking or Feeling), we have a total of sixteen possible categories. When I say I am INTP, I mean my type is Introverted, not Extraverted; Intuitive, not Sensing; Thinking, not Feeling; and Perceiving, not Judging.

So this is Myers-Briggs in a nutshell: sixteen categories and a sorting mechanism based on answers to either/or questions. Pictorially, we can represent Myers-Briggs as shown in the following diagram.

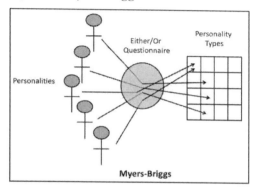

**Myers-Briggs**

## COMPARING THE I CHING TO MYERS-BRIGGS

I will discuss the I Ching much more in the following chapters. Here, I am going to describe it in the context of being a categorization framework. At a high level, the I Ching looks much like Myers-Briggs.

Both map items to categories. Myers-Briggs maps personalities to personality types. The I Ching maps situations to situational archetypes.

Both have a grid of possibilities to which a particular item can map. Myers-Briggs has a grid of sixteen personality types. The I Ching has a grid of sixty-four situational archetypes.

Both have a sorting mechanism to determine which items map to which categories. Myers-Briggs uses a questionnaire made up of either/or questions. The I Ching uses a "random event," such as those discussed in the last chapter.

Both claim that once an item has been mapped to a category, you gain unique insight into that item. Myers-Briggs claims that you can make broad predictions about the personality that was mapped. The I Ching claims that you can discern God's Wisdom with respect to the situation being mapped.

Pictorially, we can represent the I Ching as shown in the following diagram:

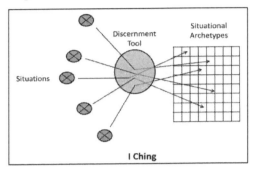

If you compare the pictorial diagrams of the I Ching and Myers-Briggs, you will see how similar these two categorization frameworks are.

## VALIDATING MYERS-BRIGGS

Some categorization frameworks make rather mundane claims. The zip code system claims only to sort mail into categories that simplify the delivery of mail. This is easy to believe and easy to test.

Other categorization frameworks make rather incredible claims. Myers-Briggs claims to accurately predict how people will behave in a large range of situations. The I Ching claims to accurately predict how any situation can be understood within the context of God's will. Such claims require a more thoughtful validation.

Let's see what we can learn about validating such frameworks based on how Myers-Briggs is evaluated. Why is Myers-Briggs so widely accepted? There are four reasons.

The first reason Myers-Briggs is widely accepted is because it has been used by many people, most of whom find that it gives them useful insight into their own and others' personalities. In other words, it works because many people see that it works. How many people have used Myers-Briggs is impossible to say, since the quality of the usage ranges from amateur Internet sites to highly qualified professionals. It seems likely that those who have worked through Myers-Briggs with the help of some reasonably qualified individual are numbered in the hundreds of thousands, perhaps as high as a million.

The second reason Myers-Briggs is widely accepted is that it has stood the test of time. It has been around for seventy years. If anything has survived for as long as seventy years, we assume it has value.

The third reason Myers-Briggs is widely accepted is that it was developed by some bright people, namely Katharine Cook Briggs and her daughter, Isabel Briggs Myers.

The fourth reason Myers-Briggs is widely accepted is its Jungian pedigree. Myers-Briggs is based on the work of the great psychologist Carl Jung. He first established the idea of categories of personalities. He called these categories *archetypes*. Myers-Briggs is based on Jung's personality archetypes.

So again, let me repeat the four reasons Myers-Briggs is considered valid. First, it has been taken by lots of people, and most have found that it gives them good insight into their own and others' personalities. Second, it has been around for seventy years. Third, it was developed by some bright people. Fourth, it is based on the work of Carl Jung. For these four reasons, and only for these four reasons, Myers-Briggs is widely accepted in the United States and other Western countries, and it is taught in almost every training program for spiritual directors.

How does this compare to the I Ching?

The I Ching, like Myers-Briggs, has been used and validated by many people. China is reported to have had ten billion people tread its earth over its long history. A conservative estimate is that 10 percent of those people have consulted the I Ching and found its advice helpful. So we can assume that the validation numbers for the I Ching have easily reached the billion-person mark.

The I Ching, like Myers-Briggs, has stood the test of time. It's hard to know exactly when the I Ching was composed, but most scholars assume that it dates to at least three thousand years ago.

The I Ching, like Myers-Briggs, was developed by bright people. We know that many of the most influential minds in Asian history have studied and contributed to the I Ching. Among these were Confucius and Lao Tzu.

## CARL JUNG AND THE I CHING

The I Ching, like Myers-Briggs, has a connection to Carl Jung. Carl Jung believed strongly in the principle that he called *synchronicity*. This means understanding divine will through events that logic (Ego) tells us are random. Jung would have appreciated my butterfly story of chapter one and given it great significance. Of all the possible uses of "random" events to discern God's Wisdom, none interested Jung more than the I Ching.

Jung studied the I Ching extensively and used it frequently in his practice. When Richard Wilhelm translated the I Ching into German, Jung wrote a lengthy foreword to the book. Jung called his foreword a "testimonial of my individual experience with this great and singular book." Jung wrote:

For more than thirty years I have interested myself in this oracle technique, or method of exploring the unconscious, for it has seemed to me of uncommon significance.

—Foreword by Carl Jung to the I Ching by Wilhelm and Baynes

Many in the Western world, if they know of the I Ching at all, dismiss it as superstitious fortune telling. Jung strongly disagreed.

The I Ching insists upon self-knowledge throughout. The method by which this is to be achieved is open to every kind of misuse, and is therefore not for the frivolous-minded and immature; nor is it for intellectualists and rationalists. It is appropriate only for thoughtful and reflective people who like to think about what they do and what happens to them.

—Foreword by Carl Jung to the I Ching by Wilhelm and Baynes

In Jung's autobiography, he wrote again of his lifelong fascination with the I Ching.

Sometimes I sat for hours under a thousand year old pear, I Ching at hand, exercising the technique, by putting into it a kind of question and answer game—the successive oracles. They gave, unmistakably, remarkable results which I couldn't explain within my own realm of thought.

—Carl Jung, *Memories, Dreams, Reflections*

The fact that the I Ching is even known to the English-speaking world is due in large part to Carl Jung's influence. While there are today dozens of English translations of the I Ching, the one that sparked the original interest was the one by Richard Wilhelm. This is the translation for which Jung wrote the foreword from which I quoted earlier. Wilhelm was a close friend of Jung and translated the I Ching in 1923, seven years before Wilhelm's death. However, Wilhelm translated the I Ching into German, not English. Jung was instrumental in convincing Cary F. Baynes to translate the German into English, a project that was finally completed in 1950. It is the Baynes English translation of the Wilhelm German translation that is still today considered the definitive English translation and the one by which all others are measured. This translation is usually referred to as the Wilhelm/Baynes I Ching. It is this translation that I have used as my primary source.

## APPLYING MYERS-BRIGGS VALIDATION CRITERIA TO THE I CHING

So let's go back to the problem of validating the I Ching based on the four tests widely used to validate Myers-Briggs. The first test is numbers—how many have found the framework useful. I credit at most a million people with validating Myers-Briggs compared with at least a billion validating the I Ching. The I Ching wins this contest by a factor of at least a thousand.

The second test is time—how long the framework has been in use. Myers-Briggs is approximately seventy years old, compared to an estimated three thousand years for the I Ching. Compared to the I Ching, Myers-Briggs is still wet behind the ears.

The third test is authorship respect. The authors of Myers-Briggs were undeniably bright and intuitive; however, they had no formal training in psychology or Jungian analysis. The authors of the I Ching are shrouded in legend, but we know they included many of China's greatest philosophers. While Katharine Cook Briggs and Isabel Briggs Myers were certainly clever, I doubt anybody would place them in the same category as Confucius or Lao Tzu.

The fourth test is Jungian pedigree. Although Myers-Briggs was based on Jung's work on personality archetypes, there is no evidence that Jung endorsed or had even heard of Myers-Briggs. On the other hand, his lifelong fascination with the I Ching is well documented.

By any reasonable standard, the I Ching should have at least as much acceptance as Myers-Briggs. But whereas Myers-Briggs is widely taught and used extensively in the Western world, the I Ching is virtually unknown. Whereas Myers-Briggs is looked upon with reverence, the I Ching, if it is known at all, is looked upon with suspicion. OK, I know I'm an INTP, but this just doesn't seem right!

## WESTERN NEGATIVITY TOWARD THE I CHING

How can we explain this Western attitude toward the I Ching? There seem to me to be two possible explanations.

The first explanation is that we, as scientific rationalists, are suspicious of discernment events, which by their very nature defy rationality. One of the few differences between Myers-Briggs and the I Ching has to do with the sorting mechanism. Myers-Briggs uses an either/or questionnaire. The I Ching uses a discernment event. We are much more comfortable with either/or questionnaires. They seem rational and predictable. Discernment events seem unpredictable.

Can we accept discernment events as valid guides to discerning God's will? For Christians, the answer to this depends on how we feel about the Bible. It is clear that the Bible presents numerous examples of the use of discernment events to understand God's will. Do we believe the Bible is wrong about this? Outdated? Metaphorical?

Rational science tells us that discernment events are random events that have no inherent meaning. The Bible (and many other Wisdom literatures) tells us everything has meaning. A coin toss does not occur in a void; it occurs within the context of God, because everything occurs within the context of God. My "complex" decision on whether or not to accept a job therefore occurs within the same context as the coin's "simple" decision on whether it should come up heads or tails. The more we can understand about the common context, the better we can use observations of the simple to guide our decision about the complex.

The approach of understanding the complex through observations of the simple is similar to using observations about a stick floating in a river to guide our decision on how best to navigate a boat through that same river. We can do this not because the stick is magical or because it is similar to our boat but because both the stick and the boat exist in and are influenced by a common context, the river.

Similarly, the Bible tells us that we exist in the same context as discernment events: the context of God. The I Ching is a framework for understanding this common context; it is our guide to the river.

If we accept the Bible's judgment on the validity of discernment events, then the only other likely explanation for the rejection of the I Ching is a xenophobic prejudice among Christians against forms of Wisdom that originate from non-Christian, non-Western sources.

But Wisdom existed long before Christianity and is not limited to any geography, as Wisdom herself makes clear.

> The Lord possessed me at the beginning of his work,
> the first of his acts of old.
> Ages ago I was set up,
> at the first, before the beginning of the earth.

—Proverbs 8:22–23

The voice that tells us that ancient non-Western sources of Wisdom are somehow suspect is not the voice of God. It is the voice of Ego.

I hope you are now interested in at least exploring the I Ching and willing to do so with an open mind. For those who find Myers-Briggs helpful, you owe it to yourself to delve into this far more ancient and venerable framework. Imagine yourself underneath that same thousand-year-old pear tree with Carl Jung, exploring Wisdom as she speaks to you through the mysterious and mystical language of the I Ching. In the next chapter, I will take a closer look at this I Ching that so captivated Carl Jung and billions of others.

# Chapter 4: Overview of the Christian I Ching

The best way to get an idea of how you might use the I Ching is to observe it being used. So let me give you an example of a recent dialogue I held with the I Ching.

## I CHING DIALOGUE: WRITING WISDOM'S WAY

As I was thinking about writing this book, I had a number of concerns. Most Christians I discussed the idea with reacted with skepticism. It was clear they thought the I Ching had no place in a Christian life. Yet I felt drawn to this project. I believed (and still believe) the I Ching has much to offer Christianity and perhaps can be a bridge between Western and Asian philosophies. But I was getting little encouragement from others.

So I did what I often do when faced with a difficult decision. I opened it to an I Ching dialogue. I asked God this question through the I Ching: what outcome should I expect from a Christian I Ching book project?

Of course, *The Christian I Ching* didn't exist at that point, so I used the Wilhelm/Baynes translation of the I Ching that I discussed in the last chapter. I'll take you through my dialogue with the I Ching regarding my question. When reading the I Ching text, you will notice many problems with the writing. The images are difficult to interpret. The language is archaic. There are allusions to historic Chinese events that are not part of our cultural background. And the discussion is usually sexist. But keep in mind that Wilhelm's German translation was written over ninety years ago and Baynes's English translation of that over sixty years ago. In *The Christian I Ching*, I will address all these issues and more. So please set these issues aside for the moment and look instead at the deep currents of wisdom that flow through the I Ching.

So again, my question: what outcome should I expect from a Christian I Ching book project? The I Ching responded with a judgment and an image.

THE JUDGMENT
SHOCK brings success.
Shock comes—oh, oh!
Laughing words—ha, ha!
The shock terrifies for a hundred miles,
And he does not let fall the sacrificial spoon and chalice.

In the Wilhelm/Baynes I Ching, we have this commentary:

The shock that comes from the manifestation of God within the depths of the earth makes man afraid, but this fear of God is good, for joy and merriment can follow upon it. When a man has learned within his heart what fear and trembling mean, he is safeguarded against any

terror produced by outside influences. Let the thunder roll and spread
terror a hundred miles around: he remains so composed and reverent
in spirit that the sacrificial rite is not interrupted.

This is the spirit that must animate leaders and rulers of men—a
profound inner seriousness from which all terrors glance off
harmlessly.

The image was as follows:

THE IMAGE

Thunder repeated: the image of SHOCK.
Thus in fear and trembling
The superior man sets his life in order
And examines himself.

The Wilhelm/Baynes I Ching follows this with a commentary:

The shock of continuing thunder brings fear and trembling. The
superior man is always filled with reverence at the manifestation of
God; he sets his life in order and searches his heart, lest it harbor any
secret opposition to the will of God. Thus reverence is the foundation
of true culture.

How do I interpret this? To start with, the judgment ("SHOCK brings
success. Shock comes—oh, oh! Laughing words—ha, ha! The shock terrifies
for a hundred miles") tells me that the book will be successful. It also tells me
what this success is likely to look like. Many people will be shocked and many
will ridicule the book.

Most Christians, if they have heard of the I Ching at all, dismiss it as a
fortune-telling device. So when I come out with a book that claims the I
Ching has an important role to play in Christian discernment, it is easy to
believe the book will be met with shock and derision. But, of course, people
must read the book before they can be shocked by it. So financially, the book
is likely to be successful.

However, there may be two kinds of shock associated with this book. The
first is shock as in "I am shocked at what he is saying." The other shock is a
much deeper and more profound shock, the shock of recognition that comes
when God's word is made manifest and one realizes that one's life can never
be the same. This kind of shock seems to be what the Wilhelm commentary
describes: "The shock that comes from the manifestation of God within the
depths of the earth makes man afraid, but this fear of God is good, for joy
and merriment can follow upon it." I pray that this shock will also come from
this book.

The remainder of the judgment ("And he does not let fall the sacrificial spoon and chalice") is reassuring to me. It is talking about items used in a religious context. From the context of my question, these items seem to be representative of Christianity as an institution. The I Ching is telling me that this book will not "let fall" the institution of Christianity. I would be heartbroken if this were not so. I am deeply Christian. My goal in writing this book is not to take anything away from Christianity, but, on the contrary, to enrich Christianity by giving Christians a wonderful tool for discerning God's Wisdom. I pray nobody will turn away from Christianity because of this book, but will instead be drawn to its fullest mystical potential. These words from the I Ching give me hope for success in this.

The I Ching isn't finished with me. It next tells me how to deal with the fallout from the book's success: "Thus in fear and trembling the superior man sets his life in order and examines himself." I am far from immune from the siren call of Ego, and the book's success (assuming the I Ching is correct) will be a great temptation to let Ego run amok. I must approach this success not with pride, but with "fear and trembling." Can I do this? It won't be easy; I have a boisterous Ego. I will need your prayers as well as mine. And I'm sure I will need help recognizing when I have failed.

## ARCHETYPES AND THE I CHING

This gives you some sense of a typical dialogue with the traditional I Ching. Now let's look more closely at the underlying philosophy of *The Christian I Ching*.

In the last chapter I talked about categorization frameworks. I gave the example of the postal service's zip code system, which can take a practically infinite number of letters coming in and sort them into one of forty-three thousand zip code categories. I also talked about Myers-Briggs, which can take a practically infinite number of human beings and sort them into one of sixteen personality types.

The I Ching is like these, except that it maps questions or concerns into one of sixty-four universal situational archetypes. An archetype is like a fundamental pattern. So, at a deep level, the I Ching claims that it has found sixty-four fundamental situational patterns, and that any situation you can ever imagine can be mapped to one of these sixty-four patterns. The details of any particular situation will, of course, be different, but the basic features and the energy of that situation can be understood by understanding which situational archetype the situation maps to. These archetypes were identified, refined, and validated over three thousand years. So the developers had plenty of time to test new situations and make sure that they were addressable by one of the sixty-four archetypes.

When we call upon God's Wisdom through the I Ching, we are asking God to direct us to the archetype that contains the understandings we need.

It is then up to us to interpret these ancient archetypes and hear how they speak to us. Jung described this process of interpretation thusly:

> These interpretations formulate the inner unconscious knowledge that corresponds to the state of consciousness at the moment.

—Carl Jung, *Synchronicity*

When I asked about the likely outcome from this book project, the I Ching told me the situation corresponds to archetype number 51. The name of this archetype is, in the Wilhelm/Baynes I Ching, *The Arousing*, and in this book, *Thunder*. This is the archetype I described earlier in this chapter.

## THREE I CHING DIALOGUES

I'll give you three more examples of actual I Ching dialogues that illustrate the mapping of situations to situational archetypes.

A friend lived an hour away from her work. She wanted to move closer to work, but she was worried about the impact of this move on her two daughters. I facilitated a dialogue between her and Wisdom through the I Ching. The I Ching directed her to archetype number 50. The Wilhelm/Baynes name of this archetype is *The Soup Pot*. It is an archetype that describes the act of providing nourishment. The message was that this move would be nourishing to her daughters. Now, two years later, it is clear that the I Ching was correct. Both of her daughters have flourished in their new home.

A friend had recently gone through a pain-filled divorce. She had a large sum of money from her share of selling the house. Everybody (including me) was advising her to take the money and buy her own house. Property values could only go up. She was nervous about doing this. I facilitated a dialogue with the I Ching to ask Wisdom's advice on the subject. The reply was archetype number 53, named *Gradual Progress*. This archetype discusses the need to move slowly and not to take on more than one can handle. The message was that purchasing a house would be a drain on her emotional reserves that she could ill afford. She followed the advice and did not purchase a house. Now, three years later, she has completed a master's degree in education and has a teaching certificate. Although she did extremely well in the program, the program was psychologically taxing. It is clear in retrospect that the added burden of worrying about home ownership would have made this program impossible to complete. Now she is in a position to be self-supporting for the first time in her life. And, by the way, property values did not go up. They went down.

A close friend of mine was dying. She lived with her niece, with whom I was also close. My friend hated being the center of attention and made her niece promise not to let anybody know she was dying. I was the only one of her friends who knew the situation. I lived far away, so I could give limited support. Her niece was getting burned out trying to be her sole support. How could she reconcile my friend's insistence on secrecy with my friend's need for almost constant support in her final journey? We asked this question of Wisdom through the I Ching. We were directed to archetype number 7, named *The Army*. The archetype describes a general leading a great army. The message was that my niece needed to ignore my friend's wishes and lead an "army" of her friends to share in the joy of supporting her. Her niece followed this advice. Because of this, my friend was blessed with a peace-filled death surrounded by many close friends who loved and cherished her.

You can see that these situational archetypes, while universal and therefore generic, are still able to provide amazingly detailed advice. You can also see why Jung was so drawn to the I Ching. Jung studied and wrote about the archetypes that describe our personalities. He believed in a "collective unconscious" that was shared throughout the world and linked us all together through its ebbs and flows. For him, the I Ching was a living, breathing tool for exploring this spiritual world and dialoging with the Wisdom it offered.

## MAPPING SITUATIONS INTO SITUATIONAL ARCHETYPES

Like all categorization frameworks, the I Ching includes sorting mechanisms. For the I Ching, the sorting mechanisms assign situations that you care about to situational archetypes that the I Ching knows about. There are several sorting mechanisms that are used with the I Ching. I will describe two in the next chapter. All of the I Ching sorting mechanisms share an important common feature: they are based on discernment events that Ego is powerless to control.

The situation that will be mapped into archetypes includes everything about the situation. This includes the subject, question, and the frame of mind of the one in dialogue. In my question about the future of this book, the subject was the book, the question was about the likely outcome of the book, and the frame of mind was mine at the time of the query. If I ask exactly the same query again, the situation will have changed. Before, my mind-frame was characterized by doubt and uncertainty about this book project. If I repeat the question, my mind-frame will have changed to one of doubt and uncertainty about the I Ching. The mind-frame is a key part of the situation, so we would expect the I Ching to respond with a different situational archetype, perhaps one that expresses annoyance at being doubted.

## ENERGY FLOWS IN THE I CHING

There is an aspect of the I Ching that does not have an analogy in either the zip code or the Myers-Briggs frameworks. This is the idea of transformation. Both the zip code and the Myers-Briggs frameworks map to static categories.

Zip codes don't change. Personality types don't change, or at least they don't change in any way that is predicted by the Myers-Briggs framework.

The situational archetypes of the I Ching are all subject to flows of energy, and this energy has the power to change any situational archetype into any other situational archetype. So the I Ching will tell you not only which archetype your situation maps to but also what energy flows are part of your situation and therefore what archetype transformation is likely to occur. I will come back to this idea of transformation once I have explained the basic situational archetypes in more detail.

## THE STRUCTURE OF THE CHRISTIAN I CHING

Part Two of *The Christian I Ching* is divided into sixty-four sections, one for each of the sixty-four situational archetypes recognized by the traditional I Ching. Each one of these sections has a name, a number, and a hexagram associated with it.

The archetype name is a short mnemonic that helps us remember the archetype meaning. In the traditional translations, this name is often an obscure translation of some ancient Chinese word. When I asked the question about this book's outcome, the name of the situational archetype was, in the Wilhelm/Baynes I Ching, *The Arousing*. Not too informative, is it? I will try to do better in *The Christian I Ching*.

The archetype number serves as an index. When I asked my question about this book, I was directed to archetype number 51. Once I know that my archetype is number 51, I can quickly look it up in the I Ching. So the archetype number is important. The archetype number is also the only way to compare archetype descriptions across different versions of the I Ching. While the different versions do not agree on the name of the archetype, the archetype number is standard across all versions.

The archetype hexagram is a pictogram that represents the situational archetype. This archetype hexagram is useful, especially to those who are highly trained in using the I Ching. Even for those of us who will be using the I Ching informally, a basic understanding of the hexagram is helpful. So let's take a look at this next.

A hexagram, in the context of the I Ching, is a stack of six lines. *Hex* means "six" in Greek. Any one of these lines can be either solid or open. The hexagram associated with the situational archetype I received (number 51) looks like this:

```
━━━━    ━━  ━━
━━━━    ━━  ━━
━━━━━━━━━━━  ━━  ━━
━━━━    ━━  ━━
━━━━    ━━  ━━
━━━━━━━━━━━━━━━━━━
```

**Hexagram 51**

If you are mathematically inclined and figure out how many hexagrams can be constructed using six lines, any of which can be either solid or open, you will find that there are exactly sixty-four possible hexagrams. These correspond to the sixty-four situational archetypes of the I Ching.

The most basic element in a hexagram is a single line, either solid or open. A solid line is called a *yang* line and is considered to represent the male energy. The open line is called a *yin* line and is considered to represent the female energy. You have probably heard of the concept of yin and yang. This is a fundamental concept in Chinese philosophy.

```
━━━━    ━━━━    Yin Line
━━━━━━━━━━━━━━  Yang Line
```

The I Ching does not assign more importance to either the yang or the yin. They are just different, and they complement each other. As we will see later, either can transform into the other, so what started as a yang line representing male energy can transform into a yin line representing female energy. The idea of male and female energy should not be seen as mapping to a man and a woman. Yin and yang does not describe a sex; it describes a type of energy. If you are a Carl Jung devotee, you may think of the yin as representing the *anima* and the yang as representing the *animus*.

Just to be sure we are clear on this, look again at the hexagram associated with my situational archetype, number 51. The six lines starting from the bottom and working up are yang, yin, yin, yang, yin, and yin.

```
━━━━    ━━━━    Yin Line
━━━━    ━━━━    Yin Line
━━━━━━━━━━━━━━  Yang Line
━━━━    ━━━━    Yin Line
━━━━    ━━━━    Yin Line
━━━━━━━━━━━━━━  Yang Line
```

## THE TRIGRAMS

The next unit of organization in the hexagram is the trigram. *Tri* comes from the Greek word for "three," so a trigram is a collection of three lines. In this perspective, we think of a hexagram as consisting of two trigrams, one lower trigram and one upper trigram. Hexagram 51 can be thought of as these two trigrams:

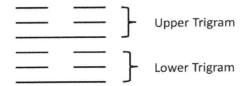

Notice that in this particular case, the lower and upper trigrams are the same. This is true for eight of the sixty-four hexagrams. The rest have different lower and upper trigrams.

So far, we have seen three numbers standing out in the description of a hexagram: one, three, and six.

One represents the individual line, which can consist of either male or female energy. In Christian theology, this one corresponds to the Unity, to God, which contains everything, both male and female.

Three is the number of lines in the trigram. In Christian theology, this number represents the Trinity.

And finally, six represents the complete hexagram. In Christian theology, six represents the number of days it took God to complete the universe.

So even at this level of detail, we can see parallels between the I Ching and Christian theology. Wisdom, apparently, does not recognize geographic, temporal, or theological boundaries.

In traditional translations of the I Ching, the hexagram is not seen as distinct from the archetype it represents. If I were using the language of traditional translations, I would say that in response to my query about this book, I received hexagram 51. Of course, my goal in this book is not to create another version of the traditional I Ching, but to reinterpret the I Ching within the context of contemporary Christianity. From this perspective, the situational archetype is much more meaningful than the pictographic representation of that archetype. So, rather than say that I received hexagram 51, I will say that I was directed to archetype 51.

There is one more aspect of the lines of a hexagram that we need to understand. This is the energy state of each of the lines. A line can have either low energy or high energy. Recall that earlier I said lines are fluid. The yang (solid) line can turn into the yin (open) line, and visa versa. A line that has low energy is in a state of rest. A line that has high energy is moving, or in a state of flux. If a line is in flux, it is getting ready to turn into its opposite. Lines that are in flux are often called *moving lines*. The protocol you use to determine the lines in your hexagram will also tell you which of the lines are in flux, or moving.

## DIALOGUING WITH THE I CHING

Now that we understand the hexagram, let's look at how a typical I Ching dialogue unfolds within the context of Christian discernment.

First, you will need a query. Think carefully about what you want to ask. My query is, "What is the likely outcome of this book project?" Because I am asking this within the context of Christian discernment, I understand this question to mean, "Is this project something that God wills?" Or, using the stream analogy, "Is this project going with the flow of God's stream?" If God wills this project, then it will have a positive outcome. If God does not will this project, then it will have a negative outcome. As a Christian, I don't want to invest a lot of time doing something God doesn't want done. There are easier ways to make my life miserable.

The reply to your query will be in the form of an archetype number and a set of energy points (moving lines). As Christians, we understand this as Wisdom's voice telling us that the answer to our reply will be found by pondering that particular archetype and those particular energy points.

## FORMING THE QUERY

Forming a good query is critical to getting a good response. If the query is muddled, the response will be difficult to interpret. Here are a few basic guidelines to keep in mind in forming the query.

Do not ask trivial questions. Ask about situations with which you are truly struggling. Jung describes these situations as "having an element of impossibility." There seems to be no way out. In such situations, according to Jung, "archetypal dreams are likely to occur which point out a possible line of advance one would never have thought of oneself. It is this kind of situation that constellates the archetype with the greatest regularity." (*Synchronicity* by Carl Jung).

Do not ask yes/no questions. The I Ching does not give absolute answers, and it has no language for yes or no. So instead of asking, "Should I take this job?" ask, "What would be the consequences of taking this job?" Even better is the question formulated from a Christian perspective: "God, how are you calling me to move forward with respect to this job offer?"

Do not ask the I Ching to predict the future. So do not ask, "Will this stock do well?" I discussed the prohibition on fortune telling in Chapter 2.

Do not ask either/or questions. Such questions presuppose that you already know the answer must be one of two choices. The I Ching needs the flexibility to show you possibilities you haven't thought of. So instead of asking, "Should I do A or B?" ask two questions: "God, how are you calling me to move forward with respect to A?" and "How are you calling me to move forward with respect to B?"

Do not ask for help violating God's laws. So do not ask, "How can I best hide my affair from my wife?" Ask for wisdom that will help you keep God's laws. So you might ask, "Why do I want to have an affair?"

Do not repeat a question just because you didn't like the answer. If you don't understand a previous answer, then ask further questions to clarify the answer.

A good rule of thumb is not to ask the I Ching questions you wouldn't ask a wise teacher. When you use the I Ching, you are asking for God's advice. And God is your wisest of teachers.

Once you have your query, write it down. Frequently the interpretation of God's response through the I Ching will hinge on the specific wording you used. If Ego doesn't like the answer (which it probably won't), then it will try to convince you that the question you asked was really something else. Best to have written proof.

## PREPARATION FOR DIALOGUE

Before dialoguing with the I Ching, prepare the atmosphere both physically and spiritually. These are my recommendations, but feel free to modify them to feel right to you. First, clear the space you will need for whatever protocol you are following. Light some incense and three candles. The candles represent the Trinity. If you are in the season of Lent (that is, between Ash Wednesday and Easter Sunday), then the middle candle representing Christ is not lit.

Clear your mind by meditating. This is a time when you are letting go of Ego. The length of the meditation depends on your comfort with meditating. Ideally this time period will last twenty minutes, but even a few minutes will be helpful. As you feel more comfortable with meditation, this time period can be lengthened.

During the meditation period, sit in a chair with your back straight. Start a timer. Close your eyes and silently repeat a mantra of your choice. I personally recommend the mantra that is commonly used in the World Community for Christian Meditation, "Maranatha." Maranatha means "Come, Holy Spirit" in the ancient language of Aramaic, the language Jesus spoke. Maranatha was a common prayer, and one we assume Jesus said. It was used several times as a closing in Paul's letters.

Maranatha is pronounced with four syllables: *mar* (rhyming with *bar*), *a* (rhyming with *la*), *nath* (rhyming with the English pronunciation of *bath*), and *a* (rhyming with *la* again). Say this word slowly and silently, in time with your breathing.

*Marra natha*   Mara Natha

bar  la  recte  lc

During meditation, thoughts will come to you. This is Ego speaking; Ego doesn't like to be silenced. When this happens, silently say to Ego, "Not right now." Then go back to repeating your mantra. You may need to do this a dozen times in a two-minute meditation. No problem.

At the end of your meditation, hold on to the silence you have created. If you have some specific prayers or psalms that you like, feel free to say them. Include a prayer that God send you Wisdom.

## RECEIVING A RESPONSE

Once you have your query and have completed your preparations, you present your query to God and request a response through the I Ching. There are several possible protocols you can use to receive that answer. Each is similar to the biblical (God-directed, Egoless) protocols discussed earlier. I will describe the two most common protocols in the next chapter.

Regardless of which protocol you use, you will receive a response consisting of the six lines of the hexagram and information as to which of those lines are in flux, or "moving." The hexagram, remember, is the pictographic representation of the situational archetype. The moving lines are pictographic representations of the energy state of the archetype. Let's start by considering just the lines without their energy states.

Your response will consist of the six hexagram lines, any of which can be either yin (open) or yang (solid). In response to my book question, I was given the following hexagram:

At this point, you have been given a pictographic representation of the archetype that contains Wisdom's answer to your query. But there are sixty-four archetypes. Which one does this hexagram point to?

To find the correct archetype, you start by dividing the hexagram into two halves, an upper half and a lower half. These halves are called *trigrams*. My hexagram response is divided as shown here:

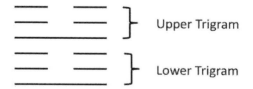

Notice that in this particular case, the upper and lower trigrams are identical. In most cases, this will not be true, but this doesn't change how we map hexagrams to archetypes.

Now that we have the upper and lower trigram, we can use these as indices in the hexagram index table. The standard hexagram index table is shown here and is reprinted in Appendix 5:

| | Upper Trigram | | | | | | | |
|---|---|---|---|---|---|---|---|---|
| | 1 | 34 | 5 | 26 | 11 | 9 | 14 | 43 |
| | 25 | 51 | 3 | 27 | 24 | 42 | 21 | 17 |
| | 6 | 40 | 29 | 4 | 7 | 59 | 64 | 47 |
| | 33 | 62 | 39 | 52 | 15 | 53 | 56 | 31 |
| | 12 | 16 | 8 | 23 | 2 | 20 | 35 | 45 |
| | 44 | 32 | 48 | 18 | 46 | 57 | 50 | 28 |
| | 13 | 55 | 63 | 22 | 36 | 37 | 30 | 49 |
| | 10 | 54 | 60 | 41 | 19 | 61 | 38 | 58 |

(Lower Trigram indicated along the left side)

**Hexagram Table**

To use a hexagram index table, use the lower and upper trigrams of your hexagram as indices. Find the lower trigram in the first column of the hexagram index table. Find the upper trigram in the first row of the hexagram index table. Look for the intersection of the row containing your lower trigram with the column containing your upper trigram. Inside the intersection is the index number of the situational archetype that corresponds to this hexagram.

When I followed this process for my hexagram response, I found that my archetype was number 51 by looking at the intersection of the second row (containing my lower trigram) with the second column (containing my upper trigram).

| | | | | | | | |
|---|---|---|---|---|---|---|---|
| 1 | 34 | 5 | 26 | 11 | 9 | 14 | 43 |
| 25 | 51 | 3 | 27 | 24 | 42 | 21 | 17 |
| 6 | 40 | 29 | 4 | 7 | 59 | 64 | 47 |
| 33 | 62 | 39 | 52 | 15 | 53 | 56 | 31 |
| 12 | 16 | 8 | 23 | 2 | 20 | 35 | 45 |
| 44 | 32 | 48 | 18 | 46 | 57 | 50 | 28 |
| 13 | 55 | 63 | 22 | 36 | 37 | 30 | 49 |
| 10 | 54 | 60 | 41 | 19 | 61 | 38 | 58 |

The hexagram index is important when comparing discussions of the archetypes in this book with descriptions of the same archetypes in other versions of the I Ching. Although the names of the archetypes differ from version to version, the hexagram index is standard across all versions. So what I call "archetype 51" will correspond to what other versions will call "hexagram 51" regardless of the name assigned to that archetype/hexagram.

Now let's return to the topic of energy patterns. Each of the lines in my hexagram can be in a state of low or high energy. High-energy lines are in flux, or moving. These are lines that are undergoing transformation into their opposite line. A high-energy yin (open) line is about to transform into a yang (solid) line. A high-energy yang line is about to transform into a yin line.

There are two reasons you need to know about the lines that are in flux. First, the archetype description in the I Ching will include specific information related to those lines. Second, the archetype itself undergoes a transformation into a second archetype called a *resultant* archetype. The resultant archetype's hexagram has the same lines as the original archetype's hexagram except for those lines that are in flux. These lines all change into their opposite.

When I was given the response to my book question, I was not only given archetype 51, I was also told that lines 1, 5, and 6 are in flux. Since we count lines starting at the bottom of the hexagram and working up, this means that the bottom line and the top two lines are in flux. When I write the response, I put an asterisk after lines that are in flux. Then I draw an arrow pointing to the new resultant archetype. So the response I drew in response to my question looks like this:

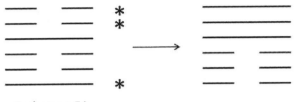

Archetype 51

You can see in the above figure that the new hexagram is exactly the same as hexagram 51 except for lines 1, 5, and 6. These lines are reversed. These were the lines that I was told were in flux.

Next you find the index number of the resulting hexagram. You use the same process you used to find the index number of the original hexagram; you divide the hexagram into a lower and upper trigram and use these as indices to the hexagram index table. For my dialogue, my resulting archetype was number 12, as shown here:

| Lower Trigram | Upper Trigram | | | | | | | |
|---|---|---|---|---|---|---|---|---|
| 1 | 34 | 5 | 26 | 11 | 9 | 14 | 43 |
| 25 | 51 | 3 | 27 | 24 | 42 | 21 | 17 |
| 6 | 40 | 29 | 4 | 7 | 59 | 64 | 47 |
| 33 | 62 | 39 | 52 | 15 | 53 | 56 | 31 |
| 12 | 16 | 8 | 23 | 2 | 20 | 35 | 45 |
| 44 | 32 | 48 | 18 | 46 | 57 | 50 | 28 |
| 13 | 55 | 63 | 22 | 36 | 37 | 30 | 49 |
| 10 | 54 | 60 | 41 | 19 | 61 | 38 | 58 |

Now I have complete information as to Wisdom's response. I know the original archetype is 51. I know the resultant archetype is 12. And I know that lines 1, 5, and 6 are in a high-energy state (in flux, or moving). I complete my drawing of this response as shown here:

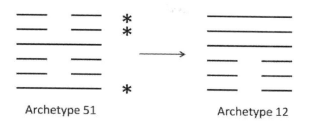

Archetype 51                          Archetype 12

## INTERPRETING THE RESPONSE

Next you go to Part II of *The Christian I Ching* itself. The I Ching is divided into sixty-four sections, one for each archetype. Each section has the following structure:

- The index number and name of the archetype
- The pictographic representation (hexagram) of the archetype
- A biblical reading that captures the sense of the archetype
- A discussion of how the reading relates to the archetype
- The Hexagram: a discussion of how the hexagram pictorially represents the archetype
- The Archetype: a discussion of the message this archetype is meant to deliver
- The Lines: six sections, one for each line. Each of these sections has a discussion of the message that a moving line is meant to convey.
- Notes: A brief look at three other translations of the I Ching

When you dialogue with the I Ching, you start with the original archetype (before the lines are changed). This is the starting point for Wisdom's response. You read the entire description, stopping when you reach the sections on the lines. Then you read the descriptions of those lines (and only those lines) you are told are in flux. Next you read the section on the resulting archetype, the one derived by changing the high-energy lines. The resultant archetype is interpreted as where the situation is headed given the flow of energy in the original archetype. You read the entire section for the resulting archetype, except for the discussions on the lines. You have already read about the high-energy lines, so you ignore this section in the resulting archetype.

Not all responses will have high-energy lines. When that happens, your archetype is considered stable. You do not read any of the line discussions, and you do not have a resultant archetype.

For my dialogue, I start at the section of the I Ching that describes archetype 51. I will read the general description and the specific discussion relating to lines 1, 5, and 6. Then I will look up archetype 12 and read that description, ignoring the section on changing lines since I have already read about these in the first hexagram.

The final step in the dialogue is meditating on the answer. Sometimes the answer is immediately obvious. Other times the truth takes time to materialize. Even the most obvious answer will yield subtleties when allowed to ripen. God, whether speaking through the Bible or the I Ching, speaks in the slow-moving right-brain languages of imagery, metaphors, irony, and poetry to deliver the profound truths that defy literal left-brain interpretations. Pay attention to the name of the archetype, the Bible readings, the discussion on the readings, the description of the hexagram, the discussion of the archetype, and even the notes. Which of these speaks to you? What part do you play in the readings? Where do you feel the tingle of recognition?

When you are finished with the session, blow out your candles and offer a prayer of thanks to God for giving you this answer. Promise God you will reflect carefully on God's Wisdom.

You should take notes on every I Ching session and save them. If you keep a spiritual journal, that would be a good place to keep these notes. For every reading, you should note the date, the query, the hexagram, the moving lines, and the resultant hexagram. Make a note of any thoughts you had on any of the replies. You will often find that the use of the I Ching triggers dreams related to either the question or the response or both. Make a note of these as well. Don't waste any communications from God.

## INCORPORATING OTHER VERSIONS OF THE I CHING

You will find it useful to consult other versions of the I Ching alongside *The Christian I Ching*. I have taken a specific approach to interpreting the I Ching that involves looking at the archetype beneath the words and then looking for biblical stories that I believe better express the meaning of the archetype to a modern Christian. I have found this approach speaks in a meaningful way to people who are grounded in Christian contemplative/mystical theology. But sometimes the traditional words will contain meanings that augment or even improve upon my interpretations.

For example, in archetype 5, *Waiting*, I use the reading describing the Wedding at Cana. I believe this reading captures the tension of waiting for something important to happen when its time has not yet arrived. However, the traditional language for this archetype includes a description of crossing a great water or river. The water is, I believe, a metaphor for accomplishing something great in the face of danger.

Is the image of the great water important to you? It may be if, for example, you have been having dreams about crossing a river. And if it is important, you won't find it in *The Christian I Ching*. You will find it in most other versions of the I Ching. On the other hand, if you have been feeling pressured to accomplish something, you won't find any imagery in a traditional I Ching that is as poignant as the story of Mary and Jesus at the Wedding at Cana.

So the question is not which I Ching is better, but how you can use both. I have designed this book so that it is easy to incorporate other versions of the I Ching. *The Christian I Ching*, that is, Part II of this book, is independent of the rest of the book. All of Part I, which describes how the I Ching fits into contemporary Christian theology, can be applied to any version of the I Ching. The discernment protocols I have described can be used with any I Ching. All the appendices, with the exception of those that are specific to the readings I have chosen, apply to all versions. So, for example, the probability analysis that constitutes Appendix 1 of this book is valid for all versions of the I Ching. I have also used the standard numbering scheme for the archetypes, so that you can easily compare my interpretation of archetype 5 with another version's interpretation of what it will call hexagram 5. And for three of these other I Chings, I have even given you the names they use for this archetype in the notes section.

The three other versions of the I Ching that I describe and recommend are these:

- *The I Ching, or Book of Changes*, the Richard Wilhelm German translation rendered into English by Cary F. Baynes and published by Princeton University Press. This version is referred to here as Wilhelm/Baynes.
- *I Ching: Walking Your Path, Creating Your Future* by Hilary Barrett, published by Arcturus and referred to here as Barrett
- *The Original I Ching: An Authentic Translation of the Book of Changes* by Margaret J. Pearson, published by Tuttle Publishing and referred to here as Pearson

Each of these translations/interpretations has strengths. The Wilhelm/Baynes version is the gold standard for I Chings and the one that has most spoken to me over the last forty years. It has been my primary source in preparing this book. Barrett's version is the most pragmatic and presents the I Ching in a highly approachable way that focuses on its relevance to life's issues. Pearson's version strives to give an accurate translation of the I Ching imagery with minimal interpretation. I think you will find all three of these to be valuable additions to your study of the I Ching.

This completes the basic ideas of the I Ching. You ask the questions. God provides the answers. The I Ching provides the medium.

> Ask, and it will be given to you; seek, and you will find; knock, and it will be opened to you. For everyone who asks receives, and the one who seeks finds, and to the one who knocks it will be opened.

—Matthew 7:7–8

# Chapter 5: Hexagram Protocols

## INTRODUCTION TO PROTOCOLS

If you have gotten this far in the book, you must be ready to consult the I Ching. Congratulations! I assume that you have read the previous chapter about constructing a question and setting the stage. In this chapter I will discuss the two main protocols you can use to receive a hexagram.

By whatever protocol you use, you are going to receive six numbers, one for each line of the hexagram. Each of these numbers will have the value 6, 7, 8, or 9. Each of these values refers to a type of line (yin or yang) and a level of energy (static or in flux). The numbers are interpreted as follows:

| Number | Line | Energy |
|--------|------|--------|
| 6 | yin (open) | in flux (moving) |
| 7 | yang (solid) | static (not moving) |
| 8 | yin (open) | static (not moving) |
| 9 | yang (solid) | in flux (moving) |

Notice that the odd numbers (7 and 9) refer to the yang (solid) line and the even numbers (6 and 8) refer to the yin (open) line. Also notice that the smallest possible number (6) and the largest possible number (9) refer to high-energy lines (lines in flux) and that the middle numbers (7 and 8) refer to low-energy lines (static lines).

In the last chapter, I discussed my dialogue with the I Ching regarding the likely outcome of *The Christian I Ching*. I said I received hexagram 51 with lines 1, 5, and 6 in flux. Since I did not mention lines 2, 3, and 4, they are assumed to be static.

| | |
|---|---|
| ▬▬  ▬▬ | Yin line (flux) |
| ▬▬  ▬▬ | Yin line (flux) |
| ▬▬▬▬▬ | Yang line |
| ▬▬  ▬▬ | Yin line |
| ▬▬  ▬▬ | Yin line |
| ▬▬▬▬▬ | Yang line (flux) |

The lines of my hexagram 51 response are, from bottom to top: yang, yin, yin, yang, yin, yin. If we add the energy descriptions, I received a yang (flux), yin, yin, yang, yin (flux), and yin (flux). So you can assume that by whatever protocol I was using, I received a 9, 8, 8, 7, 6, and 6.

All protocols have some action or group of actions that is repeated six times, one for each line in the hexagram. As each line is received, the hexagram is built from the bottom up. Lines are also numbered from the bottom up, so if you read a reference to line 3, it means the third line from the bottom.

I will describe two protocols, the *yarrow* protocol and the *coin* protocol. The original ancient protocols have been lost, but the "modern" yarrow and coin protocols each have at least 1,500 years of usage.

The yarrow protocol is more meditative. It is the protocol I use exclusively. I find it relaxing and calming, and that it allows time for Wisdom to let herself be known. Many people don't like this protocol because it takes "too long," that is, a little under fifteen minutes. For me this is time you are dedicating to God. We are asking God for help and symbolically offering God a sacrifice of fifteen minutes of our busy lives. That seems like a fair exchange.

The coin protocol is much faster. You can zip out a hexagram in under a minute. It is the drive-through protocol.

Let's start with my preferred protocol, the yarrow protocol.

## THE YARROW PROTOCOL

The yarrow protocol I follow (and describe here) is a combination of the protocol described by Jane English for manipulating the stalks (www.eheart.com) and the protocol described by Hilary Barrett for determining the resulting line (www.onlineclarity.co.uk).

The yarrow protocol is so named because it traditionally uses yarrow stalks. Yarrow is a weed that was widespread in ancient China and is still with us today. The dried stalks of the yarrow plant are manipulated to receive a hexagram.

Yarrow stalks with quarter (for size comparison)

There are two problems with manipulating yarrow stalks. First, the stalks are not as easily located today as they were in ancient China. Second, the protocol involves holding yarrow stalks comfortably between various fingers. While this is probably natural to those who have spent their lifetimes using chopsticks, it is much less comfortable for most Westerners.

For both of these reasons, I use a variant on the traditional yarrow protocol. I follow the same protocol used by those who use yarrow stalks, but instead of yarrow stalks, I use material that slides on a flat surface. My favorite material is Go stones, that is, the playing pieces of the ancient game of Go. Go stones are small flat stones that are pleasing to hold and easily manipulated with the fingers. If you have a good game store nearby, you should be able to buy a nice set of Go stones without spending too much money. Buy "double convex" stones if you have a choice. A standard set of Go stones includes over three hundred stones, which is overkill for what we will use (fifty stones). Perhaps you can go in with some friends.

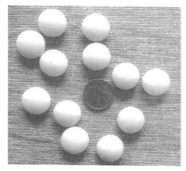

Go stones with quarter (for size comparison)

There are many other types of material you could use just as easily. You could use large dried beans, small sea-shells, beach pebbles, or beads. The basic requirements are:

- The items should not roll around.
- About 50 of the items should fit comfortably but not be lost in your two hands.
- The items should be large enough and smooth enough to easily manipulate by dragging them around with your fingers.
- The items should all look roughly similar and be similar sizes.

I name this protocol the yarrow protocol in honor of the yarrow stalks that are traditionally used. But I will describe this protocol as using "stones" by which I mean Go stones. You should read "stones" as referring to whatever material you are using.

The protocol has a number of steps, but they are all simple and repetitive. At first, you should go slowly and carefully. Soon this protocol will become quite natural, and you won't need these directions. You will require an area of about two and a half feet by a foot and a half, not including room for your candles and incense.

Here are the steps.

1. Count out 50 stones. Return 1 to your holder, leaving 49.

2. Put the 49 stones in a single layered group:

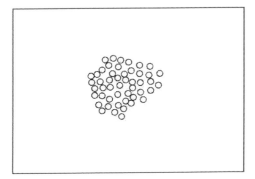

3. Meditate on your question. As you are meditating, divide your pile into a left-hand and a right-hand pile. Do this without looking at the stones and without trying to be exact:

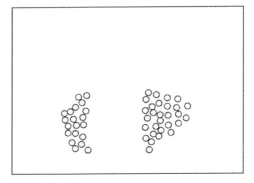

4. Take one of the stones from the left-hand pile and start the first of three piles in a holding area above your working area:

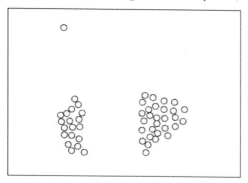

5. Count the remaining stones in the left-hand pile into groups of 4. You will have a remainder of 1, 2, 3, or 4 stones. If you have a remainder of 0, then you have a remainder of 4, and the last pile is your remainder:

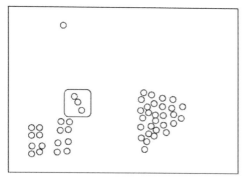

6. Take the remainder pile and place it just underneath the single stone you placed earlier:

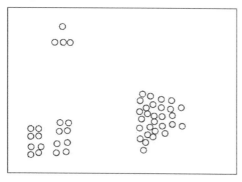

7. Repeat this counting-off operation with the right-hand pile. Once again, you will have a remainder of 1, 2, 3, or 4:

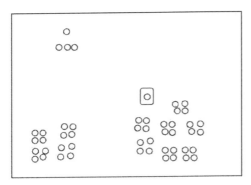

8. Place the remainder pile below the left-hand remainder pile in the holding area:

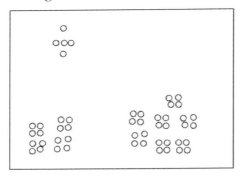

9. If you have counted correctly, there will either be 5 or 9 stones in the pile in the holding area. If there is anything other than 5 or 9 stones in the pile, then correct your error.

10. If you do have 5 or 9 stones in the holding area, then continue. Put the left-hand and right-hand piles back into a single pile, leaving the holding area as it is:

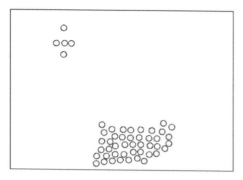

11. Meditate on your question while you once again separate the large pile into a left-hand and a right-hand pile:

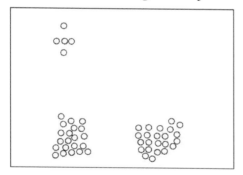

12. Repeat the previous operations with the left-hand pile. Take one stone from the left-hand pile and start a new pile in the holding area:

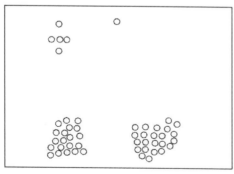

13. Count off the left-hand pile into groups of 4, leaving a remainder of 1, 2, 3, or 4 stones. Place the remainder pile below the just-placed single stone in the holding area:

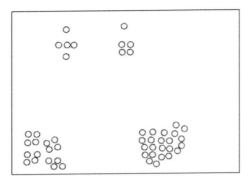

14. Count off the right-hand pile into groups of 4, leaving a remainder of 1, 2, 3, or 4 stones. Place the remainder pile below the new pile in the holding area:

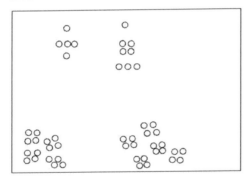

15. If you have counted correctly, you will have either 4 or 8 stones in the new pile in the holding area. (Not 5 or 9, like the first pile.) If you don't have 4 or 8 stones in the pile, then correct your error. If you do have 4 or 8 stones in the pile, then take the left-hand pile and right-hand pile and bring them together, leaving the holding area untouched:

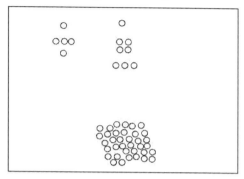

16. We will now repeat this operation a third time. Meditate on your question while dividing the pile, then take one stone from the left-hand pile and start a new pile in the holding area:

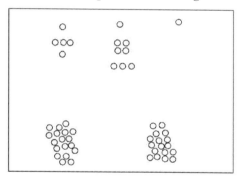

17. Count the left-hand pile into fours and put the remainder above. This is similar to what we did in previous steps, but we are now going to do one thing differently: we are going to be particularly neat in our piles of four:

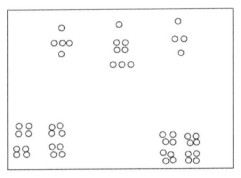

18. Do the same with the right-hand pile, again focusing on neatness:

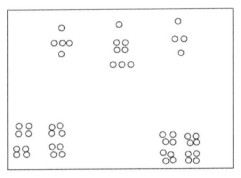

19. Once again, you will have either 4 or 8 stones in the new pile. If you have anything else, correct the error. Now count the groups of 4 you have left in the left-hand and right-hand sides. If you have done everything correctly, you will have no remainders, and you will have 6, 7, 8, or 9 groups of 4. The reason I wanted you to be neat earlier is to make this counting as easy (and accurate) as possible.

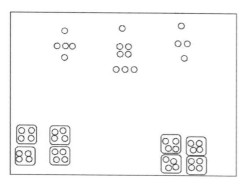

20. The number of groups of four you have is the number of the line in the hexagram. As I said earlier, the numbers are interpreted as follows:

**6** means a changing yin line (open line moving to solid).
**7** means a static yang line (solid line not moving).
**8** means a static yin line (open line not moving).
**9** means a changing yang line (solid moving to open).

In our case, we have 8 groups, so we have been given a static yin line. You now have the bottom (first) line of your hexagram. You will now put all 49 stones back into a single pile and repeat this entire procedure starting with step 2. You will do this five more times, one for each of the remaining five lines of the hexagram. Build your hexagram from the bottom up.

Many books on the I Ching give an alternative approach to interpreting the yarrow protocol. Instead of counting the groups of four that are left at the end, they recommend looking at the three piles at the top. They call a pile containing four or five stones (or yarrow stalks) a "small" pile and a pile containing eight or nine stones a "large" pile.

Then the piles are interpreted as follows. If all three piles are small, a changing yang line is indicated. If all three piles are large, a changing yin line is indicated. If two piles are small and one is big, a static yin line is indicated. And if two piles are large and one is small, a static yang line is indicated. Using this approach, the last picture has two small piles and one large pile, indicating a static yin line. This is the same result we got by counting piles of four. It makes no difference which method you use; you will get the same result in either case. Use whichever approach for the final reckoning you prefer. I like counting piles of four, because there is nothing to remember.

## THE COIN PROTOCOL

The coin protocol is much faster and much easier than the yarrow protocol. This is either its major advantage or its major disadvantage, depending on your attitude toward time.

This protocol requires less than a square foot, not including an area for your candles and incense. Oh, heck, why bother with candles and incense—who has time for that?

The only materials you need for the coin protocol are three of the same coins.

1. Throw the three coins.

2. Assign a two for each coin that comes up tails and a three for each coin that comes up heads. Count up the three numbers.

3. The resulting number will be a 6, 7, 8, or 9. This is the number of your bottom line.

4. Repeat this operation five more times and build up your hexagram from the bottom up.

See how much easier this is than the yarrow protocol? But somehow, it just doesn't feel right to me. Nevertheless, this is the most widely used protocol today. In a world in which fast food restaurants are the norm, I'm not surprised.

## PROBABILITIES

Part of the debate between proponents of the two different protocols has to do with probabilities. It turns out that the probabilities of various results from the coin method are different than the probabilities of the yarrow method. The following table shows a summary of these probabilities. For those interested, I will derive these numbers in Appendix 1 and give much more information about probabilities and the I Ching. For now, trust me.

| Line | Coin | Yarrow |
| --- | --- | --- |
| yang, rest | 6 in 16 | 5 in 16 |
| yin, rest | 6 in 16 | 7 in 16 |
| yang, flux | 2 in 16 | 3 in 16 |
| yin, flux | 2 in 16 | 1 in 16 |

Of course, these probabilities are only valid if we assume the outcome of the I Ching is random, and if we thought it was random, we wouldn't be using it. Still, there are some facts worth looking at.

The coin protocol is symmetric. There is an equal chance of getting a yin line as a yang line. There is an equal chance of getting a resting yang line as a resting yin line, and an equal chance of getting a moving yang line as a moving yin line.

The yarrow protocol is semisymmetric. There is still an equal chance of getting a yin line as a yang line, but beyond that, things get odd. A resting yin line has an almost 50 percent higher probability of showing up as a resting yang line, whereas a moving yang line has three times the probability of showing up as a moving yin line.

Extrapolating this to archetypes, it means that the more yin lines that are in an archetype's hexagram, the more stable that archetype is. Or, conversely, the more yang lines there are in an archetype's hexagram, the more likely it is that hexagram will have at least one moving line.

All of this seems to reflect an I Ching philosophy that the female nature (the yin line) is the stable energy and the male energy (the yang line) is the unstable energy. I doubt that many women disagree with this philosophy.

? female is Chaos ?
Male is order .

# Chapter 6: The Trigrams

We tend to focus on the hexagrams as the basic unit of communications. But if you pay attention not only to the hexagrams but also to the trigrams, you will be surprised at how much information can be packed into three little lines. I'll give you two examples.

## EXAMPLES OF TRIGRAM ANALYSIS

Earlier I discussed a dialogue between a friend and the I Ching concerning her struggle with a decision on whether or not to make a move. She was commuting a long distance to and from work, and the time and the cost of gas was draining her. Her only concern was the effect the move would have on her two daughters. We entered into a dialogue with God via the I Ching to ask what impact her contemplated move would have on her two daughters. As I mentioned, the response came through as archetype 50, which is about offering nourishment. This in itself seemed to imply that God looked favorably on the move. But it is even more remarkable when you look at the two trigrams.

Upper Trigram: Christ

Lower Trigram: Spirit

Hexagram 50
Preparing Nourishment

So far, this doesn't appear remarkable, until you look at the descriptions of the upper (Christ) and lower (Spirit) trigrams. When you look at these descriptions from a family perspective, the Christ trigram represents the second daughter, and the Spirit trigram represents the first daughter. You will see this in the descriptions that follow. So the I Ching replied not only with an archetype about providing nourishment, but it did so in language that explicitly included her two daughters.

Could this have been a "random" event? It seems highly unlikely. There are only two hexagrams that are made up of the trigrams for first and second daughter. The chances of getting either one of these is only 1 in 32, which is about the same odds you have of being dealt three of a kind in a poker game. And the other possibility, hexagram 37, is a description of a family, not an effect on a family.

I had some interesting trigrams when I asked about the outcome of this book project. Remember, the response was hexagram 51 with lines 1, 5, and 6 in flux. With these lines in flux, hexagram 51 transforms into hexagram 12.

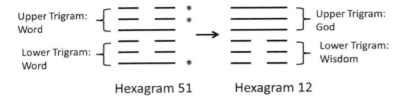

Hexagram 51          Hexagram 12

Hexagram 51 is a doubling of the trigram Word, which seems appropriate since I was specifically asking about a book. And the resulting hexagram is made up of the two trigrams for Wisdom and God. So if we just look at the answer to my question from the perspective of trigrams, we have Words resulting in God and Wisdom. What more could I hope for?

There is actually one thing I could have hoped for. That would be the reversal of these two trigrams in the resulting archetype. Had God been on the bottom and Wisdom on the top, then I would have had the resultant archetype 11 (*Peace*) instead of the resultant archetype 12 (*Resignation*). Archetype 11 is much more positive, a true Disneyland archetype with spring flowers everywhere and Bambi cavorting in the meadow. The negative archetype 12 is more ominous, in line with the shock and ridicule that archetype 51 promised would accompany the success of this book project. I discussed this in Chapter 4.

Oh, well. I'll take God and Wisdom any way I find them. Forewarned is forearmed. And, in any case, I suspect Resignation is the way most Prophets end up feeling after their bouts with God and Wisdom. At least I'll be in good company.

# THE EIGHT TRIGRAMS OF THE I CHING
Here are the eight trigrams of *The Christian I Ching*.

| | |
|---|---|
| God | Wisdom |
| Christ | Chaos |
| Stillness | Wonder |
| Spirit | Word |

Let's look at these in more detail. For each of these, I'll also give the Chinese name (as given in the Wilhelm/Baynes I Ching) in case you ever want to compare these to the Chinese equivalents. I will also follow the descriptions by a summary chart showing the most important attributes of each trigram.

## God

Chinese name: Ch'ien
Wilhelm translation: The Creative

The image of God is Heaven. God represents purity, strength, firmness, power, and endurance. In the family, this trigram represents the father. In the body, it represents the head. Its shape is the straight line.

## Wisdom

Chinese name: K'un
Wilhelm translation: The Receptive

The image of Wisdom is Earth. Earth is covered with life. Wisdom represents nurturing, devotion, yielding, multitude, fertility, and simplicity. In the family, this trigram represents the mother. In the body, it represents the belly. Its shape is level.

## Christ

Chinese name: Li
Wilhelm translation: The Clinging

The image of Christ is Fire. Fire brings light and allows us to see truth. Christ is characterized by firmness on the outside and yielding on the inside. In the family, this trigram represents the second daughter. In the body, it represents the eye.

## Chaos

Chinese name: K'an
Wilhelm translation: The Abysmal

The image of Chaos is Water. Water winds its way around. It penetrates everything. It can destroy anything. It is associated with melancholy and sneakiness. In the family, this trigram represents the second son. In the body, it represents the ear.

## Stillness

Chinese name: Ken
Wilhelm translation: Keeping Still

The image of Stillness is the Mountain. The mountain keeps watch. It is associated with resting. In the family, this trigram represents the third son. In the body, it represents the hand.

## Wonder

Chinese name: Tui
Wilhelm translation: The Joyous

The image of Wonder is the Lake. The lake rests and is joyful to behold. In the family, it is associated with the third daughter. In the body, it is associated with the mouth. It is also associated with autumn, a time when things are opening and breaking apart.

## Spirit

Chinese name: Sun
Wilhelm translation: The Gentle

The image of Spirit is a Gentle Wind. The wind penetrates everything, not in a destructive way like water, but in a sustaining way. In the family, this trigram is associated with the first daughter. In the body, it is associated with the thighs.

## Word

Chinese name: Chen
Wilhelm translation: The Arousing

The image of the Word is Thunder. It is decisive and frightening. It brings new things into being. In the family, this trigram represents the eldest son. In the body, it represents the foot.

| Trigram | Name | Image | Attribute | Family |
|---------|------|-------|-----------|--------|
| ☰ | God | Heaven | Strength | Father |
| ☷ | Wisdom | Earth | Devotion | Mother |
| ☲ | Christ | Fire | Light | Second Daughter |
| ☵ | Chaos | Water | Danger | Second Son |
| ☶ | Stillness | Mountain | Resting | Third Son |
| ☱ | Wonder | Lake | Joy | Third Daughter |
| ☴ | Spirit | Gentle Wind | Penetrating | First Daughter |
| ☳ | Word | Thunder | Life Giving | First Son |

## Summary of Trigrams

These eight trigrams are the alphabet of *The Christian I Ching*. Now let's look at some of the rich communications that are possible using this simple alphabet.

# Part II. The Christian I Ching

# Archetype 1: God

In the beginning when God created the heavens and the earth, the earth was a formless void and darkness covered the face of the deep, while a wind from God swept over the face of the waters. Then God said, "Let there be light"; and there was light. And God saw that the light was good.

—Genesis 1:1–3

## THE READING

The reading describes the awesome creative force that we call God. Nothing can be more creative than God, because God is the ground of all that is. This is a force that cannot be contained by space or time, because space and time are themselves only manifestations of its creativity.

## THE HEXAGRAM

| | Trigram | Name | Image | Attribute | Family |
|---|---|---|---|---|---|
| Upper | ☰ | God | Heaven | Strength | Father |
| Lower | ☰ | God | Heaven | Strength | Father |

The hexagram consists of a doubling of the God trigram, resulting in six solid lines. These solid lines symbolize the divine power that is the ultimate creative, loving force. This is a hexagram of power, energy, and love. It represents the paternal.

## THE ARCHETYPE

There is a time...

- To persevere, anticipating success.
- To draw strength from the boundless and eternal power we call God.
- To create great works that will last for generations.
- To deliver on God's promise of justice, peace, and love.

Now is that time.

## THE LINES

### MOVING LINE IN THE FIRST POSITION

A moving line in the bottom position indicates a creative force that is hidden and unrecognized but remains true to its calling. This is not the time to worry about how the world defines success. It is the time to listen to how Wisdom defines success. It is a time for patience and knowing that God's work happens in God's time. That time is coming.

### MOVING LINE IN THE SECOND POSITION

A moving line in the second position indicates a new light dispelling the darkness. A wise one comes forth to offer guidance and help. The wise one seems powerless, but power is not always obvious. This one has the power of authority, recognized expertise, and great character. This is the power of faith. When one has faith the size of a mustard seed, mountains can be moved (Luke 17:6). This is the time to embrace the wise one.

### MOVING LINE IN THE THIRD POSITION

A moving line in the third position indicates a new sphere of influence. Fame is increasing, and people come with hopeful hearts. But Ego is fed by the popular adoration, ambition, and desire for power. One must not be seduced by Ego. One must remain centered, focused, and attentive to Wisdom. Great things are going to be accomplished. Do not worry. Do not be sidetracked.

### MOVING LINE IN THE FOURTH POSITION

A moving line in the fourth position points to a divergence. A choice is being offered. One may choose to emerge and become a hero, or one may choose to withdraw and become holy. Either could be the right choice. The right decision will be reached by listening attentively to the voice of Wisdom.

### MOVING LINE IN THE FIFTH POSITION

A moving line in the fifth position indicates one who has taken on the light of God. The holy one's influence spreads throughout the world and blesses all whose presence it graces.

### MOVING LINE IN THE SIXTH POSITION

A moving line in the top position warns how easy it is to lose touch with humanity. Ego calls: "You are chosen, you are the one, you can do anything!" But listening to Ego can only lead to isolation, failure, and destruction. Listen to Wisdom, who will show what can be accomplished within the limitations of your abilities and power.

Notes
Wilhelm/Baynes and Pearson both call this archetype *The Creative*. Barrett calls this archetype *Creative Force*. Pearson comments, "This first hexagram has been associated with extremely auspicious times and people, with creativity and leadership."

# Archetype 2: Wisdom

The Lord created me at the beginning of his work,
the first of his acts of long ago.
Ages ago I was set up,
at the first, before the beginning of the earth…
Happy is the one who listens to me,
watching daily at my gates,
waiting beside my doors.
For whoever finds me finds life
and obtains favor from the Lord.

—Proverbs 8:22–29

## THE READING

This reading describes Wisdom. This is not the wisdom you acquire by
studying or reading books; it is a Wisdom you acquire by being fully receptive
to the Holy Spirit. Wisdom is traditionally named Sophia, after the Greek
goddess of Wisdom. In the Bible, Wisdom is always referred to in the
feminine gender. Wisdom is associated with receptivity, earth, and nature.
Wisdom is not God, but she is inseparable from God. She is God's
companion, perhaps even God's lover. Wisdom does not compete with
God's creative power; Wisdom guides that power. Creative power without
Wisdom's guidance leads to chaos. For this reason, Wisdom was the first of
God's creations.

## THE HEXAGRAM

|        | Trigram | Name   | Image | Attribute | Family |
|--------|---------|--------|-------|-----------|--------|
| Upper  | ☷       | Wisdom | Earth | Devotion  | Mother |
| Lower  | ☷       | Wisdom | Earth | Devotion  | Mother |

This hexagram is made by doubling the Wisdom trigram, resulting in six open
lines. These open lines symbolize the open, yielding, receptive power of the
feminine. This is a hexagram of devotion and great holiness. The force of this
hexagram is associated with the reproductive power of the earth and the
maternal.

# THE ARCHETYPE
There is a time...

- To draw strength from the earth.
- To embrace silence, solitude, and receptivity.
- To mobilize the resources, wisdom, and power that will be needed for the effort.
- To nurture.
- To dance in the presence of God.
- To feel a great love that is not bound by place or space.
- To seek a wise guide.
- To persevere with gentleness and devotion.
- To learn from nature.

Now is that time.

# THE LINES

### MOVING LINE IN THE FIRST POSITION
A moving line in the bottom position warns of early signs of decay. If decay is not noticed early on, it advances to deterioration and then to death. But if the early signs of decay are noticed, a wise one can take appropriate action before the decay is irreversible.

### MOVING LINE IN THE SECOND POSITION
A moving line in the second position reminds that Wisdom must conform to God. All beings are created in God's image, and all creatures are equal. This is the wonder of nature. Nature creates what is right for all without any deception or favor. The wise one is guided by nature's example.

### MOVING LINE IN THE THIRD POSITION
A moving line in the third position warns of Ego. The wise one will be free of Ego and will avoid being conspicuous. This is a time to blend in, conceal abilities, and not attract attention prematurely. If the wise one must enter public life, it should be done with restraint. The wise one does not seek credit for what has been done in the past but focuses on the active creativity that will pay off in the future.

### MOVING LINE IN THE FOURTH POSITION
A moving line in the fourth position calls for reticence. The time is dangerous. Any degree of prominence leads to risk from powerful foes. Challenges can lead to hostility. Recognition can earn enmity. This is a time

to be reserved, blend in, and not make waves. This time can best be used to gather one's inner strength.

### MOVING LINE IN THE FIFTH POSITION
A moving line in the fifth position counsels discretion. One who is prominent but has no independence needs the utmost discretion. Now is not the time to shine. Instead, one's qualities must express themselves indirectly, reflecting the interior self.

### MOVING LINE IN THE SIXTH POSITION
A moving line in the top position warns that it is time to yield. One who tries to maintain an undeserved position risks attracting the anger of those who are stronger. No one will win this struggle; all will suffer.

### NOTES
Wilhelm/Baynes calls this archetype *The Receptive*. Pearson calls this archetype *Earth, The Receptive*. Barrett calls this archetype *Earth*. Barrett says, "The noble one has a direction to go: she is purposeful, she has a destination in mind, but this doesn't mean she has her route to it already mapped out."

# Archetype 3: Hard Beginning

Jesus, full of the Holy Spirit, returned from the Jordan and was led by the Spirit in the wilderness, where for forty days he was tempted by the devil. He ate nothing at all during those days, and when they were over, he was famished.

—Luke 4:1–2

## THE READING

This reading describes Jesus at the end of his forty days in the desert. Forty is a mystical number in the Bible. It is used to signify a period of hardship and testing resulting in new birth. Forty is the number of days and nights it rained during the Great Flood before the earth was reborn. Forty is the number of years the Israelites wandered through the desert before being reborn as the Nation of God. Forty is the number of days Moses fasted before returning with the Ten Commandments.

Forty captures the tension between what was and what is about to be. Something is about to die, and something, if it is able to surmount the difficulty, is about to be born. It is the moment the blade of grass pushes against a rock, struggling to spring forth onto the earth. It is the moment the newly formed bird beats against the eggshell, straining to be hatched. It is the moment the caterpillar pushes against the cocoon, struggling to emerge as a butterfly.

## THE HEXAGRAM

|       | Trigram | Name  | Image   | Attribute   | Family     |
|-------|---------|-------|---------|-------------|------------|
| Upper |         | Chaos | Water   | Danger      | Second Son |
| Lower |         | Word  | Thunder | Life Giving | First Son  |

The hexagram consists of the Word trigram below and the Chaos trigram above. The image of Word is Thunder, with an upward energy flow. The image of Chaos is Water, with a downward energy flow. Thus the energies of the two trigrams are in opposition to each other. Thunder and water fill the air. It is a frightening time. But eventually the rain ends, and new growth emerges from the parched earth.

## THE ARCHETYPE

There is a time…

- To recognize that the darkness and chaos before birth is a difficult time, and even more difficult because something great is struggling to be born.
- To remember that nothing can be born before its time. If the chick emerges before its struggle is complete, it will not have the strength to survive.
- To seek support from those who are wise in the ways of birth.
- To actively participate in the birth process.
- To take the time to sort through the chaos; to arrange and organize; and to separate and unite.

Now is that time.

## THE LINES

### MOVING LINE IN THE FIRST POSITION

A moving line in the bottom position reminds of the danger of prematurely pushing past that which blocks birth. This does not mean giving up. It does mean taking the time to pause, reflect, and regroup. Good helpers are needed. Finding such helpers requires humility. With the right help, the blockages can be overcome.

### MOVING LINE IN THE SECOND POSITION

A moving line in the second position gives hope. In the midst of difficulties and blockages, one appears who seems to offer an irresistible solution to all our problems. Although this seems too good to be true, the offer is genuine. That does not mean, however, that the offer should be accepted, at least at this time. The line cautions that obligations we take on could later cause new problems. There is no rush; patience is called for. Time needs to work its course. Eventually the chaos will dissipate and the goals will be achievable.

### MOVING LINE IN THE THIRD POSITION

A moving line in the third position cautions that when wandering in a strange place without a guide, it is easy to get lost. The wise one closely observes the present to know how the future will unfold. Sometimes one must step aside from one's goals rather than risk failure by relentlessly and forcefully pursuing them before the time is right.

## MOVING LINE IN THE FOURTH POSITION

A moving line in the fourth position suggests that it is our duty to act even though we lack sufficient power. We can use this opportunity to make connections. This is not the time for either Ego or false humility. Wisdom will show when it is time to take the first step, even when that step requires letting go of things. Finding the right helper will make everything much easier.

## MOVING LINE IN THE FIFTH POSITION

A moving line in the fifth position warns that this is not the time to try to express our intentions. In these conditions, our intentions will be distorted and misunderstood. We are warned to be cautious, methodical, and unobtrusive. This is not the time to force our agenda. We are to use this time for faithful and methodical work carried out unobtrusively. This work will build trust and confidence over time, and once this happens, the obstructions will disappear.

## MOVING LINE IN THE SIXTH POSITION

A moving line in the top position encourages us not to give up. Some are not strong enough to face the difficulties at the beginning of a project. They get hopelessly stuck and give up. This is unfortunate, because they will not realize their goals.

## NOTES

Wilhelm/Baynes calls this archetype *Difficulty at the Beginning*. Pearson calls this archetype *Sprouting*. Pearson describes the image of a sprout, "pallid and weak, bent over and exhausted from the effort of pushing through the earth." Barrett also calls this archetype *Sprouting*, saying, "The Creative drive of heaven and earth joins together and grows. It's tiny, scarcely born, but burgeoning with life and a great desire to attain full growth."

# Archetype 4: Youthful Exuberance

As he was setting out on a journey, a man ran up and knelt before him, and asked him, "Good Teacher, what must I do to inherit eternal life?" Jesus said to him, "Why do you call me good? No one is good but God alone. You know the commandments: 'You shall not murder; You shall not commit adultery; You shall not steal; You shall not bear false witness; You shall not defraud; Honor your father and mother.'" He said to him, "Teacher, I have kept all these since my youth." Jesus, looking at him, loved him and said, "You lack one thing; go, sell what you own, and give the money to the poor, and you will have treasure in heaven; then come, follow me."

—Mark 10:17–22

## THE READING

The reading focuses on the rich young man at the moment when he asks Jesus the secret to "eternal life," or, as we understand it, a life grounded in the eternal.

The young man is enthusiastic about following God. He has heard about this new itinerant teacher. People say that he makes the lame walk, the blind see. People say he has the secret to eternal life. When the teacher comes to his town, the young man is excited. He goes to the teacher and kneels before him and asks his question. "Teacher, what must I do?" But the answer stops him cold. Now he is frozen, indecisive on whether to move forward or backward. Whichever way he moves, he will never be the same.

## THE HEXAGRAM

| | Trigram | Name | Image | Attribute | Family |
|---|---|---|---|---|---|
| Upper | ☶ | Stillness | Mountain | Resting | Third Son |
| Lower | ☵ | Chaos | Water | Danger | Second Son |

The upper trigram is Stillness, and the lower trigram is Chaos. The image is motion caught in confusion and stopping on the brink of chaos. This is the state of mind of the rich young man in the reading.

# THE ARCHETYPE
There is a time…

- To recognize that youth lacks wisdom and needs to learn from others.
- To seek a wise guide, and for that guide to give clear teachings that are grounded in God's Wisdom.
- To understand that it is the student's place to seek the guide, not the guide's place to seek the student.
- To refrain from asking repetitive questions that annoy the guide, and, if the student persists, for the guide to respond only with silence.

Now is that time.

# THE LINES

### MOVING LINE IN THE FIRST POSITION
A moving line in the bottom position further cautions on the inexperience and carelessness of youth. Youth must be educated on the seriousness of life and the need for discipline. Discipline begins with rules and laws. Without discipline, little can be accomplished in life. But discipline must seek to enlighten and not to suffocate with mindless repetition.

### MOVING LINE IN THE SECOND POSITION
A moving line in the second position evokes an image of a wise one who has no external power but great character. A wise one treats the weaker and less experienced with kindness and love. Inner strength combined with modesty are traits that serve well in directing others and achieving goals.

### MOVING LINE IN THE THIRD POSITION
A moving line in the third position warns one who is weak, inexperienced, and struggling to make a name not to lose one's way and to become attached to false idols. There is a temptation to follow a stronger personality and sacrifice one's integrity. This will cause great loss in dignity and serves neither party well. Be true to self and to God's calling.

### MOVING LINE IN THE FOURTH POSITION
A moving line in the fourth position warns youth that it is easy to be sidetracked by flashy but false idols. The rich young man was enamored of his wealth. The more Ego clings to false idols, the more difficult it is to hear Wisdom's voice. Great inner discipline is required to keep Ego in check. A wise teacher may need to resort to humiliation to put Ego in its place so that real discernment can occur.

MOVING LINE IN THE FIFTH POSITION

A moving line in the fifth position advises the inexperienced one to set Ego aside and seek instruction from a wise teacher in an unassuming and childlike way.

MOVING LINE IN THE SIXTH POSITION

A moving line in the top position advises that it is sometimes necessary to punish wrongdoing. This punishment should never be done in rage; it should be directed at correcting a specific problem and guarding against unjustified excesses. The punishment itself must be appropriate to the transgression. Discernment is required to understand the necessary degree of punishment. Punishment can be a means of restoring balance but, if left to Ego, it can also become a path to tyranny.

## NOTES

Wilhelm/Baynes calls this archetype *Youthful Folly*. Pearson calls this archetype *New Grass*. Barrett calls this archetype *Not Knowing*. Barrett says, "To be small and ignorant is a creative, harmonious way to engage with your world."

# Archetype 5: Waiting

On the third day there was a wedding in Cana of Galilee, and the mother of Jesus was there. Jesus and his disciples had also been invited to the wedding. When the wine gave out, the mother of Jesus said to him, "They have no wine." And Jesus said to her, "Woman, what concern is that to you and to me? My hour has not yet come."

—John 2:1–4

## THE READING

This reading centers on the tension between Mary pushing Jesus forward and Jesus holding back. The young Mary was promised by God's angel that her son "will be great, and will be called the Son of the Most High, and the Lord God will give to him the throne of his ancestor David. He will reign over the house of Jacob forever, and of his kingdom there will be no end (Luke 1:32–35)."

These words sounded nice, but Jesus is now past thirty. Most men his age have grandchildren. Other than Jesus showing some precocious speaking ability and gathering a motley crew of hungry followers, Mary has seen no sign of God's promise being fulfilled. She is frustrated. She is tired of waiting. But still her son says his time has not come.

## THE HEXAGRAM

| | Trigram | Name | Image | Attribute | Family |
|---|---|---|---|---|---|
| Upper | | Chaos | Water | Danger | Second Son |
| Lower | | God | Heaven | Strength | Father |

The images of the two trigrams are Water above and Heaven below. The rain will come and nourish the entire earth. But rain comes in its own time. It cannot be hurried.

The attributes of the two trigrams are Strength below and Danger above. Strength in the face of danger waits until the time is right, whereas weakness in the face of danger grows agitated and acts too early.

## THE ARCHETYPE
There is a time…

- To wait with the inner certainty that the goal will be reached.
- To know that in the face of danger, pushing forward gains nothing.
- To wait for destiny to unfold and to not worry about or try to shape the future.
- To face things exactly as they are and wait for the path to show itself.
- To know that once the path is found and the time is right, then and only then will it be time for action.
- To spend this time preparing the body and soul for what will come.

Now is that time.

## THE LINES

### MOVING LINE IN THE FIRST POSITION
A moving line in the bottom position reassures that although there is a sense that something bad is getting ready to happen, actual danger is still in the distance. Instead of worrying, we should spend this time living as normally as possible. Worrying will just result in energy being wasted and errors being made.

### MOVING LINE IN THE SECOND POSITION
A moving line in the second position brings a warning that danger is getting closer. Disagreements begin. Conditions are ripe for general unrest, with one blaming the other. Only calmness will bring peace and harmony. Slander is not to be dignified. If we do not feed it, it will die away on its own.

### MOVING LINE IN THE THIRD POSITION
A moving line in the third position warns of a truly dangerous situation. Without strength to achieve the destination, we are trapped in a vulnerable position. Failure is not certain, but caution and a sense of the seriousness of the situation are absolutely needed to avert a disaster.

### MOVING LINE IN THE FOURTH POSITION
A moving line in the fourth position is ominous. The situation is extremely dangerous, a matter of life and death. Somebody will be hurt. Surrounded, there is no way forward and no way back. There is nothing left to do but let fate unfold. Any move will only make the situation worse.

## MOVING LINE IN THE FIFTH POSITION

A moving line in the fifth position reminds that even when danger is all around, there are intervals of relative peace. With the wisdom to withdraw from danger, these opportunities can fortify for the struggle to come. Enjoy the moment but be not deflected from the ultimate goal. People can't work without rest and recreation, but resting does not mean losing sight of the cause. Perseverance will be needed to achieve success.

## MOVING LINE IN THE SIXTH POSITION

A moving line in the top position says the time of waiting is over; the danger is now here. The worst imaginable has happened. Everything seems to have been in vain. It is time to yield to the inevitable. But things take an unforeseen turn. Outside intervention arrives. Is it good news or bad news? This is the time for alertness, not withdrawal. Greet each new turn with respect and thereby avoid danger. Sometimes salvation comes in forms that are difficult to recognize.

# NOTES

Wilhelm/Baynes, Pearson, and Barrett all call this archetype *Waiting*. Pearson says, "Waiting is rarely easy…so we should instead focus on the simple daily pleasures."

# Archetype 6: Conflict

Though I am bold enough in Christ to command you to do your duty, yet I would rather appeal to you on the basis of love—and I, Paul, do this as an old man, and now also as a prisoner of Christ Jesus. I am appealing to you for my child, Onesimus, whose father I have become during my imprisonment. Formerly he was useless to you, but now he is indeed useful both to you and to me. I am sending him, that is, my own heart, back to you. I wanted to keep him with me, so that he might be of service to me in your place during my imprisonment for the gospel; but I preferred to do nothing without your consent, in order that your good deed might be voluntary and not something forced.

—Philemon 1:9–14

## THE READING

This reading describes the conflict between Paul and Philemon, a wealthy Roman convert to Christianity. The conflict is over Onesimus, one of Philemon's slaves, whom Paul has converted to Christianity. Onesimus has fled to Paul for sanctuary. Paul wants Onesimus freed. Philemon doesn't.

Paul can use his authority to order Philemon to free Onesimus. But Philemon is wealthy and a major supporter of his local church. Paul doesn't want to offend a wealthy donor. And if Philemon is offended, it won't be Paul bearing the brunt of his anger. It will be Onesimus and the local church. So Paul doesn't attack the issue directly, but instead uses gentle persuasion and subtle guilt and appeals to higher authorities to resolve the conflict.

# THE HEXAGRAM

| | Trigram | Name | Image | Attribute | Family |
|---|---|---|---|---|---|
| Upper | ▬▬▬ | God | Heaven | Strength | Father |
| Lower | ▬ ▬ | Chaos | Water | Danger | Second Son |

The upper trigram, God, has the image of heaven. Heaven's energy moves upward. The lower trigram, Chaos, has the image of water. Water moves downward. Thus the two trigrams are moving away from each other, causing conflict.

# THE ARCHETYPE

There is a time…

- To understand that conflict occurs when one feels in the right, but is opposed.
- To be willing to meet the opponent halfway.
- To meet conflict not head-on, but with gentleness.
- To reduce conflict by taking great care and consideration of the other's feelings.
- To worry less about being right and more about being clearheaded.
- To take time to build the unity that will be needed to achieve goals.
- To ensure the spiritual needs of the individuals and the group are in harmony, thereby removing the causes of conflict before the conflict becomes manifest.
- To recognize that one who relies on cunning and determination will inevitably cause conflict.

Now is that time.

# THE LINES

## MOVING LINE IN THE FIRST POSITION
A moving line in the bottom position suggests conflict is in its initial stage, and the best thing to do is simply to drop the issue. This is especially true when facing a stronger adversary. There is too much of a risk of creating a crisis. A fire with no fuel dies out.

MOVING LINE IN THE SECOND POSITION

A moving line in the second position warns that the enemy is stronger that it seems. It is the time for retreat. Ego tells us to fight and defend our honor. Wisdom tells us that fighting against overwhelming strength brings defeat, not only on ourselves but on others who will inevitably be dragged into the conflict. Accommodation, not aggression, is called for.

MOVING LINE IN THE THIRD POSITION

A moving line in the third position suggests an expanding influence, but also an expanding danger. Wariness is called for when laying claim to things that belong to others. Things can only be held that are acquired through Wisdom and inner strength. These things can never be taken away. This is not the time to seek fame for accomplishments. It is the time to let fame go to those who care about it.

MOVING LINE IN THE FOURTH POSITION

A moving line in the fourth position points to one who is not at peace with God. Ego tempts the antagonist to escalate the conflict. This seems reasonable because of a strong position. But this will ultimately fail, because Wisdom knows who is really in the right. Therefore it is a time for acceptance of fate. Ultimately this leads to a greater grounding in God, which is more valuable than whatever could have been achieved through force.

MOVING LINE IN THE FIFTH POSITION

A moving line in the fifth position suggests a way out of the dilemma. There is an arbiter who is powerful and just and respected by both sides. The dispute can be turned over to this arbiter with confidence. Whoever is right will be vindicated. Whoever is wrong will be spared the loss of honor. All works out well.

MOVING LINE IN THE SIXTH POSITION

A moving line in the top position is ominous. This line points to one who has carried the conflict to its bitter end and has apparently triumphed. But the glory is short lived. The victor can never rest; new attacks will continuously pop up. This conflict has no end.

## NOTES

Wilhelm/Baynes and Pearson both call this archetype *Strife*. Barrett calls this archetype *Arguing*. Pearson says, "This is a time to take shelter and cut your losses."

# Archetype 7: The Army

Once when Joshua was near Jericho, he looked up and saw a man standing before him with a drawn sword in his hand. Joshua went to him and said to him, "Are you one of us, or one of our adversaries?" He replied, "Neither; but as commander of the army of the Lord I have now come." And Joshua fell on his face to the earth and worshipped, and he said to him, "What do you command your servant, my lord?" The commander of the army of the Lord said to Joshua, "Remove the sandals from your feet, for the place where you stand is holy." And Joshua did so.

—Joshua 5:13–15

## THE READING

The reading describes a vision of Joshua. Joshua was one of Moses's commanders and trusted assistants. But now Moses is dead and Joshua is the leader of the Israelites. He has been charged with leading them out of the desert into the Promised Land. His first challenge now lies directly in front of him: the city of Jericho. He has been called by God to take this city. But how? The city is surrounded by walls that seem ten miles high and a mile thick. He stares at the mammoth fortress in front of him. How can he possibly conquer this well-fortified city? He then has this vision. He sees a man. The man tells Joshua that he is a commander of the army of God.

## THE HEXAGRAM

|       | Trigram | Name   | Image | Attribute | Family     |
|-------|---------|--------|-------|-----------|------------|
| Upper |         | Wisdom | Earth | Devotion  | Mother     |
| Lower |         | Chaos  | Water | Danger    | Second Son |

This hexagram is made up of the trigrams Chaos, on the bottom, and Wisdom, on the top. The image of Wisdom is Earth, and of Chaos, Water. This is a picture of water beneath the earth, in deep underground springs of great strength that can be called upon in times of need.

## THE ARCHETYPE
There is a time…

- To bring together a great mass of people and organize them into a cohesive force.
- To discipline those people not through force, but through devotion.
- To be sure that the commander has the full trust of the ruler.
- To gather spiritual strength that will capture the love of the people and flame their enthusiasm for the difficult task at hand.
- To recognize the danger of the task and the possibility of destruction and devastation.
- To understand that war is to be used only as a last resort.
- To remember that a prosperous people are a strong people.
- To rule gently and govern humanely.
- To be merciful in victory.

Now is that time.

## THE LINES

### MOVING LINE IN THE FIRST POSITION
A moving line in the bottom position reminds that any military enterprise starts by establishing order. Once it is clear that a valid cause exists, the troops must be organized and discipline must be established. Without organization and discipline, success is impossible.

### MOVING LINE IN THE SECOND POSITION
A moving line in the second position tells how the leader should lead. The leader of the army must be in the thick of the struggle and in touch with the soldiers, sharing the good as well as the bad. The leader also needs the recognition of the ultimate authority, just as Joshua in the reading was chosen by God. When receiving a decoration, the wise commander receives it on behalf of the whole army, and thus shares in the glory.

### MOVING LINE IN THE THIRD POSITION
A moving line in the third position warns that defeat occurs when someone other than the chosen leader interferes with the command. The proper chain of command serves an important purpose. When it is bypassed, defeat results.

## MOVING LINE IN THE FOURTH POSITION

A moving line in the fourth position recommends retreat in the face of overwhelming superior strength. The alternative is conquest and chaos. It is not a sign of courage to engage in a hopeless struggle; it is a sign of Ego.

## MOVING LINE IN THE FIFTH POSITION

A moving line in the fifth position suggests a response to an invasion that has occurred without provocation. When this has occurred, defense and even punishment are justified. But punishment must never degenerate into wanton slaughter. Even when one has fought well and with bravery, unnecessary cruelty leads to misfortune. The army must be directed and held in check by an experienced and compassionate leader who understands when to fight, when to punish, and when to forgive.

## MOVING LINE IN THE SIXTH POSITION

A moving line in the top position says that victory has been won, but even in victory, there are risks. When the spoils of war are divided, there is an opportunity for unscrupulous people to build a power base. This is avoided by paying them off in money rather than in power or privileges. Thus they are treated fairly but not given an opportunity to manipulate the situation.

# NOTES

Wilhelm/Baynes and Barrett also call this archetype *The Army*. Pearson calls this archetype *With a Multitude of Followers*, saying, "It is only with a vast multitude of followers and with full unity among them that effective political action is possible."

# Archetype 8: Holding Together

For where two or three are gathered in my name, I am there among them.

—Matthew 18:20

## THE READING

This reading recounts some of Jesus's final words. Jesus is close to the end of his ministry. He knows that within a short time he will be facing his death on the cross. He knows the impact this will have on his followers. So Jesus says the words that will provide solace not only to his living followers but also to millions of followers who are yet to be born.

## THE HEXAGRAM

|         | Trigram | Name    | Image   | Attribute | Family      |
|---------|---------|---------|---------|-----------|-------------|
| Upper   |         | Chaos   | Water   | Danger    | Second Son  |
| Lower   |         | Wisdom  | Earth   | Devotion  | Mother      |

This hexagram is made up of the same two trigrams as *The Army* (archetype 7), but now the trigrams are reversed. Water is now above the earth, symbolically representing the ocean, that place where all rivers meet and become one.

## THE ARCHETYPE

There is a time…

- To unite with others, and through that union to complement and help one another.
- To form that union around a central respected person.
- To recognize the responsibility held by the central figure and the need for tremendous spirit, consistency, and strength.
- To have the humility not to take on the responsibility of guiding unless one is truly equal to the undertaking.
- To recognize the risk of chaos if a poor leader is chosen.

- To understand the importance of timing, for while a strong union attracts the uncommitted, newcomers lack the shared experiences that bond others.

- To understand that the strength of the union depends on the purpose and meaning each of the members find in the union.

This is that time.

## THE LINES

### MOVING LINE IN THE FIRST POSITION

A moving line in the bottom position reminds us that sincerity and truthfulness are the foundations of relationships. This attitude shows itself not in fancy talk but through calm inner strength grounded in Wisdom. This strength creates a magnetism that seems to attract blessings from the universe.

### MOVING LINE IN THE SECOND POSITION

A moving line in the second position tells us the way to respond to God's call is with dedication and inner conviction. This creates an inner peace and dignity that fosters positive relationships with others. Relationships driven by the hope of gain are grounded in Ego, not God. These relationships will bear poor fruit.

### MOVING LINE IN THE THIRD POSITION

A moving line in the third position shows how to deal with the inevitable company of those who do not follow Wisdom's way. At such times, we must be careful not to be drawn back into our old patterns. We can't avoid people of darkness, so the best approach is to be social without being intimate. True intimacy must be reserved for those whose path we share.

### MOVING LINE IN THE FOURTH POSITION

A moving line in the fourth position is positive. The relationship with the one who holds the union together is now well established. It is right and proper to be open about our dedication. We must remain constant in our dedication and not allow ourselves to be led astray.

### MOVING LINE IN THE FIFTH POSITION

A moving line in the fifth position depicts one of great influence. Some are attracted, some are not. It is their choice. No threats are necessary. Opinions can be expressed. Those who are meant to be part of the union will stay; those who aren't won't.

## MOVING LINE IN THE SIXTH POSITION

A moving line in the top position counsels care in the beginning. Every journey begins with a single first step. If one missteps in the beginning, there is little hope of correcting the path later. When building a union, complete and full devotion are needed from the beginning. If that opportunity is missed, by the time the error is realized it will be too late.

## NOTES

Wilhelm/Baynes calls this archetype *Holding Together (Union)*. Pearson calls this archetype *Closeness with Others*. Barrett calls this archetype *Seeking Union*. Barrett says, "To seek union is to search for connection and belonging, discovering how it all fits together and creating a new world out of relationships."

# Archetype 9: Small Gathering

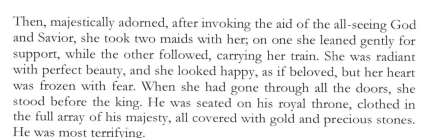

Then, majestically adorned, after invoking the aid of the all-seeing God and Savior, she took two maids with her; on one she leaned gently for support, while the other followed, carrying her train. She was radiant with perfect beauty, and she looked happy, as if beloved, but her heart was frozen with fear. When she had gone through all the doors, she stood before the king. He was seated on his royal throne, clothed in the full array of his majesty, all covered with gold and precious stones. He was most terrifying.

Lifting his face, flushed with splendor, he looked at her in fierce anger. The queen faltered, and turned pale and faint, and collapsed on the head of the maid who went in front of her.

—Esther 15:1–7

## THE READING

Esther was the Jewish queen of the Persian king Achaemenid around 460 BCE. Her cousin had refused to bow down before Prince Haman because it would have violated his beliefs as a Jew. In retaliation, Haman ordered the killing of all the Jews in the Persian Empire. Esther was determined to save her people. She planned a series of banquets during which she would soften up the king and convince him to rescind the order. But first she had to convince the king to attend the banquets. This meant appearing before the king unbidden. Appearing before the king unbidden, as Esther well knew, was a crime punishable by death.

## THE HEXAGRAM

|       | Trigram | Name | Image | Attribute | Family |
|-------|---------|------|-------|-----------|--------|
| Upper |         | Spirit | Gentle Wind | Penetrating | First Daughter |
| Lower |         | God | Heaven | Strength | Father |

This hexagram consists of the Spirit above and its image of a Gentle Wind coupled with the strength of God below.

## THE ARCHETYPE
There is a time...

- To recognize than when in a position of weakness, only gentleness can restrain and subdue strength.
- To maintain the determination that will overcome the obstacles.
- To remain inwardly grounded in God, but to outwardly be as gentle and adaptable as a soft breeze.

Now is that time.

## THE LINES

### MOVING LINE IN THE FIRST POSITION
A moving line in the bottom position suggests that when strength is pressed, resistance is encountered. It is best to return to a way suited to the situation. This may be advance. This may be retreat. Call on Wisdom, not force, to bring about a positive outcome.

### MOVING LINE IN THE SECOND POSITION
A moving line in the second position suggests that although one desires to press forward, by looking at others one can see that the way is blocked. Thus pressing forward will only result in rejection. This is the time to retreat with others who share convictions.

### MOVING LINE IN THE THIRD POSITION
A moving line in the third position suggests the opposition is underestimated. Although the opposition is individually weak, collectively they are too strong to engage with. Because of sheer numbers, power lies with the weak. Their arguments are irrational and mean spirited, but even the wisest can make no headway under these circumstances. Trying to influence people who have turned their backs on Wisdom is pointless and undignified.

### MOVING LINE IN THE FOURTH POSITION
A moving line in the fourth position suggests how a counselor to a powerful leader should behave. The counselor should restrain the leader so that bloodshed is avoided. This is not an easy task. The way to accomplish this is to simply present the truth, dispassionately and honestly. The truth is enough; emotions will only get in the way of a peaceful outcome.

## MOVING LINE IN THE FIFTH POSITION

A moving line in the fifth position describes two partners bonded by loyalty. Each complements the other. For the weaker partner, loyalty consists of devotion. For the stronger partner, loyalty consists of trustworthiness. This relationship leads to the deepest kind of wealth. This wealth is not to be hoarded but is to be generously shared with friends and thus made even greater.

## MOVING LINE IN THE SIXTH POSITION

A moving line in the top position warns us about the fragile nature of success. Goals have been reached through the accumulation of small successes won because they were in accord with Wisdom's way. But these successes are fragile because they have not yet been bound together. Nothing can be added without jeopardizing what has been won. Now is the time to be content with what has been accomplished, knowing greater successes will come in time.

## NOTES

Wilhelm/Baynes calls this archetype *The Taming Power of the Small*. Pearson calls this archetype *The Smaller Herd*. She says the archetype describes "a time of great promise not yet fulfilled." Barrett calls the archetype *Small Taming* and says, "to tame is to restrain and also to nurture."

# Archetype 10: Careful Conduct

Then the Lord said, "How great is the outcry against Sodom and Gomorrah and how very grave their sin! I must go down and see whether they have done altogether according to the outcry that has come to me; and if not, I will know."

So the men turned from there, and went toward Sodom, while Abraham remained standing before the Lord. Then Abraham came near and said, "Will you indeed sweep away the righteous with the wicked? Suppose there are fifty righteous within the city; will you then sweep away the place and not forgive it for the fifty righteous who are in it? Far be it from you to do such a thing, to slay the righteous with the wicked, so that the righteous fare as the wicked! Far be that from you! Shall not the Judge of all the earth do what is just?" And the Lord said, "If I find at Sodom fifty righteous in the city, I will forgive the whole place for their sake."

Abraham answered, "Let me take it upon myself to speak to the Lord, I who am but dust and ashes. Suppose five of the fifty righteous are lacking? Will you destroy the whole city for lack of five?" And he said, "I will not destroy it if I find forty-five there."

Again he spoke to him, "Suppose forty are found there." He answered, "For the sake of forty I will not do it." Then he said, "Oh do not let the Lord be angry if I speak. Suppose thirty are found there." He answered, "I will not do it, if I find thirty there." He said, "Let me take it upon myself to speak to the Lord. Suppose twenty are found there." He answered, "For the sake of twenty I will not destroy it."

Then he said, "Oh do not let the Lord be angry if I speak just once more. Suppose ten are found there." He answered, "For the sake of ten I will not destroy it." And the Lord went his way, when he had finished speaking to Abraham; and Abraham returned to his place.

—Genesis 18:20–33

## THE READING

Abraham is in a good mood. God has just told him that he and Sarah, his wife, are soon to have a child. Normally this would not be unusual, but Sarah and Abraham are old. Sarah has long ago gone through menopause. Sarah actually thinks this is funny and laughs at the idea, but, as God tells them, "Is anything too wonderful for the Lord?" (Gen. 18:14)

Right after this exchange, God tells Abraham of his plan to destroy the city of Sodom because of its great wickedness. Perhaps Abraham is still giddy from his good news, but for whatever reason, he decides to try to convince God to spare Sodom. But this raises an interesting question. How does puny Abraham convince Almighty God to not do something that God has decided to do? The answer is *very carefully*. One can imagine God's amusement at Abraham using a careful combination of wit, guile, and God's own words to turn God's anger aside.

## THE HEXAGRAM

|  | Trigram | Name | Image | Attribute | Family |
|---|---|---|---|---|---|
| Upper | ☰ | God | Heaven | Strength | Father |
| Lower | ☱ | Wonder | Lake | Joy | Third Daughter |

The hexagram is composed of the father above and the youngest daughter below. The small and cheerful youngest daughter is manipulating the large and strong father figure. The direction of movement of the two hexagrams is upward, so the energy of the weakest is being directed at the strongest. Normally, this could be very dangerous, but because this is being done with joy and good humor, the strong figure takes it all in good humor.

## THE ARCHETYPE

There is a time...

- To tread very carefully when one has little power.
- To move a powerful person using joy, humor, and tact.
- To know that the difference in stature between the meek and the mighty must be natural and accepted by both. If the difference is unjust, then envy and struggle result.
- To not worry about social obligations and norms, but instead to embrace a simple and undemanding attitude.

- To understand that inner strength coupled with simplicity can accomplish a great deal.
- To reach for a goal that is in keeping with God's way and not driven by Ego.

Now is that time.

## THE LINES

### MOVING LINE IN THE FIRST POSITION
A moving line in the bottom position suggests that social conventions need not bind, as long as one has true humility and simple conduct. The situation may be weak in the beginning, but by cultivating inner strength and being satisfied with simplicity and modesty, progress will be blessed. But if one is unhappy with modest circumstances and seeks only to improve material comforts, then any gains will lead to arrogance and greed. Therefore the goal must not be just an outcome, but an outcome that is in accord with Wisdom's way.

### MOVING LINE IN THE SECOND POSITION
A moving line in the second position counsels withdrawal from the bustle of life. Seek nothing, ask nothing, and accept fate as it comes, and thus travel through life safely. Seek only God's company. Be content and free of entanglements.

### MOVING LINE IN THE THIRD POSITION
A moving line in the third position warns us that progress requires vision. Ignoring weaknesses and overestimating strength exposes one to great danger. Undertaking something beyond one's strength invites disaster. The only time plunging ahead regardless of ability can be justified is when battling for a noble idea. In this case, one is not being reckless; one is offering of oneself a sacrifice.

### MOVING LINE IN THE FOURTH POSITION
A moving line in the fourth position cautions of a dangerous situation. The power to prevail is here, but this power is impeded by an overly cautious attitude. The line tells us to have confidence in our abilities and push forward.

### MOVING LINE IN THE FIFTH POSITION
A moving line in the fifth position suggests cautious resolve. There is danger in moving forward, but as long as one maintains awareness of the danger, forward movement is possible.

## MOVING LINE IN THE SIXTH POSITION

A moving line in the top position says that the work is ended. Will the work yield good results? If the tree yields good fruit, then good will result. If the tree yields bad fruit, then bad will result.

## NOTES

Wilhelm/Baynes calls this archetype *Treading (Conduct)*. Pearson calls this archetype *Stepping*, as in "stepping on the tail of a tiger." Barrett calls this archetype *Treading*. Barrett says, "Look to the power and intensity you are drawn to in the situation: its specific danger is there, and also its potential gift."

# Archetype 11: Peace

The wolf shall live with the lamb,
the leopard shall lie down with the kid,
the calf and the lion and the fatling together,
and a little child shall lead them.

—Isaiah 11:6

## THE READING
This reading describes a world at peace. War is over. Hatred and bigotry are dim memories. The Kingdom of God has arrived. And the Messiah (Anointed One) who will lead us to this kingdom is not a king or a general. Their way is the way of war, not of peace. The Messiah who will lead us to this kingdom will be a little child.

## THE HEXAGRAM

|        | Trigram | Name   | Image  | Attribute | Family |
|--------|---------|--------|--------|-----------|--------|
| Upper  |         | Wisdom | Earth  | Devotion  | Mother |
| Lower  |         | God    | Heaven | Strength  | Father |

The lower trigram, God, has the image of Heaven. The upper trigram, Wisdom, has the image of Earth. Thus we have Earth supported by Heaven. This portrays wonderful fortune and success.

## THE ARCHETYPE
There is a time...

- To set aside anger and fighting and embrace peace and harmony.
- To enjoy the knowledge that heaven has arrived on earth and the two forces complement each other perfectly.
- To encourage harmony within social divisions.
- To not worry about evil, and let it depart on its own.

- To appreciate the peace and blessings that have come to all of God's creation.
- To control the flow of energy through a process of partitioning, dividing, and adjusting so that outcomes occur in their proper time and place and thereby increase in yield.

Now is that time.

## THE LINES

### MOVING LINE IN THE FIRST POSITION

A moving line in the bottom position suggests that in times of peace and prosperity, leaders are to bring like-minded people along. This is a time when wise ones can extend their influence. It is therefore a good time for the wise to go out into the world and accomplish worthwhile acts.

### MOVING LINE IN THE SECOND POSITION

A moving line in the second position suggests that both the great and the not so great can be used effectively. Wisdom shows us how to make use of those with lesser abilities; everybody can contribute something. In a time of peace, people come together and work as a cohesive whole, but if this results in cliques, peace is weakened. In times of prosperity, we can afford to undertake projects that make us apprehensive, such as visiting with those who are different and whom we have traditionally avoided. Peace is a time to attend to both immediate and future needs and to not allow the carefree times to tempt us to lower our diligence. Such laziness will increase the risk of danger later.

### MOVING LINE IN THE THIRD POSITION

A moving line in the third position reminds us that everything is subject to change. Times of peace are followed by times of discord. Evil can be held in check, but it always returns. Is this defeatist? No, it is just being aware of the way things are. Complacency is dangerous. Use this time to maintain diligence, build inner strength, and cultivate Wisdom.

### MOVING LINE IN THE FOURTH POSITION

A moving line in the fourth position reminds us that in times of peace, people of all social ranks interact with each other easily and spontaneously. This happens not by force, but because people have the inner conviction to follow God's will.

MOVING LINE IN THE FIFTH POSITION
A moving line in the fifth position suggests that in times of peace, social rank is no longer meaningful, and equality brings happiness and blessings.

MOVING LINE IN THE SIXTH POSITION
A moving line in the top position is a warning that the bad times mentioned in the third line have begun. The defenses have been breached. Armed resistance will be futile and will result in further collapse and chaos. The hour of doom has truly arrived. At such times, one must submit to fate, trust in God, and look to one's intimate friends for strength.

## NOTES
Wilhelm/Baynes and Pearson also call this archetype *Peace*. Barrett calls this archetype *Flow*, saying, "Creative force flows through the earth."

# Archetype 12: Despair

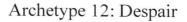

Then he [Jesus] said to them, "I am deeply grieved, even to death; remain here, and stay awake with me." And going a little farther, he threw himself on the ground and prayed, "My Father, if it is possible, let this cup pass from me; yet not what I want but what you want." Then he came to the disciples and found them sleeping.

—Matthew 26:38–41

## THE READING
This reading describes Jesus at his darkest moment. He knows he is about to die a horrible death. He has no idea if the seeds he has sown have fallen on fertile or barren ground. His closest disciples have shown over and over again how little they understand of his message. Very soon, it will fall on their shoulders to carry on his work, yet he can't even trust them to stay awake and keep him company in his hour of despair.

## THE HEXAGRAM

|       | Trigram | Name | Image | Attribute | Family |
|-------|---------|------|-------|-----------|--------|
| Upper | ☰ | God | Heaven | Strength | Father |
| Lower | ☷ | Wisdom | Earth | Devotion | Mother |

This hexagram has the same trigrams as the previous hexagram (*Peace*), but now the trigrams are reversed. The energy of God is upward, and that of Wisdom is downward. Whereas before their energy was directed toward each other, thus reinforcing each other, now their energy is pulling away from each other, and a great emptiness is left in between.

## THE ARCHETYPE

There is a time...

- To exist in a dark night of the soul, a time when it seems even God has deserted us.
- To feel abandoned, empty, and desolate.
- To understand that in times of darkness and confusion people are unable to hear Wisdom.
- To disengage from the darkness and build the light within.
- To realize that the weak and the harsh are now coming to power and to resist both their influences and temptations.

Now is that time.

## THE LINES

### MOVING LINE IN THE FIRST POSITION

A moving line in the bottom position counsels that when it is impossible to make one's influence count, the best thing to do is to simply withdraw. Others may follow. God is with those who hold true to their spiritual core.

### MOVING LINE IN THE SECOND POSITION

A moving line in the second position describes the way to deal with gridlock. Lesser people adjust by attempting to flatter and endure those in power. The wise one does not act this way. The wise one withdraws from the riffraff and is willing to suffer to remain true to principles.

### MOVING LINE IN THE THIRD POSITION

A moving line in the third position describes those who have risen to power despite ineptitude. Eventually they will recognize their inadequacy. Humiliation tames Ego. Once Ego has been brought under control, improvement can begin.

### MOVING LINE IN THE FOURTH POSITION

A moving line in the fourth position is auspicious. The time of gridlock is coming to an end, and positive progress is once again possible. What is needed now is a leader who is inspired by God rather than inspired by Ego. God's inspiration will lead to order, whereas Ego's inspiration can only lead to further disorder.

## MOVING LINE IN THE FIFTH POSITION

A moving line in the fifth position announces that the chosen one has arrived. The possibility of restoring order exists. But periods of transition are precarious, and success requires great caution. Caution is appropriate; failure would be terrible. There are still many risks, each of which requires a contingency.

## MOVING LINE IN THE SIXTH POSITION

A moving line in the top position reassures us that the period of gridlock does not last forever. But it also tells us that it will not end by itself. A wise one is needed to bring it to an end, and ongoing effort is required to bring about peace. But through creativity and Wisdom, the negative energy can be reversed, and despair can be transformed into peace.

# NOTES

Wilhelm/Baynes calls this archetype *Standstill (Stagnation)*. Pearson calls this archetype *Obstruction (Stagnation)*, and translates, "This is a time of great losses and small gains." Barrett calls this archetype *Blocked*, saying this is a time when "your very best and strongest efforts come to nothing."

# Archetype 13: Fellowship

Day by day, as they spent much time together in the temple, they broke bread at home and ate their food with glad and generous hearts, praising God and having the goodwill of all the people. And day by day the Lord added to their number those who were being saved.

—Acts 2:43–47

## THE READING
This reading describes a holy center unifying a committed fellowship of people. A center that asks little and offers much ("my yoke is easy and my burden light") gives stability to the fellowship.

## THE HEXAGRAM

|        | Trigram | Name   | Image  | Attribute | Family          |
|--------|---------|--------|--------|-----------|-----------------|
| Upper  | ☰       | God    | Heaven | Strength  | Father          |
| Lower  | ☲       | Christ | Fire   | Light     | Second Daughter |

The lower trigram is Christ whose attribute is Light. The upper trigram is God, whose attribute is Strength. This gives us Strength grounded in Light. The strength is in the people who make up the fellowship. The light is the foundation that holds the fellowship together.

## THE ARCHETYPE
There is a time…

- To align a strong fellowship to God's purpose.
- To choose a leader who carries God's light faithfully and whose core is yielding and soft.
- To know that a fellowship built around such a leader can accomplish great things.
- To know the difference between a united fellowship and a random gathering of individuals.

Now is that time.

# THE LINES

### MOVING LINE IN THE FIRST POSITION

A moving line in the bottom position teaches that a fellowship grows out of shared experiences, aims, and visions. If the fellowship allows cliques to form, discord soon follows. The challenge is to ensure that the core values of the fellowship remain inclusive, and that transparency in the organization of the fellowship is maintained.

### MOVING LINE IN THE SECOND POSITION

A moving line in the second position warns of factions forming based on Ego-serving interests. Such factions are exclusive; instead of welcoming all, they unite some groups while excluding others. Because these factions are driven by Ego rather than God's purpose, they cannot lead anywhere but failure.

### MOVING LINE IN THE THIRD POSITION

A moving line in the third position is unfortunate: the fellowship is unraveling. Members do not trust each other, and cliques are planning secret ambushes. In such a situation, a problem member cannot be approached by the normal rules of engagement. The doubts of the few will spread to the many, and this will threaten the stability of the fellowship. The longer this continues, the worse the situation becomes.

### MOVING LINE IN THE FOURTH POSITION

A moving line in the fourth position brings good news. The quarreling described in the previous line is coming to an end. Reconciliation is closer. There are still divisions and confrontations, but the issues creating the discord have been addressed. There are still challenges ahead, but instead of causing further discord, these challenges will help unite the fellowship.

### MOVING LINE IN THE FIFTH POSITION

A moving line in the fifth position reassures two people who are separated but whose hearts are still one. Circumstances are keeping them apart. Yet despite all the obstacles, they remain true to each other and allow nothing to get in the way of their commitment to each other.

## MOVING LINE IN THE SIXTH POSITION

A moving line in the top position warns the fellowship lacks dedication and is splintering into factions. The original fellowship now includes only those who share physical proximity. While the ultimate goal of the fellowship has not yet been reached, progress is still possible. It is time to set Ego aside and join together in a greater community.

## NOTES

Wilhelm/Baynes calls this archetype *Fellowship with Men*. Pearson calls this archetype *Friendship*. Barrett calls this archetype *People in Harmony*. Pearson translates, "You should observe differences in all things, even in friendship."

# Archetype 14: Wealth

God said to him, "Because you have asked this, and have not asked for yourself long life or riches, or for the life of your enemies, but have asked for yourself understanding to discern what is right, I now do according to your word. Indeed I give you a wise and discerning mind; no one like you has been before you and no one like you shall arise after you. I give you also what you have not asked, both riches and honor all your life; no other king shall compare with you."

—1 Kings 3:10–14

## THE READING

This reading describes King Solomon at this early point in his reign. Solomon has a dream in which he meets God. God promises to grant Solomon whatever he wants. Solomon doesn't ask for wealth or power. Instead he says, "I am but a little child. I do not know how to go out or come in. And your servant is in the midst of your people whom you have chosen, a great people, too many to be numbered or counted for multitude. Give your servant therefore an understanding mind to govern your people that I may discern between good and evil" (1 Kings 3:7–9). At this pivotal moment, Solomon chooses wisdom over wealth and thereby will be granted both. However, it is his great wisdom for which he will be remembered.

## THE HEXAGRAM

|       | Trigram | Name  | Image  | Attribute | Family          |
|-------|---------|-------|--------|-----------|-----------------|
| Upper |         | Christ | Fire  | Light     | Second Daughter |
| Lower |         | God   | Heaven | Strength  | Father          |

The trigrams indicate that strength, the attribute of God, and light, the attribute of Christ, are now united. This indicates a time favoring strength on the inside and clarity and culture on the outside. Strength is present, but it is expressed as light.

## THE ARCHETYPE
There is a time…

- To feel the alignment of strength and light and know that the light shines far.
- To feel the synergy between strength and clarity.
- To fight against evil and to promote Wisdom's way.
- To understand that a true leader's strength is tempered with kindness, modesty, and wisdom.
- To manage great wealth with great wisdom and use it in accordance with God's will.

Now is that time.

## THE LINES

### MOVING LINE IN THE FIRST POSITION
A moving line in the bottom position tells us that wealth is coming but is still in its early phases. Therefore it has not yet been challenged, and one must not be overconfident; there are still many difficulties to be overcome. One can overcome these difficulties if one stays diligent, but if one gives in to Ego, conceit and waste are likely to follow.

### MOVING LINE IN THE SECOND POSITION
A moving line in the second position counsels that wealth has value only if it is used effectively and for good purposes. Able and willing helpers are needed, and, once found, they can be given substantial responsibility. This will help achieve desired outcomes.

### MOVING LINE IN THE THIRD POSITION
A moving line in the third position tells us that the one with wealth must be generous. Possessions are not to be seen as personal property, but as God's property that has been loaned to us to help us accomplish God's will. Possessions thought of in this way have great energy. Possessions hoarded for private use wither and disappear. The petty person cannot understand this and becomes possessed by the possessions.

### MOVING LINE IN THE FOURTH POSITION
A moving line in the fourth position warns that when one is caught between the conflicting whims of the rich and powerful, one is in a dangerous position. One can only survive this by remaining fully centered and not giving in to Ego.

MOVING LINE IN THE FIFTH POSITION

A moving line in the fifth position is very favorable. People are willing to be led by an honest and sincere leader. But the dedication of the people can degenerate into insolence, and once insolence gains a foothold, it can quickly spread. But force is not the correct response to insolence; dignity is.

MOVING LINE IN THE SIXTH POSITION

A moving line in the top position portrays one who, though in full possession of wealth and at the height of power, remains modest, helps others, and gives honor to God. When success is approached this way, God's blessings will come in abundance.

## NOTES

Wilhelm/Baynes calls this archetype *Possession in Great Measure*. Both Pearson and Barrett call this archetype *Great Possession*. Pearson says, "With great possessions come great responsibilities to one's neighbors, and to the highest powers."

# Archetype 15: Modesty

"And whenever you pray, do not be like the hypocrites; for they love to stand and pray in the synagogues and at the street corners, so that they may be seen by others. Truly I tell you, they have received their reward. But whenever you pray, go into your room and shut the door and pray to your Father who is in secret; and your Father who sees in secret will reward you."

—Matthew 6:5–6

## THE READING

Jesus is telling us not to make public displays of prayer. Prayer is not about trying to impress others; it is about deepening our relationship with God. When we tell others how wonderful we are because we are better Christians than they are, we are not using prayer to deepen our relationship with God. We are using prayer to deepen our relationship with Ego.

This same admonition applies to charitable work. Charitable work is the public manifestation of faith. This includes taking care of the poor, healing the sick, and visiting those in prison. Are we doing these as a public manifestation of faith or as a public manifestation of Ego? Work done as a manifestation of faith nurtures faith. Work done as a manifestation of Ego nurtures Ego.

As Christians, we understand that our abilities are not our abilities; they are abilities given to us for a purpose.

## THE HEXAGRAM

|       | Trigram | Name | Image | Attribute | Family |
|-------|---------|------|-------|-----------|--------|
| Upper | ☷ | Wisdom | Earth | Devotion | Mother |
| Lower | ☶ | Stillness | Mountain | Resting | Third Son |

The hexagram is made up of the trigrams Stillness below and Wisdom above. Stillness is the foundation of Wisdom. This is the picture of modesty.

## THE ARCHETYPE

There is a time…

- To embrace modesty.
- To meditate on the lesson of nature: God makes full that which is empty and empties that which is full.
- To reduce the extremes that cause social discontent.
- To understand that the nature of modesty doesn't mean not doing great things, but not doing them to feed Ego.
- To remain modest despite a high position and thereby shine with wisdom.

Now is that time.

## THE LINES

### MOVING LINE IN THE FIRST POSITION
A moving line in the bottom position warns that a dangerous task is even more dangerous when Ego's self-serving claims, demands, and considerations are allowed to muddy the waters. Ego must be checked at the door. This must be attended to quickly, simply, and with attention to God's will.

### MOVING LINE IN THE SECOND POSITION
A moving line in the second position teaches that when modesty is reflected in speech and behavior, God's blessings follow. Then one can resist interference and have a lasting influence.

### MOVING LINE IN THE THIRD POSITION
A moving line in the third position contains the essence of this archetype. When one achieves great things, one earns recognition and distinction. Fame feeds Ego. Ego tells us to take on a superior attitude. Nobody loves or supports us when we act superior. Therefore it is critical to maintain modesty despite our achievements.

### MOVING LINE IN THE FOURTH POSITION
A moving line in the fourth position admonishes those who would use modesty as an excuse for not doing God's work. Moses tried this: "Who am I that I should go to Pharaoh and bring the Israelites out of Egypt?" (Exod. 4:11) Modesty is not about avoiding, but simply doing what needs to be done and recognizing all who have contributed.

MOVING LINE IN THE FIFTH POSITION

A moving line in the fifth position reminds that modesty is not to be confused with weakness. When one holds an important position, one must at times act forcefully. But that doesn't give one a license for boasting. The forceful actions are to be used only to achieve God's will, not to gratify one's Ego.

MOVING LINE IN THE SIXTH POSITION

A moving line in the top position says that modesty must be made manifest. This requires energy. When difficulties arise, Ego tells us to lay the blame on others. When Ego feels under attack, we draw back, feeling fear and self-pity. Ego tries to hide behind modesty. But true modesty inspires us to create order, to tame Ego, and provide discipline to ourselves and those around us. True modesty gives us the courage to stand up to Ego. Only then can we embrace the path God has set before us and accomplish that which God has chosen us to do.

## NOTES

Wilhelm/Baynes and Pearson both call this archetype *Modesty*. Barrett calls this archetype *Integrity*. Pearson says of this archetype, "Modesty is the crucial quality that enables us to remember our own limits and to value all we can learn from others."

# Archetype 16: Enthusiasm

A very large crowd spread their cloaks on the road, and others cut branches from the trees and spread them on the road. The crowds that went ahead of him and that followed were shouting,
"Hosanna to the Son of David!
Blessed is the one who comes in the name of the Lord!
Hosanna in the highest heaven!"

—Matthew 21:8–9

## THE READING
This reading describes the energy level of the crowd as they watch Jesus enter Jerusalem on a donkey. They can feel the great love Jesus has for them. They are excited and ebullient. Their devotion to Jesus is contagious.

## THE HEXAGRAM

|       | Trigram | Name   | Image   | Attribute   | Family    |
|-------|---------|--------|---------|-------------|-----------|
| Upper | ☰ ☰     | Word   | Thunder | Life Giving | First Son |
| Lower | ☷ ☷     | Wisdom | Earth   | Devotion    | Mother    |

The lower trigram is Wisdom, whose image is Earth. Earth, in this hexagram, refers to one who is grounded. The upper trigram is Word, whose image is Thunder. Thunder is the sound of Enthusiasm.

# THE ARCHETYPE

There is a time...

- To watch devotion gain momentum and erupt into enthusiasm.
- To understand that enthusiasm is directed at one who holds the interests of the people most dear.
- To take advantage of the enthusiasm to unify popular movements, to invigorate helpers, and to achieve great goals.
- To encourage enthusiasm by treating others with respect.
- To recognize the power of music to bring people together joyfully and unleash bursts of creative energy.

Now is that time.

# THE LINES

### MOVING LINE IN THE FIRST POSITION
A moving line in the bottom position warns of an arrogant person who tries to get ahead by boasting about connections. When enthusiasm is rooted in Ego, it degenerates into arrogance. Arrogance leads away from God and causes disunity among the people.

### MOVING LINE IN THE SECOND POSITION
A moving line in the second position warns not to be misled by illusions or dazzled by enthusiasm but to remain centered and cultivate Wisdom. One must not flatter those higher or ignore those lower. It is important to watch for signs of good fortune or discord, and when either occurs, to take appropriate action immediately.

### MOVING LINE IN THE THIRD POSITION
A moving line in the third position describes a time of seeking a great leader and warns against ambivalence. There is a right time for approaching the leader, and when that moment occurs, there should be no hesitation.

### MOVING LINE IN THE FOURTH POSITION
A moving line in the fourth position describes one who is able to awaken enthusiasm through sureness and action. Self-confidence and sincerity attract people. But the enthusiasm must run in both directions; as the people are enthusiastic about the leader, the leader must also be enthusiastic about the people.

## MOVING LINE IN THE FIFTH POSITION

A moving line in the fifth position describes enthusiasm that is being obstructed. This obstruction is not necessarily bad. It may be offering protection from squandering energy at a time when energy is needed to maintain survival.

## MOVING LINE IN THE SIXTH POSITION

A moving line in the top position warns about being deluded by enthusiasm and having one's vision distorted. But if this happens, all is not lost. If one awakens from the delusion, change is possible and the right path can be found again.

## NOTES

Wilhelm/Baynes and Barrett call this archetype *Enthusiasm*. Pearson calls this archetype *Excess*. Barrett says, "The energetic charge of enthusiasm can be used to set great things in motion."

# Archetype 17: Following

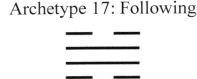

Now before the festival of the Passover, Jesus knew that his hour had come to depart from this world and go to the Father. Having loved his own who were in the world, he loved them to the end. The devil had already put it into the heart of Judas son of Simon Iscariot to betray him. And during supper Jesus, knowing that the Father had given all things into his hands, and that he had come from God and was going to God, got up from the table, took off his outer robe, and tied a towel around himself. Then he poured water into a basin and began to wash the disciples' feet and to wipe them with the towel that was tied around him.

—John 13:1–5

## THE IMAGE

Jesus is getting ready to go to his death. His death will only have meaning if his disciples carry his message of love, forgiveness, and reconciliation to the world. But will they follow through? Jesus knows that Judas will soon betray him. Peter will deny him, not once but three times. Most of his disciples will abandon him to die alone. What can he do to impress upon them how much he needs them and how important their work is? Should he browbeat them and tell them how worthless they have been? Should he threaten them with damnation if they do not follow through? But Jesus does none of these things. He gets up and washes their feet.

# THE HEXAGRAM

| | Trigram | Name | Image | Attribute | Family |
|---|---|---|---|---|---|
| Upper | | Wonder | Lake | Joy | Third Daughter |
| Lower | | Word | Thunder | Life Giving | First Son |

This hexagram is composed of the trigram Wonder above and the trigram Word below. The image of Word is Thunder, which denotes great power. The image of Wonder is Lake, which denotes receptivity. So we have the powerful thunder in the lower position, subservient to the "weaker" trigram above. This is the picture of this archetype, a great leader deferring to a weaker follower.

# THE ARCHETYPE

There is a time...

- To learn to serve so that one may learn to rule.
- To understand that by serving others, one builds commitment in one's followers.
- To know that those who follow willingly and joyfully will remain true, whereas those who follow from fear will soon fall away.
- To build one's following by adapting to the needs of the moment.
- To take the time to rest and regain strength.

Now is that time.

# THE LINES

## MOVING LINE IN THE FIRST POSITION
A moving line in the bottom position suggests that it is appropriate for the relationship between leader and follower to switch. The leader must empathize with and listen to the opinions of others. An effective leader cannot associate only with those who are of like mind. This does not mean giving up principles. It does mean being open to others' ideas.

## MOVING LINE IN THE SECOND POSITION
A moving line in the second position warns that one must be careful in choices for friends and close relationships. One can surround oneself with either positive or negative influences; one cannot do both.

MOVING LINE IN THE THIRD POSITION

A moving line in the third position suggests that when one connects with those who are wiser, one will lose connections with those who are inferior and superficial. This is part of the human growth process. But one must remain grounded in God. Otherwise it is easy to be led astray by impulsive desires.

MOVING LINE IN THE FOURTH POSITION

A moving line in the fourth position cautions that those who are attracted to an Ego-driven leader are not useful followers. They will gladly feed the Ego, but this leads only to further separation from God. Cultivate Wisdom, and see these people for who they are.

MOVING LINE IN THE FIFTH POSITION

A moving line in the fifth position reminds us that all people need something to follow that is beautiful and good.

MOVING LINE IN THE SIXTH POSITION

A moving line in the top position refers to a holy one who has set aside the demands of the world and embraced an interior peace. This line predicts that a follower appears who is simpatico with the holy one and will not leave until the holy one agrees to help. An eternal bond is formed between the holy one and the follower, and the holy one returns to help the follower further God's purpose.

## NOTES

Wilhelm/Baynes, Pearson, and Barrett all call this archetype *Following*. Barrett says, "Energy flows strongly into life's landscapes, bringing a great creative drive from the source through toward fulfillment."

# Archetype 18: Restoration

And all the people responded with a great shout when they praised the Lord, because the foundation of the house of the Lord was laid. But many of the priests and Levites and heads of families, old people who had seen the first house on its foundations, wept with a loud voice when they saw this house, though many shouted aloud for joy, so that the people could not distinguish the sound of the joyful shout from the sound of the people's weeping, for the people shouted so loudly that the sound was heard far away.

—Ezra 3:11–13

## THE READING

The First Temple was built by King Solomon and is described in 1 Kings 6. It was a magnificent affair, requiring the labors of over thirty thousand workers. The temple served as a holy worship place for God. Over time, a succession of kings appeared who allowed the temple to degenerate into idol worship. The people lost their divine vision and were weakened. Jerusalem was no longer able to defend itself effectively and was attacked repeatedly by the Babylonians. In 586 BCE, the Babylonians overwhelmed Jerusalem, burned the city, and destroyed Solomon's Temple. This left a great stain on the soul of the Israelites that would remain for seventy years, until the Second Temple was built on the same site. This reading describes the rebuilding of this temple.

## THE HEXAGRAM

|       | Trigram | Name | Image | Attribute | Family |
|-------|---------|------|-------|-----------|--------|
| Upper | ☶ | Stillness | Mountain | Resting | Third Son |
| Lower | ☴ | Spirit | Gentle Wind | Penetrating | First Daughter |

The upper trigram is Stillness, with the image of the rigid Mountain. The lower trigram is Spirit, with the image of Gentle Wind. Both trigrams are relatively passive. The inactivity results in decay, which now must be restored.

# THE ARCHETYPE
There is a time…

- To rebuild that which has been allowed to spoil.
- To realize that the rebuilding will take effort and will involve danger.
- To understand that the cause of the decay is the abuse of human freedom.
- To not move forward until the causes of decay are well understood.
- To stir up public opinion and reground the people in God.

Now is that time.

# THE LINES

### MOVING LINE IN THE FIRST POSITION
A moving line in the bottom position suggests that rigid adherence to tradition is the root cause of the decay. Fortunately, the decay has not progressed far and can still be remedied. This will take dedication and may involve danger, but now is the time to deal with the issue.

### MOVING LINE IN THE SECOND POSITION
A moving line in the second position tells us that mistakes made through weakness are the cause of the decay. In this case, gentler consideration and deeper reflection are called for.

### MOVING LINE IN THE THIRD POSITION
A moving line in the third position warns that we shouldn't be overly enthusiastic about the restoration. This enthusiasm has already resulted in discord. While not ideal, too much enthusiasm is better than too little. The future still looks good.

### MOVING LINE IN THE FOURTH POSITION
A moving line in the fourth position describes one who is too weak to take the necessary steps to stop the decay. Even though the decay is just starting to be visible, nothing can be done to stop it until it runs its course.

### MOVING LINE IN THE FIFTH POSITION
A moving line in the fifth position describes one who is confronted with corruption through neglect. This person is not strong enough alone to correct the decay, but with the help of others can at least address the corruption. This is a good start.

MOVING LINE IN THE SIXTH POSITION

A moving line in the top position suggests that not all are called to take an active role in correcting the problems of the world. Some are called instead to cultivate an inner Wisdom. This does not imply sitting around and criticizing what others are doing. It means cultivating the human values that will provide a foundation for the future.

## NOTES

Wilhelm/Baynes calls this archetype *Work on What Has Been Spoiled (Decay)*. Pearson calls this archetype *Branching Out*. Barrett calls this archetype *Corruption*. Pearson says, "We are urged here to encourage others in the development of their capabilities, to feed their desire for what is sound, and have virtue in themselves and in what they can do."

# Archetype 19: Approach

Moses was keeping the flock of his father-in-law Jethro, the priest of Midian; he led his flock beyond the wilderness, and came to Horeb, the mountain of God. There the angel of the Lord appeared to him in a flame of fire out of a bush; he looked, and the bush was blazing, yet it was not consumed. Then Moses said, "I must turn aside and look at this great sight, and see why the bush is not burned up." When the Lord saw that he had turned aside to see, God called to him out of the bush, "Moses, Moses!" And he said, "Here I am." Then he said, "Come no closer! Remove the sandals from your feet, for the place on which you are standing is holy ground." He said further, "I am the God of your father, the God of Abraham, the God of Isaac, and the God of Jacob." And Moses hid his face, for he was afraid to look at God.

—Exodus 3:1–6

## THE READING

There are a number of images captured in this reading.

First, we have Moses about to transition from lowness to greatness. Moses had been saved from infanticide as a baby, was adopted by a princess of Egypt, and became a trusted high official. Then he killed an Egyptian and had to flee for his life. He had been reduced to tending the flock of his father-in-law. But in this reading, God has called him to a new greatness that will far exceed anything Moses has yet experienced.

The second image captured in this reading is the idea of approach, especially the approach of that which is lower (Moses) to that which is greater (God).

Finally, we have a bit of condescension between the greater toward the lesser. "Do not come any closer," God tells Moses, "and remove your sandals." Moses does so, and hides his face.

# THE HEXAGRAM

| | Trigram | Name | Image | Attribute | Family |
|---|---|---|---|---|---|
| Upper | ☷ | Wisdom | Earth | Devotion | Mother |
| Lower | ☱ | Wonder | Lake | Joy | Third Daughter |

The lower trigram is Wonder. The upper trigram is Wisdom. Wonder approaches Wisdom with reverence.

# THE ARCHETYPE

There is a time...

- For the wise one to approach those who need wisdom and care.
- To look forward to the approach of spring.
- To remember that spring does not last forever and to prepare for the changes before they come.
- To master evil before it becomes manifest.

Now is that time.

# THE LINES

### MOVING LINE IN THE FIRST POSITION

A moving line in the bottom position suggests Wisdom is beginning to prevail and will strike a chord in upper circles. This encourages the able. It is appropriate to join in the momentum, but one must stay grounded in Wisdom and not allow Ego to get out of control.

### MOVING LINE IN THE SECOND POSITION

A moving line in the second position says that when one is invited to approach by God and is grounded in strength and Wisdom, a good outcome is likely. There is no need to worry about the future. Of course, everything is transitory, and what goes up must eventually come down. This is just the way things are. For now, things are moving in a positive direction, and as long as they remain guided by Wisdom, things will move forward. Everything suggests the path will be traversed swiftly, honestly, and bravely.

MOVING LINE IN THE THIRD POSITION

A moving line in the third position suggests caution. Although things are going well and a positive outcome is still likely, there is a danger of complacency. Ego says we can be easy-going and careless. If this happens, one must understand what has happened, turn away from Ego, and take one's responsibility seriously. Take action, but don't panic. It is not too late to make things right.

MOVING LINE IN THE FOURTH POSITION

A moving line in the fourth position observes that those in the higher position are favorable to the ideas of those in the lower position. The time is right for an able one to be drawn into the circle of influence.

MOVING LINE IN THE FIFTH POSITION

A moving line in the fifth position advises those with authority to recognize their limitations and to look to others who have the necessary expertise. Once these experts are on board, they must be given freedom and not be micromanaged. This is the way to build successful teams.

MOVING LINE IN THE SIXTH POSITION

A moving line in the top position describes a wise one who has put the world behind and withdrawn from life. This line suggests that it may be time for the wise one to return to active participation in life. The wise one's insight is needed. And the wise one also benefits through this interaction.

## NOTES

Wilhelm/Baynes also calls this archetype *Approach*. Pearson calls this archetype *The Forest* and describes the strength of the forest and the great perspective the forest implies. Barrett calls this archetype *Nearing*, saying, "There are two strands of meaning here: the approach of a greater spirit or presence in an ongoing process of growth, and your approach as the one who pays attention and takes responsibility."

# Archetype 20: Contemplation

In the morning, while it was still very dark, he got up and went out to a deserted place, and there he prayed.

—Mark 1:35

## THE READING

This reading describes Jesus going off by himself and inviting Wisdom through deep contemplation. Jesus frequently went by himself to pray in silence. This is the role model he offers for our own relationship with God.

## THE HEXAGRAM

|       | Trigram | Name | Image | Attribute | Family |
|-------|---------|------|-------|-----------|--------|
| Upper |         | Spirit | Gentle Wind | Penetrating | First Daughter |
| Lower |         | Wisdom | Earth | Devotion | Mother |

The upper trigram is Spirit, with the attribute of Penetrating. The lower trigram is Wisdom, with the attribute of Devotion. This is the image of contemplation: a deep penetration into the nature of God. In this way, we show our devotion.

## THE ARCHETYPE

There is a time…

- To gather information and cultivate wisdom in silence and deep inner concentration.
- To observe what is in a detached, Egoless manner.
- To refrain from activity, making decisions, and pursuing goals.
- To reconnect with the divine and mysterious presence of God.
- To inspire others through concern for their well-being.
- To reconnect with the lives of the people.
- To hear God speaking in the silence of the present moment.
- To cultivate great clarity of thought and purpose through meditation.

Now is that time.

## THE LINES

### MOVING LINE IN THE FIRST POSITION

A moving line in the bottom position portrays a wise one who is not recognized. However, all benefit from the wisdom, even those who do not recognize its source. It is acceptable for the ignorant masses to fail to recognize the source of divine wisdom, but it is not acceptable for those who have the capacity to understand. Jesus calls out, "Let those who have ears, hear."

### MOVING LINE IN THE SECOND POSITION

A moving line in the second position suggests contemplation is being limited by Ego, by the tendency to relate everything to oneself rather than to understand others. For a follower, this is understandable. But for a leader, such a narrow, Ego-driven way of seeing things leads to harm.

### MOVING LINE IN THE THIRD POSITION

A moving line in the third position indicates one who is ready to make the transition from education to Wisdom. One is finally able to understand that the world one sees is the world one creates, and if one wants true Wisdom, one must start by creating purity in oneself. But beware! This does not mean preoccupation with oneself; it means understanding one's full capacity to help bring about God's kingdom on earth and acting accordingly.

### MOVING LINE IN THE FOURTH POSITION

A moving line in the fourth position describes one who, through Wisdom, understands how to build and nurture an organization. Such a person should be given a leadership role and be granted autonomy.

### MOVING LINE IN THE FIFTH POSITION

A moving line in the fifth position suggests self-examination. Self-examination does not mean self-preoccupation. It means examining the effects one produces. As Jesus says, "A good tree cannot bear bad fruit, nor can a bad tree bear good fruit" (Matt 7:18). One should first of all examine the fruit one is producing, and only then worry about the nature of the tree.

## Moving Line in the Sixth Position

A moving line in the top position indicates one who has completely let go of Ego, who stands outside the petty affairs of the world. Liberation from Ego leaves one fully open to Wisdom and living a life grounded in God. This way of life is the highest ideal.

## NOTES

Wilhelm/Baynes calls this archetype *Contemplation (View)*. Pearson calls this archetype *Gazing (Contemplation)*. Barrett calls this archetype *Seeing*. Pearson says, "This hexagram describes a time for gaining a broader perspective, a wider view."

# Archetype 21: Justice

Cain said to his brother Abel, "Let us go out to the field." And when they were in the field, Cain rose up against his brother Abel and killed him. Then the Lord said to Cain, "Where is your brother Abel?" He said, "I do not know; am I my brother's keeper?"

And the Lord said, "What have you done? Listen; your brother's blood is crying out to me from the ground! And now you are cursed from the ground, which has opened its mouth to receive your brother's blood from your hand. When you till the ground, it will no longer yield to you its strength; you will be a fugitive and a wanderer on the earth."

Cain said to the Lord, "My punishment is greater than I can bear! Today you have driven me away from the soil, and I shall be hidden from your face; I shall be a fugitive and a wanderer on the earth, and anyone who meets me may kill me."

Then the Lord said to him, "Not so! Whoever kills Cain will suffer a sevenfold vengeance." And the Lord put a mark on Cain, so that no one who came upon him would kill him. Then Cain went away from the presence of the Lord, and settled in the land of Nod, east of Eden.

—Genesis 4:8–16

## THE READING

This reading describes Cain, who has brutally murdered his brother. This is a crime against not only his brother but also God's holy plan for a world grounded in peace and love. Cain must be removed, and justice must be restored. However, God's justice is not vindictive; it is justice tempered by mercy.

# THE HEXAGRAM

| | Trigram | Name | Image | Attribute | Family |
|---|---|---|---|---|---|
| Upper | ▬ ▬ | Christ | Fire | Light | Second Daughter |
| Lower | ▬ ▬ | Word | Thunder | Life Giving | First Son |

The upper trigram is Christ, the light of the world. The lower trigram is Word, whose image is Thunder. Thunder represents the fear of attribution, of justice. Society must be based on justice. Justice must always be guided by Wisdom.

# THE ARCHETYPE

There is a time…

- To look to the law for protection against criminals and liars.
- To promptly take the necessary steps to protect oneself and others from injury.
- To find a middle ground between cruelty and softness.
- To ensure the laws are clear, the penalties fair, and the corrections swift.
- To take vigorous measures to break through obstructions.

Now is that time.

# THE LINES

### MOVING LINE IN THE FIRST POSITION
A moving line in the bottom position reminds us we are not punishing for the sake of punishment or humiliation, but to bring about a correction. Therefore, the first transgressions should be met with a mild response.

### MOVING LINE IN THE SECOND POSITION
A moving line in the second position describes a situation in which one can easily discriminate between right and wrong but may be overcome by anger. Anger blots out Wisdom, and under anger's influence, it is easy to get carried away in the punishment. The line suggests that even if this has happened, the punishment is justified, and no great harm has been done.

### MOVING LINE IN THE THIRD POSITION
A moving line in the third position suggests that the punishment is being carried out by someone who lacks the necessary authority. This makes a correction unlikely. The evil that has been done has a long history, and dealing with it is difficult. The punishment is likely to arouse great resentment. The enforcer should be reassured by knowing that the punishment was necessary and the outcome inevitable.

### MOVING LINE IN THE FOURTH POSITION
A moving line in the fourth position suggests that the obstacles that must be overcome are very large. Powerful opponents need to be punished. This is difficult; the effort will succeed only if undertaken by one who is both tough and honest. If one understands the difficulty and follows through, success will eventually be achieved.

### MOVING LINE IN THE FIFTH POSITION
A moving line in the fifth position tells us the case at hand is difficult, but what needs to be done is clear. There is a natural inclination to leniency. A good decision in this case requires impartiality and an awareness of the great responsibility one has undertaken. One must also be careful, because with the responsibility comes danger.

### MOVING LINE IN THE SIXTH POSITION
A moving line in the top position is the opposite of a moving line in the bottom place. A moving line in the first position describes a first-time offender who can still be corrected. A moving line in the top position describes a longtime offender who is hardened and unwilling to repent. Correction is therefore impossible, and failure is likely. There is little hope in this situation.

## NOTES
Wilhelm/Baynes and Barrett both call this archetype *Biting Through*, since the Chinese descriptions refer to an obstruction between the teeth that requires forceful biting. Pearson calls this archetype *Taking a Bite*. Pearson says, "The situation described here is one in which you are forced to deal decisively with others' acts of cruelty to others."

# Archetype 22: Elegance

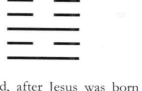

In the time of King Herod, after Jesus was born in Bethlehem of Judea, wise men from the East came to Jerusalem, asking, "Where is the child who has been born king of the Jews? For we observed his star at its rising, and have come to pay him homage."...When they saw that the star had stopped, they were overwhelmed with joy. On entering the house, they saw the child with Mary his mother; and they knelt down and paid him homage. Then, opening their treasure chests, they offered him gifts of gold, frankincense, and myrrh.

—Matthew 2:1–11

## THE READING
This reading describes the birth of Jesus using a number of rich metaphors. There are wise ones coming from far-off lands to meet a newly born king. There is a star rising, as it seems, from the secret depths of the earth and illuminating and beautifying the earth. And there are three gifts (gold, frankincense, and myrrh) associated with divinity (e.g., 1 Kings 6:22), lovers (e.g., Song of Solomon 5:13), and priests (e.g., Leviticus 2:15). These gifts are made in homage to the baby who will eventually reunite the human race with God.

## THE HEXAGRAM

|       | Trigram | Name      | Image    | Attribute | Family          |
|-------|---------|-----------|----------|-----------|-----------------|
| Upper | ☶       | Stillness | Mountain | Resting   | Third Son       |
| Lower | ☲       | Christ    | Fire     | Light     | Second Daughter |

The lower trigram is Christ, whose image is Fire. The upper trigram is Stillness, whose image is Mountain. Thus we have Fire lighting up the Mountain with its shining presence.

## THE ARCHETYPE
There is a time...

- To appreciate the graceful beauty that ornaments something of importance.
- To recognize the limitations of ornamentation.
- To remember that the ornamentation is ultimately not what is important.
- To realize that ornamentation used indiscriminately loses its value.
- To recognize that while the ornamentation adds beauty, it cannot resolve important questions.
- To gain Wisdom by observing the forms existing in nature.
- To not be distracted by ornaments when deciding important matters.

Now is that time.

## THE LINES

### MOVING LINE IN THE FIRST POSITION
A moving line in the bottom position describes a subordinate who needs to advance. There may be sleazy opportunities offered for advancement, but this is not the path of Wisdom. It is best to advance with humility and honesty.

### MOVING LINE IN THE SECOND POSITION
A moving line in the second position advises us not to confuse form and function. The contents of the book are what give it value, not its fancy cover. It is vain to focus on ornaments at the expense of content.

### MOVING LINE IN THE THIRD POSITION
A moving line in the third position cautions us that we may be falling under the intoxicating spell of ornament. Ornaments can make things beautiful, but ornaments can also weigh things down. Now is not the time to fall into frivolity, but to remain constant in perseverance.

### MOVING LINE IN THE FOURTH POSITION
A moving line in the fourth position points to one who is struggling with a choice between ornamentation and simplicity. The answer is already known. Confirmation from the outside points to simplicity. Renouncing the comfortable life is difficult. But in the end, the choice of simplicity will enable a deep and satisfying friendship.

MOVING LINE IN THE FIFTH POSITION

A moving line in the fifth position suggests one who withdraws from those who value superficiality and instead seeks solitude. In the process, one finds another whose friendship is tempting. One feels that the gifts one has to offer are unworthy. This line reminds us that we have something even more valuable to offer: the depth of our being.

MOVING LINE IN THE SIXTH POSITION

A moving line in the top position describes the highest stage of development, at which time ornamentation is no longer needed. A thing of value can now be fully revealed and the simplicity of its form made manifest.

## NOTES

Wilhelm/Baynes call this archetype *Grace*. I chose not to use this description because the word has a specific meaning within Christian theology that does not match this archetype. Pearson also calls this archetype *Elegance*. Barrett calls this archetype *Beauty*, saying, "This is about natural beauty, like the beauty of a plant, whose form is the perfect, simple expression of its nature."

# Archetype 23: Destruction

He [King Nebuchadnezzar] burned the house of the Lord, the king's house, and all the houses of Jerusalem; every great house he burned down…The bronze pillars that were in the house of the Lord, as well as the stands and the bronze sea that were in the house of the Lord, the Chaldeans broke in pieces, and carried the bronze to Babylon. They took away the pots, the shovels, the snuffers, the dishes for incense, and all the bronze vessels used in the temple service, as well as the firepans and the basins. What was made of gold the captain of the guard took away for the gold, and what was made of silver, for the silver.

—2 Kings 25:8–15

## THE READING
The reading describes the destruction of the Temple of Solomon. The "First Temple" was built around 1000 BCE and then destroyed by Nebuchadnezzar II around 600 BCE. As portrayed in the Bible, the destruction of the Temple of Solomon was not an isolated act of war; it was the result of a long series of poor choices by various kings of Judah that alienated the people from God. Without a firm grounding in God, the kingdom could not stand against its enemies.

## THE HEXAGRAM

|        | Trigram | Name      | Image    | Attribute | Family    |
|--------|---------|-----------|----------|-----------|-----------|
| Upper  | ☶       | Stillness | Mountain | Resting   | Third Son |
| Lower  | ☷       | Wisdom    | Earth    | Devotion  | Mother    |

The hexagram shows a single strong line supported by five weaker lines. Collapse is coming.

# THE ARCHETYPE
There is a time…

- To understand how that which is strong is undermined by that which is weak, not directly, but by a gradual and almost imperceptible undermining until the strong eventually collapses.
- To accept that the strong are not in a position to accomplish anything. The strong are simply overwhelmed by the sheer numbers of the weak and the nature of the times.
- To not feel resentment against the times, but to accept the natural ebb and flow.
- To cultivate personal virtues such as generosity, especially to subordinates, knowing this will eventually pay off.

Now is that time.

# THE LINES

### Moving Line in the First Position
A moving line in the bottom position warns of a dangerous situation. Mediocre people are on the rise. They are undermining the necessary foundations. Those who remain loyal are being hurt by slander and intrigue. The situation is not good, but there is nothing to do but wait.

### Moving Line in the Second Position
A moving line in the second position warns that the power of the mediocre is growing. There are clear indications that the danger is coming closer. Isolation is increasing. Extreme caution is called for. This is not the time for stubborn perseverance; this leads only to disaster. This is the time to be flexible and avoid danger.

### Moving Line in the Third Position
A moving line in the third position suggests one who is in a bad place but unable to extricate oneself because of commitments. Mediocre people are all around, but there is also a wise one who can bring stability. Naturally, the mediocre ones will not take kindly to the wise one. That is to be expected.

### Moving Line in the Fourth Position
A moving line in the fourth position suggests the disaster is now affecting not only the environment but also the one trapped in the environment. The danger has reached a peak and can no longer be avoided. It is a bad time.

## Moving Line in the Fifth Position

A moving line in the fifth position suggests a turn for the better. The nature of the dark force is undergoing a change. It no longer opposes the strong principle but now submits to its guidance voluntarily. This bodes well for both the dark and the light. All will end well.

## Moving Line in the Sixth Position

A moving line in the top position brings relief. The corner has been turned. Danger has spent itself, and better times are on the horizon. Those in power now embrace wisdom and effectiveness. Evil ones still battle, but now they battle against themselves. A house divided cannot stand. God's law is at work: evil eventually destroys itself. The mediocre are advised to submit to the control of the wise.

# NOTES

Wilhelm/Baynes calls this archetype *Splitting Apart*. Pearson calls this archetype *Peeling*. Barrett calls this archetype *Stripping Away*. Pearson doesn't see this archetype as quite as dark as does Wilhelm/Baynes, but still describes the situation thusly: "Peeled away from others, you can accomplish little."

# Archetype 24: Returning

Then Jesus said, "There was a man who had two sons. The younger of them said to his father, 'Father, give me the share of the property that will belong to me.' So he divided his property between them.

A few days later the younger son gathered all he had and travelled to a distant country, and there he squandered his property in dissolute living. When he had spent everything, a severe famine took place throughout that country, and he began to be in need.

So he went and hired himself out to one of the citizens of that country, who sent him to his fields to feed the pigs. He would gladly have filled himself with the pods that the pigs were eating; and no one gave him anything. But when he came to himself he said, 'How many of my father's hired hands have bread enough and to spare, but here I am dying of hunger! I will get up and go to my father, and I will say to him, "Father, I have sinned against heaven and before you; I am no longer worthy to be called your son; treat me like one of your hired hands."'

So he set off and went to his father. But while he was still far off, his father saw him and was filled with compassion; he ran and put his arms around him and kissed him. Then the son said to him, 'Father, I have sinned against heaven and before you; I am no longer worthy to be called your son.' But the father said to his slaves, 'Quickly, bring out a robe—the best one—and put it on him; put a ring on his finger and sandals on his feet. And get the fatted calf and kill it, and let us eat and celebrate; for this son of mine was dead and is alive again; he was lost and is found!'

And they began to celebrate."

—Luke 15:11–24

## THE READING

This reading is the story of the Prodigal Son. Prodigal, in the context of this story, means extremely wasteful. The boy was given a great deal. The boy was given love. He used it to insult his father, telling him he couldn't wait any longer for the father to die. The boy was given an inheritance. He spent it, we can assume, on wine, partying, and loose women. The boy's Ego was controlling his life. But the flame couldn't burn forever. Eventually he ran through his money. What would he do now? Return to his father? Not so long as his Ego had a say. He would take a job, even the most menial job imaginable, tending pigs. Pigs are unclean animals, according to Jewish law. A pig-tender is looked down upon by everybody. The boy is paid next to nothing for this degrading job and can't even feed himself. Eventually, close to starving, his Ego is humiliated. And he is able to listen to the voice of Wisdom. He returns to his father.

The story now takes an odd twist. What would the listeners of Jesus expect the father to do? Perhaps tell the boy to get lost. After the insulting treatment the boy gave the father, that would be completely understandable. At best, the father might throw the boy a few scraps of food and give him an opportunity to prove he has learned his lesson.

Instead, the father does something completely unexpected. He welcomes his son back with joyous arms. Even the boy's older brother is horrified. This is unfair. But the father only sees that his son, who has been lost in so many ways, has returned. The darkness that has clouded his life has been lifted.

## THE HEXAGRAM

|        | Trigram | Name   | Image   | Attribute   | Family    |
|--------|---------|--------|---------|-------------|-----------|
| Upper  | ☷       | Wisdom | Earth   | Devotion    | Mother    |
| Lower  | ☳       | Word   | Thunder | Life Giving | First Son |

In the symbolism of lines, the yin line (open) is symbolic of darkness, and the yang line (closed) is symbolic of light. In this hexagram we have a single line of light pushing up into the darkness, symbolic of the return of the time of light.

## THE ARCHETYPE

There is a time…

- To welcome back the light that has been banished for so long.
- To let the return happen of its own accord and to not rush it before its time.
- To give the newly vitalized energy time to emerge.
- To treat things tenderly and with care, so that the return will lead to a great flowering.

Now is that time.

# THE LINES

### MOVING LINE IN THE FIRST POSITION
A moving line in the bottom position suggests the necessity for a slight detour, but tells us to return to the path as soon as possible. When Ego temptations occur, put them aside before they take hold and gain control. These precautions will lead to a good result.

### MOVING LINE IN THE SECOND POSITION
A moving line in the second position calls for a decision based on carefully listening to the voice of Wisdom. A support system is helpful. This is a time to be guided by those who have compassion and wisdom.

### MOVING LINE IN THE THIRD POSITION
A moving line in the third position warns against giving in to inner insecurity and flip-flopping positions. It is natural to feel apprehensive, but this can be overcome by always returning to Wisdom's way.

### MOVING LINE IN THE FOURTH POSITION
A moving line in the fourth position describes a situation in which one is in the company of obsequious people but still connected with a strong and wise friend. This friend should be trusted to return one to the path of Wisdom. There is no need to offer rewards or threaten punishments. A path guided by Wisdom is a reward in itself.

### MOVING LINE IN THE FIFTH POSITION
A moving line in the fifth position counsels us that when the time for return has come, you should look within and seek Wisdom. You should not make flimsy excuses for what you have done. If you have done something wrong, admit it and apologize. Then repent by turning away from Ego and resolving to follow Wisdom's way.

### MOVING LINE IN THE SIXTH POSITION
A moving line in the top position warns that if one misses the opportune time for return, misfortune will be the result. Ego is a poor substitute for Wisdom. Beware of Ego hardened into obstinacy.

# NOTES
Wilhelm/Baynes calls this archetype *Return (The Turning Point)*. Pearson and Barrett both call this archetype *Returning*. Pearson says, "When our lives are shaken to their foundation, we must return to what gives us sustenance.

# Archetype 25: Innocence

*Virgin*

And Mary said,
"My soul magnifies the Lord,
and my spirit rejoices in God my Savior,
for he has looked with favor on the lowliness of his servant.
Surely, from now on all generations will call me blessed;
for the Mighty One has done great things for me,
and holy is his name."

—Luke 1:46–49

## THE READING

This reading portrays Mary, mother of Jesus, the symbol of one who is innocent and without guile. Her mind is natural and true, devoid of Ego, fully aligned with and accepting God's will. This reading also describes the unexpected. Mary doesn't know what is going to happen, but she is putting herself in God's hands. And, indeed, all generations will call her blessed.

## THE HEXAGRAM

|        | Trigram | Name | Image | Attribute | Family |
|--------|---------|------|-------|-----------|--------|
| Upper  |         | God  | Heaven | Strength | Father |
| Lower  |         | Word | Thunder | Life Giving | First Son |

The trigram God is above. Below is Word. All things came into being from the Word (John 1:1). Things are born innocent and pure. They are protected by God above, like a mother bird protects her chicks (2 Esd. 1:30).

# THE ARCHETYPE
There is a time…

- To marvel in the essential goodness of human nature.
- To remember that all people are made in the image of God, and, because of this, all have that inner voice that is able to hear the call of Wisdom.
- To follow Wisdom's way without thought of reward or advantage.
- To know that following Wisdom's way leads to divine success.
- To remember how easily Ego can tempt one away from Wisdom's way.
- To remember that only those with the innocence of children will be able to share in the Kingdom of God.
- To understand that a good ruler is one who nurtures life and all people.

Now is that time.

# THE LINES

### MOVING LINE IN THE FIRST POSITION
A moving line in the bottom position affirms that one's first impulses are aligned with Wisdom's way and can be trusted.

### MOVING LINE IN THE SECOND POSITION
A moving line in the second position says we should complete tasks as time and place allow and not be focused on future outcomes. The completion of tasks is its own reward. This is the way to build true value.

### MOVING LINE IN THE THIRD POSITION
A moving line in the third position reminds us that sometimes bad things happen to good people. There is no point in getting upset. Let it go.

### MOVING LINE IN THE FOURTH POSITION
A moving line in the fourth position says if something really belongs to us, we cannot lose it. Even if we throw it away, it will still be ours. There is no point in getting upset. All we need to do is to stay grounded and remain true to Wisdom's way.

### MOVING LINE IN THE FIFTH POSITION
A moving line in the fifth position warns that an unexpected evil may appear. If it does not originate from one's own Ego, then it need cause no worry. Stay grounded and let nature take its course. Everything will work out.

## Moving Line in the Sixth Position

A moving line in the top position suggests that the time may not be right for action. Now is the time to wait quietly, listening for Wisdom's voice. There is nothing to be gained by acting thoughtlessly and steamrolling ahead. This will accomplish nothing.

## NOTES

Wilhelm/Baynes calls this archetype *Innocence (The Unexpected)*. Pearson calls this archetype *Not False*. Barrett calls this archetype *Without Entanglement* and says, "Freedom from entanglement brings extraordinary energy."

# Archetype 26: Power of the Great

And Jesus rebuked the demon, and it came out of him, and the boy was cured instantly. Then the disciples came to Jesus privately and said, "Why could we not cast it out?" He said to them, "Because of your little faith. For truly I tell you, if you have faith the size of a mustard seed, you will say to this mountain, 'Move from here to there,' and it will move; and nothing will be impossible for you."

—Matthew 17:18–20

## THE READING

This reading shows the strength of Jesus in confronting evil. But his strength is not a traditional strength. He doesn't have big muscles. He doesn't bully. He doesn't have an army. His strength comes from a strong sense of purpose, restraint, and his readiness to care for others.

## THE HEXAGRAM

|  | Trigram | Name | Image | Attribute | Family |
|---|---|---|---|---|---|
| Upper | ☶ | Stillness | Mountain | Resting | Third Son |
| Lower | ☰ | God | Heaven | Strength | Father |

The top trigram is Stillness, and the bottom trigram, God. The attribute of God is Strength. The strength described by this archetype is a restrained strength, a combination of strength and stillness.

## THE ARCHETYPE
There is a time…

- To use one's strength to hold back.
- To use one's strength to hold together.
- To use one's strength to nourish and care.
- To realize the need for one who is strong, firm, and honored by those in power.
- To use periods of rest to gather strength, renew faith, and cultivate character.
- To cultivate the right kind of power, a power that is Egoless, that is fully aligned with God's will, and that is used purely to help others.
- To internalize lessons from the past, and, by applying those lessons, strengthen character.

Now is that time.

## THE LINES

### MOVING LINE IN THE FIRST POSITION
A moving line in the bottom position describes an obstacle that is preventing a desired advance. This is not the time to try to force an advance. This is the time to compose oneself and wait patiently until one's energies can be used effectively.

### MOVING LINE IN THE SECOND POSITION
A moving line in the second position describes a restraining force that is absolutely superior. Struggle is pointless. Now is the time for waiting, accumulating energy, building character, and preparing for a vigorous advance at a later time.

### MOVING LINE IN THE THIRD POSITION
A moving line in the third position describes an obstacle that has been cleared away. A path has opened. Another has appeared who is also strong willed, and a partnership is possible. But danger still threatens. The wise one remains wary. This is the time to cultivate the skill needed to move forward and to protect oneself from unexpected attacks. One must have a clear goal for which one is striving.

### MOVING LINE IN THE FOURTH POSITION
A moving line in the fourth position counsels us that the best way to restrain wild force is to tame it while it is still young.

## MOVING LINE IN THE FIFTH POSITION

A moving line in the fifth position suggests that there is an impetuous force that must be restrained indirectly. If the power of one's enemies poses a danger, don't try to neutralize that power. Instead, eliminate it at its source.

## MOVING LINE IN THE SIXTH POSITION

A moving line in the top position is auspicious. It tells us the time of obstruction is past. The energy that has been restrained for so long has now burst forth and is able to achieve great success. This line points to one who is now honored and whose ideas shape the world.

# NOTES

Wilhelm/Baynes calls this archetype *The Taming Power of the Great*. Pearson calls this archetype *Great Nurturing*. Barrett calls this archetype *Great Taming*. Pearson says, "This hexagram reminds us that we continue to need to learn from the past when we are doing well."

# Archetype 27: Nourishment

As he went ashore, he saw a great crowd; and he had compassion for them, because they were like sheep without a shepherd; and he began to teach them many things.

When it grew late, his disciples came to him and said, "This is a deserted place, and the hour is now very late; send them away so that they may go into the surrounding country and villages and buy something for themselves to eat." But he answered them, "You give them something to eat." They said to him, "Are we to go and buy two hundred denarii worth of bread, and give it to them to eat?" And he said to them, "How many loaves have you? Go and see." When they had found out, they said, "Five, and two fish."

Then he ordered them to get all the people to sit down in groups on the green grass. So they sat down in groups of hundreds and of fifties. Taking the five loaves and the two fish, he looked up to heaven, and blessed and broke the loaves, and gave them to his disciples to set before the people; and he divided the two fish among them all.

And all ate and were filled; and they took up twelve baskets full of broken pieces and of the fish.

—Mark 6:34–43

## THE READING

This reading describes the Feeding of the Five Thousand. This is the only miracle described in all four of the gospels. Jesus is offering the people two types of nourishment: spiritual and physical. His disciples are happy to offer spiritual nourishment (Jesus is, after all, doing all the work), but when it comes to offering physical nourishment, this sounds too much like real effort. We don't have enough, they say. We can't afford to feed them, they whine. Send them away to find their own food, they plead. Jesus replies emphatically, "*You* give them something to eat!" This reading is not denigrating spiritual nourishment. It is only pointing out that giving people spiritual food is not helpful if they are physically starving. Both spiritual food and physical food are necessary for people to thrive.

# THE HEXAGRAM

| | Trigram | Name | Image | Attribute | Family |
|---|---|---|---|---|---|
| Upper | ☶ | Stillness | Mountain | Resting | Third Son |
| Lower | ☳ | Word | Thunder | Life Giving | First Son |

This hexagram is composed of Stillness above and Word below. When Stillness is stacked above Word, the resulting hexagram looks like an open mouth, with the solid upper and lower lines representing the lips.

# THE ARCHETYPE

There is a time...

- To provide nourishment to others, both to their bodies and to their souls.
- To choose carefully the people who are to be nourished. If one cares for those who will care for others, one's care is magnified.
- To offer only that which is truly nourishing and only as much as is really needed.
- To remember that one can only nourish others if one also nourishes oneself.
- To observe how people care for themselves and others and thus learn how to best nourish their inner nature.
- To not confuse nourishment with indulgence.

Now is that time.

# THE LINES

## MOVING LINE IN THE FIRST POSITION

A moving line in the bottom position describes an independent person who has turned away from self-reliance and is now consumed by envy of those who have more material possessions. Others have no sympathy for such a person. Why should they?

## MOVING LINE IN THE SECOND POSITION

A moving line in the second position describes one who is not willing to be self-reliant and instead accepts favors from those higher up. This creates a feeling of guilt, since self-reliance is integral to being human. This is a bad situation and must be ended.

## MOVING LINE IN THE THIRD POSITION

A moving line in the third position describes one who craves nourishment but does not offer nourishment to others. This leads to a spiritual emptiness that one seeks to fill with material possessions and pleasure. But this is a vicious cycle. The goods and pleasure temporarily dull the pain but soon leave one even emptier. Now a larger fix of goods and pleasure must be sought. The only way to break this cycle is to turn back to God.

## MOVING LINE IN THE FOURTH POSITION

A moving line in the fourth position describes one who occupies a high place and is striving to do God's work. This requires the right helpers, since the work that needs to be done is beyond the capacity of a single person. This person may be over-zealous, but at least the goals are worthwhile.

## MOVING LINE IN THE FIFTH POSITION

A moving line in the fifth position describes one who should be there to serve others but is incapable. This can be resolved by seeking counsel and help from one who, though grounded in Wisdom, seems from the outside unremarkable. This is not the time to try to reach for lofty goals, but instead to learn and gather.

## MOVING LINE IN THE SIXTH POSITION

A moving line in the top position describes one who is truly wise and able to help others. This is not an enviable position, since it carries such heavy responsibilities. But if the one is able to stay focused, the greatest goals will be achieved and many will benefit.

## NOTES

Wilhelm/Baynes calls this archetype *Corners of the Mouth (Providing Nourishment)*. Pearson calls this archetype *Jaws*. She says, "This may be a time for restrained nurturing rather than for decisive action." Barrett calls this archetype *Nourishment*. She says, "A noble one pays careful attention to both giving and receiving: how he nourishes others, and what he will accept as nourishment."

# Archetype 28: The Breaking Point

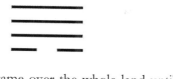

From noon on, darkness came over the whole land until three in the afternoon. And about three o'clock Jesus cried with a loud voice, "Eli, Eli, lema sabachthani?" that is, "My God, my God, why have you forsaken me?"

—Matthew 27:45–46

## THE READING

Jesus has reached the end. Up until now, he has been able to take the torment. Not anymore. He has reached the breaking point.

## THE HEXAGRAM

| | Trigram | Name | Image | Attribute | Family |
|---|---|---|---|---|---|
| Upper | | Wonder | Lake | Joy | Third Daughter |
| Lower | | Spirit | Gentle Wind | Penetrating | First Daughter |

This hexagram consists of Wonder above and Spirit below. These trigrams are mirror images of each other. Putting the two together gives four strong lines in the center surrounded by weak lines at the end. This indicates that even though there is great strength in the center, that strength has reached its breaking point.

## THE ARCHETYPE

There is a time…

- To accept that even the greatest strength cannot bear the load any longer.
- To recognize that one is in an extraordinary and momentous time and that extraordinary measures are needed.
- To recognize that things cannot continue, and that a transition must be found if success is to be achieved.

- To understand that force will not be effective; what is needed is understanding.
- To stand firm, even when standing alone.

Now is that time.

## THE LINES

### MOVING LINE IN THE FIRST POSITION
A moving line in the bottom position warns that this is a time for exceptional caution.

### MOVING LINE IN THE SECOND POSITION
A moving line in the second position suggests that it is possible to move forward by uniting with those of a lower position.

### MOVING LINE IN THE THIRD POSITION
A moving line in the third position indicates one who is pushing forward despite the obstacles and refusing advice from those wiser. When one refuses advice, one cannot expect support. This is not sustainable. Eventually the situation will collapse, and the more forcefully one pushes, the sooner this will happen. Now is the time to hold back.

### MOVING LINE IN THE FOURTH POSITION
A moving line in the fourth position indicates that an alliance with those in a lower position has resulted in mastering the situation. But the line also warns one not to take advantage of the situation by giving in to one's own Ego-driven desires.

### MOVING LINE IN THE FIFTH POSITION
A moving line in the fifth position warns not to abandon the relationships with those in a lower position in favor of those in a higher position.

### MOVING LINE IN THE SIXTH POSITION
A moving line in the top position indicates that a climactic time has been reached. Courage is needed, and great danger is around the corner. The task at hand is so important that even losing one's life is a price worth paying.

## NOTES
Wilhelm/Baynes calls this archetype *Preponderance of the Great*. Barrett calls this archetype *Great Exceeding*. Pearson calls this archetype *Greatly Surpassing*. Pearson says, "The image of the hexagram, as a whole, stresses the need for emotional equilibrium in those times when we must stand alone."

# Archetype 29: Meeting Danger

"See, I am sending you out like sheep into the midst of wolves; so be wise as serpents and innocent as doves. Beware of them, for they will hand you over to councils and flog you in their synagogues; and you will be dragged before governors and kings because of me, as a testimony to them and the Gentiles. When they hand you over, do not worry about how you are to speak or what you are to say; for what you are to say will be given to you at that time; for it is not you who speak, but the Spirit of your Father speaking through you."

—Matthew 10:16–20

## THE READING

Jesus is sending his disciples out into a hostile environment. They will face great dangers. If they can stay completely grounded and not give way to their fear, they will achieve success.

## THE HEXAGRAM

| | Trigram | Name | Image | Attribute | Family |
|---|---|---|---|---|---|
| Upper | | Chaos | Water | Danger | Second Son |
| Lower | | Chaos | Water | Danger | Second Son |

This hexagram consists of a doubling of the Chaos trigrams. The image of Chaos is Water, and its attribute is Danger. In the beginning, "the earth was a formless void and darkness covered the face of the deep, while a wind from God swept over the face of the waters" (Gen. 1:2). In the Christian creation mythos, the image of water upon water represents the ultimate in chaos and danger. With Chaos doubled, we also have the idea of danger repeated. Thus we are not just facing danger, but the repetition of danger.

## THE ARCHETYPE

There is a time...

- To recognize the danger one faces and not to shrink from what must be done.
- To understand the danger will be repetitious in nature and to take advantage of this by learning from the experiences.
- To circumvent the danger by remaining sincere and true to one's inner values.
- To call on Wisdom for a deep understanding of the danger faced.
- To remember that sometimes danger can be turned into protection, as when a raging river provides a buffer from one's enemies.
- To move slowly but surely through the danger and not become trapped in it.
- To understand the value of repetition and constancy in teaching others.

Now is that time.

## THE LINES

### MOVING LINE IN THE FIRST POSITION
A moving line in the bottom position warns against being seduced by the evil one faces.

### MOVING LINE IN THE SECOND POSITION
A moving line in the second position suggests that sometimes it isn't possible to escape danger immediately. One must simply avoid being overwhelmed by the danger. Then one can weigh the possibilities and address the situation step by step.

### MOVING LINE IN THE THIRD POSITION
A moving line in the third position warns that there is no path that leads away from danger. Any attempt to escape will lead to deeper danger. There is nothing to do except wait until a path shows itself.

### MOVING LINE IN THE FOURTH POSITION
A moving line in the fourth position suggests that this is not a time for ceremony; it is a time to embrace simplicity and sincerity. When enlightening another, the best place to start is with that which is most clear. Then proceed simply and logically from that point.

## MOVING LINE IN THE FIFTH POSITION

A moving line in the fifth position advises that the way out of danger is to follow the path of least resistance. This is a time not to try to achieve great goals but to be content with escaping danger.

## MOVING LINE IN THE SIXTH POSITION

A moving line in the top position is ominous. It describes one who is no longer grounded and has become lost in the trappings of Ego. From such a situation, escape is impossible.

## NOTES

Wilhelm/Baynes describes this archetype as *The Abysmal (Water)*. Pearson calls this archetype *The Abyss*. Barrett calls this archetype *Repeating Chasms*. Barrett says, "The chasms repeat: there is no detour that would take you round them, so you must practice and learn the way of these deep places."

# Archetype 30: The Light

The true light, which enlightens everyone, was coming into the world. He was in the world, and the world came into being through him; yet the world did not know him. He came to what was his own, and his own people did not accept him. But to all who received him, who believed in his name, he gave power to become children of God, who were born, not of blood or of the will of the flesh or of the will of man, but of God.

—John 1:9–13

## THE READING

Jesus the Christ is sent to bring us light. It is the light that will bring us out of darkness. It is the light of knowing we are all children of God. It is a light so bright that no evil can long stand against it.

## THE HEXAGRAM

|       | Trigram | Name   | Image | Attribute | Family          |
|-------|---------|--------|-------|-----------|-----------------|
| Upper |         | Christ | Fire  | Light     | Second Daughter |
| Lower |         | Christ | Fire  | Light     | Second Daughter |

The hexagram is a doubling of the Christ trigram. The Christ trigram is composed of an open line within two solid lines. The openness signifies the empty space. The open space is about being receptive. We are empty so that we can be filled. It is only in emptying ourselves that we are able to receive Christ's light.

## THE ARCHETYPE
There is a time…

- To offer oneself totally to the light, so that the light may continue burning.
- To cling to what is right.
- To be bearers of the light to all we meet.
- To accept the limitations of corporeal existence and embrace one's calling as a child of God.
- To open the hearts of people to the beauty of God's light.

Now is that time.

## THE LINES

### MOVING LINE IN THE FIRST POSITION
A moving line in the bottom position signifies an awakening to the work that is now to be done. But one must not jump into the work without taking adequate time to invite Wisdom's guidance. Wisdom will bring composure and the clarity that will be needed to sort through the onslaught of new ideas. Wisdom will provide a solid foundation for all that is to come.

### MOVING LINE IN THE SECOND POSITION
A moving line in the second position describes culture and art, the harmony of which requires one to pay close attention to the balance found between the extremes.

### MOVING LINE IN THE THIRD POSITION
A moving line in the third position indicates the end of the day, a time when we remember the fragile nature of life. Some believe they must enjoy all life has to offer while it lasts. Others become depressed at the thought of growing old. But neither attitude is correct. Wisdom means knowing that it is not how long we live that matters, but how we use the time we have.

### MOVING LINE IN THE FOURTH POSITION
A moving line in the fourth position warns that fire brings clarity to wood, but also consumes it. Some who see the light become too impatient to understand the light and too anxious to spread it. These people produce nothing of lasting importance.

### Moving Line in the Fifth Position
A moving line in the fifth position indicates the height of the day, the zenith of life. This is the time to put aside Ego. Understand that hope and fear and worrying are products of Ego. Those who seek wisdom and clarity of mind will accomplish God's work.

### Moving Line in the Sixth Position
A moving line in the top position warns us to chastise sparingly. The goal is not to punish, but to discipline. Eliminate bad habits, but tolerate those that are harmless. Remove the source of the poison, but don't punish those who were poisoned. Even asceticism must find a middle way.

## NOTES
Wilhelm/Baynes calls this archetype *The Clinging (Fire)*. Pearson calls it *The Net*. Barrett calls it *Clarity*. Barrett says, "We weave a net of concepts to grasp the message and hold its meaning in awareness."

# Archetype 31: Joyful Receptivity

Now as they went on their way, he entered a certain village, where a woman named Martha welcomed him into her home. She had a sister named Mary, who sat at the Lord's feet and listened to what he was saying. But Martha was distracted by her many tasks; so she came to him and asked, "Lord, do you not care that my sister has left me to do all the work by myself? Tell her then to help me." But the Lord answered her, "Martha, Martha, you are worried and distracted by many things; there is need of only one thing. Mary has chosen the better part, which will not be taken away from her."

—Luke 10:38–42

## THE READING

Mary sits at Jesus's feet. She is fully absorbed in the wonder of his being. She doesn't speak or respond to her sister's complaints. It isn't that she is ignoring her sister. It is that Mary has found a place of profound stillness, a place in which there is room for nothing but the experience of being with Jesus. In that place of serenity, the boundaries between her and Jesus dissolve.

## THE HEXAGRAM

| | Trigram | Name | Image | Attribute | Family |
|---|---|---|---|---|---|
| Upper | ☱ | Wonder | Lake | Joy | Third Daughter |
| Lower | ☶ | Stillness | Mountain | Resting | Third Son |

The upper trigram is Wonder, whose attribute is Joy. The lower trigram is Stillness, whose attribute is Resting. Thus we have a Joy that is in a peaceful, rested state. This is the joy of one who is alive in God. From a social perspective, the upper trigram represents a youngest daughter, and the lower trigram a youngest son. There is a natural attraction between these two, with the potential for young love and courtship.

## THE ARCHETYPE

There is a time...

- To hold oneself in stillness, and in that stillness, experience joy from without.
- To not allow joy to distract from the stillness or the stillness to snuff out the joy.
- To participate in the natural rituals of courtship and enjoy the depth time adds to the relationship.
- To understand the difference between courtship, in which the strong becomes subservient to the weak, and seduction, in which the strong dominates the weak.
- To appreciate the universal law of attraction: that two synergistic parts will be naturally and even joyfully attracted to each other.
- To keep the mind humble and free, and thus receptive to the voice of Wisdom.

Now is that time.

## THE LINES

MOVING LINE IN THE FIRST POSITION

A moving line in the bottom position indicates an influence that is present but not yet apparent. Since the influence is not visible in the world, it is mere potential.

MOVING LINE IN THE SECOND POSITION

A moving line in the second position indicates one whose movement is not controlled from within. This is an undesirable situation. The wise one remains in silence until compelled into action by events.

MOVING LINE IN THE THIRD POSITION

A moving line in the third position warns against giving in to emotions. Three suggestions are made by this line:

- The wise one does not prematurely try to influence others.
- The wise one does not give in to the whims of those being served.
- The wise one knows when the best action is no action.

MOVING LINE IN THE FOURTH POSITION

A moving line in the fourth position points to the soul of the individual. Actions that are guided by the soul have the greatest vitality, but it is most important that the soul be guided by Wisdom. Actions that arise from a soul guided by Wisdom produce results that are in accord with God's will. The wise one is subtle in influencing others. Efforts to manipulate, rather than influence others, are limited in their effect and produce resistance that will be exhausting.

MOVING LINE IN THE FIFTH POSITION

A moving line in the fifth position suggests that the will is to remain firm. The wise one is not likely to succumb to confusion, and actions guided by inner spirit are not likely to lead to remorse. The actions must be guided by observations of the flows occurring in the outside world. Thus there is a unification of inner Wisdom and outside observation.

MOVING LINE IN THE SIXTH POSITION

A moving line in the top position teaches of the pointlessness of idle talk that leads to nothing of significance.

## NOTES

Wilhelm/Baynes calls this archetype *Influence (Wooing)*. Pearson calls it *Reciprocity, Respect*. Barrett calls it *Influence*. Barrett says, "Influence is what moves people, and how people are open and available to be moved—by emotion or inspiration, physical responses, or visiting spirits."

# Archetype 32: Duration

But Naomi said to her two daughters-in-law, "Go back each of you to your mother's house. May the Lord deal kindly with you, as you have dealt with the dead and with me. The Lord grant that you may find security, each of you in the house of your husband." Then she kissed them, and they wept aloud. They said to her, "No, we will return with you to your people."

But Naomi said, "Turn back, my daughters, why will you go with me? Do I still have sons in my womb that they may become your husbands? Turn back, my daughters, go your way, for I am too old to have a husband. Even if I thought there was hope for me, even if I should have a husband tonight and bear sons, would you then wait until they were grown? Would you then refrain from marrying? No, my daughters, it has been far more bitter for me than for you, because the hand of the Lord has turned against me." Then they wept aloud again. Orpah kissed her mother-in-law, but Ruth clung to her.

So she said, "See, your sister-in-law has gone back to her people and to her gods; return after your sister-in-law." But Ruth said,

"Do not press me to leave you
or to turn back from following you!
Where you go, I will go;
where you lodge, I will lodge;
your people shall be my people,
and your God my God.
Where you die, I will die—
there will I be buried.
May the Lord do thus and so to me,
and more as well,
if even death parts me from you!"

When Naomi saw that she was determined to go with her, she said no more to her.

—Ruth 1:8–18

# THE READING

Naomi's husband and sons have died. Only her two daughters-in-law, Orpah and Ruth, remain. This leaves the three of them in a very precarious position; they have no male family members to provide for them in a time when women have few options for self-support. Naomi has heard that there is food available in Moab and so decides to migrate there. She releases her two daughters-in-law to find new husbands and start new lives. Orpah leaves, but Ruth can't bear to leave Naomi. Their bond is eternal and is forged by God. Ruth and Naomi do not know what the future will hold, but they know they will face it together.

# THE HEXAGRAM

|       | Trigram | Name   | Image       | Attribute    | Family         |
|-------|---------|--------|-------------|--------------|----------------|
| Upper | ☳       | Word   | Thunder     | Life Giving  | First Son      |
| Lower | ☴       | Spirit | Gentle Wind | Penetrating  | First Daughter |

The hexagram consists of the strength of the Word supported by the gentleness of the Spirit. There is great synergy between these two. They act as a single unit, moving together in a dance: forward, backward, growing, shrinking, but always together, and together enduring through all hardships.

# THE ARCHETYPE

There is a time...

- To honor the state of duration as a self-contained and self-renewing union, guided by God's laws and beginning anew as each ending is reached.
- To meet life by contraction and expansion, contracting when reaching the end, and meeting each new beginning with expansion.
- To follow the example of God, whose love for us will endure forever.
- To understand the enduring laws of change and transformation: death and new life, winter and spring, night and day.
- To hold the meaning in one's life as an enduring value.
- To recognize that one must sometimes be flexible about the path, even if one is sure of the destination.

Now is that time.

## THE LINES

### MOVING LINE IN THE FIRST POSITION
A moving line in the bottom position warns the wise one not to expect too much at first. That which endures needs to be built up patiently and gradually.

### MOVING LINE IN THE SECOND POSITION
A moving line in the second position suggests a force of character that exceeds physical strength. This is a time to seek the guidance of Wisdom. By showing restraint and avoiding excess, positive movement is possible.

### MOVING LINE IN THE THIRD POSITION
A moving line in the third position describes one who is at the mercy of mood swings between hope and fear. One is being buffeted by the unpredictable forces of the world, resulting in distress. But it isn't just the world that is at fault. This is a time to look deeply into one's own nature.

### MOVING LINE IN THE FOURTH POSITION
A moving line in the fourth position suggests that one's goals can only be achieved by appropriate actions. One cannot seek treasure where there is none. Treasure can only be found where the treasure is. No amount of looking in the wrong place can result in success.

### MOVING LINE IN THE FIFTH POSITION
A moving line in the fifth position points back to Naomi and Ruth. It is Naomi's role to lead with Wisdom, flexibility, and adaptability. She provides the attribute of endurance. It is Ruth's role to follow and to support Naomi with her love and faithfulness. Both roles are necessary.

### MOVING LINE IN THE SIXTH POSITION
A moving line in the top position warns against busy activity that is not guided by Wisdom. One who is restless can accomplish little of value. Restlessness coupled with authority is a particularly lethal combination.

## NOTES
Wilhelm/Baynes and Pearson call this archetype *Duration*. Barrett calls it *Lasting*. Pearson says, "Seeking duration alone is not encouraged here, even though persistence is often praised in the *Changes*."

# Archetype 33: Retreat

After some time had passed, the Jews plotted to kill him, but their plot became known to Saul. They were watching the gates day and night so that they might kill him; but his disciples took him by night and let him down through an opening in the wall, lowering him in a basket.

—Acts 9:23–25

## THE READING
This reading describes the early days of the career of Saul, better known to us as Paul. Saul has had a conversion experience. He has become transformed from a persecutor of the early Christians to one of their great evangelists. But in this reading, his forward momentum has been thwarted. The power of the darkness is upon him. The only way he can remain safe is to retreat.

## THE HEXAGRAM

|  | Trigram | Name | Image | Attribute | Family |
|---|---|---|---|---|---|
| Upper | | God | Heaven | Strength | Father |
| Lower | | Stillness | Mountain | Resting | Third Son |

The upper trigram is God, the attribute of which is Strength. The lower trigram is Stillness, the attribute of which is Resting. The pictogram represents a period of withdrawal and resting for gathering strength.

## THE ARCHETYPE
There is a time…

- To recognize when the forces of darkness are gathering strength and advancing.
- To withdraw into safety instead of being drawn into an exhausting struggle with darkness.
- To maintain resistance while retreating, thus hindering evil's ability to advance.

- To understand the retreat not as a surrender, but as a preparation for a later advance.
- To respond to adversaries not with hatred, which serves the purpose of evil, but with dignity and courage, which serves the purposes of God.

Now is that time.

## THE LINES

### MOVING LINE IN THE FIRST POSITION
A moving line in the bottom position indicates one who, while in retreat, is in immediate contact with the enemy. This is particularly dangerous, and nothing should be undertaken. More than ever, stillness must be embraced.

### MOVING LINE IN THE SECOND POSITION
A moving line in the second position indicates a pursuer who holds tightly to the wise one who is in retreat. The pursuer cannot be shaken off. The wise one must remain strong, and in doing so will reach the goal.

### MOVING LINE IN THE THIRD POSITION
A moving line in the third position counsels how to deal with the unpleasant and dangerous times when one's retreat is held back. The best course is to create allies of those who are preventing the retreat. This is not ideal, because such allies are not trustworthy. But it is the best one can do under the circumstances.

### MOVING LINE IN THE FOURTH POSITION
A moving line in the fourth position describes the difference between a wise one and an inferior one in how they approach retreat. The wise one retreats voluntarily and without anger. Thus there is no conflict between actions and convictions. The inferior one retreats in anger and frustration, separated from the counsel of the wise.

### MOVING LINE IN THE FIFTH POSITION
A moving line in the fifth position counsels that the timing of retreat is critical. If the timing is right, the retreat will be carried out without violence or even acrimony. But even though the retreat is done in a positive manner, it still requires resolve. Without resolve, one can be distracted from what needs to be done.

## MOVING LINE IN THE SIXTH POSITION

A moving line in the top position suggests that the time is right. Wisdom has spoken. The wise one has listened. The time to depart is now, without doubt, without sorrow, and with clarity of vision.

## NOTES

Wilhelm/Baynes, Pearson, and Barrett all call this archetype *Retreat*. Barrett says, "Retreat means withdrawing from what can harm you, or what might swallow you up; it is a way to keep yourself whole."

# Archetype 34: Strength in Greatness

But Moses said to God, "If I come to the Israelites and say to them, 'The God of your ancestors has sent me to you,' and they ask me, 'What is his name?' what shall I say to them?" God said to Moses, "I am who I am." He said further, "Thus you shall say to the Israelites, 'I am has sent me to you.'"

—Exodus 3:13–14

## THE READING
Moses has known the power of the pharaoh. He has seen the might of the Egyptian army. But now he is confronted by a new kind of power, a power so great it cannot even be named. It is this strength that will guide Moses in freeing his people from the injustice of Egyptian slavery.

## THE HEXAGRAM

|        | Trigram | Name | Image | Attribute | Family |
|--------|---------|------|-------|-----------|--------|
| Upper  | ☳ | Word | Thunder | Life Giving | First Son |
| Lower  | ☰ | God | Heaven | Strength | Father |

This hexagram consists of the Word issuing out from God. This is the ultimate manifestation of the greatness of God's strength.

## THE ARCHETYPE
There is a time…

- To unite movement and strength.
- To call on inner worth and outer force and thereby actualize great power.
- To not become intoxicated by power and thereby forget to be guided by Wisdom.
- To remain true to the fundamental principles of right and justice.
- To patiently seek the right time to move forward.

Now is that time.

# THE LINES

### MOVING LINE IN THE FIRST POSITION

A moving line in the bottom position warns against allowing power that is not grounded in Wisdom to gain momentum.

### MOVING LINE IN THE SECOND POSITION

A moving line in the second position points to gates that are beginning to open. Resistance has diminished, and the path forward is clear. However, there is a risk of overconfidence. One can guard against this only by remaining grounded in Wisdom.

### MOVING LINE IN THE THIRD POSITION

A moving line in the third position warns the wise one not to boast about having power. This is the way of an inferior person. The wise one remains cautious and does not make empty threats.

### MOVING LINE IN THE FOURTH POSITION

A moving line in the fourth position suggests that this is the time for perseverance, for quietly working at the removal of obstacles. The real power is internal and invisible. This power can manage the heaviest of loads. When one resorts to external strength, a much greater effort is required.

### MOVING LINE IN THE FIFTH POSITION

A moving line in the fifth position suggests that resistance is in the past and everything is easy. There is no longer a need to appear belligerent or stubborn.

### MOVING LINE IN THE SIXTH POSITION

A moving line in the top position warns that we may have gone too far and come to a deadlock. Any movement now just makes the situation more complicated. The wise one takes the time to sit quietly and wait for things to right themselves in their own time.

## NOTES

Wilhelm/Baynes calls this archetype *The Power of the Great*. Pearson calls it *Great Strength*. Barrett calls it *Great Vigor*. Pearson says, "Having power over others is like thunder in the sky: it sounds really impressive, but it doesn't last very long."

# Archetype 35: Progress

Sometime afterwards Joash decided to restore the house of the Lord…A proclamation was made throughout Judah and Jerusalem to bring in for the Lord the tax that Moses the servant of God laid on Israel in the wilderness. All the leaders and all the people rejoiced, and brought their tax and dropped it into the chest until it was full…The king and Jehoiada gave it to those who had charge of the work of the house of the Lord, and they hired masons and carpenters to restore the house of the Lord, and also workers in iron and bronze to repair the house of the Lord. So those who were engaged in the work labored, and the repairs went forward at their hands, and they restored the house of God to its proper condition and strengthened it. When they had finished, they brought the rest of the money to the king and Jehoiada, and with it were made utensils for the house of the Lord, utensils for the service and for the burnt-offerings, and ladles, and vessels of gold and silver.

—2 Chronicles 24:4–14

## THE READING

Joash was a king of Judah around 800 BCE. Jehoiada was his uncle and his priest. Before Joash, God's temple was allowed to fall into disarray. Jehoiada was a man of God and a strong influence on Joash. The two together formed a holy partnership. Jehoiada convinced Joash to restore God's temple. This was a massive undertaking, but the work was undertaken with great joy. People contributed willingly, and the effort exceeded their hopes.

# THE HEXAGRAM

| | Trigram | Name | Image | Attribute | Family |
|---|---|---|---|---|---|
| Upper | ⚎ | Christ | Fire | Light | Second Daughter |
| Lower | ☷ | Wisdom | Earth | Devotion | Mother |

The upper trigram is Christ, whose image is Fire. The lower trigram is Wisdom, whose image is Earth. The Fire dances on the Earth and makes rapid progress.

# THE ARCHETYPE

There is a time...

- To make rapid, easy progress.
- To gather those in similar positions of power to work together for a common goal.
- To dedicate the alliance to God.
- To be careful not to abuse one's influence, but to use that influence for God's work.
- To form a partnership between an enlightened ruler and an obedient servant.
- To know that human nature wants to be aligned with God, but that this desire can be forgotten in the daily grind of life.

Now is that time.

# THE LINES

### MOVING LINE IN THE FIRST PLACE
A moving line in the first place suggests that we are worried about rejection, but we should simply continue doing what we know is right. If we meet with those who do not believe in our goals, there is nothing to be gained by trying to win them over. It would be easy to give in to anger, but this accomplishes nothing. The best course is to remain calm and stay grounded in Wisdom.

### MOVING LINE IN THE SECOND POSITION
A moving line in the second position describes a situation in which progress has been halted, and one is prevented from meeting with those in authority. This blockage causes grief. But the line counsels perseverance. Good news eventually comes from a loving source, like a grandmother soothing a troubled child. The happiness is well deserved because one has stayed true to God's will.

## MOVING LINE IN THE THIRD POSITION
A moving line in the third position describes one who continues to move forward with the support of others. There is nothing wrong with depending on others for help against adversity.

## MOVING LINE IN THE FOURTH POSITION
A moving line in the fourth position suggests that sometimes people acquire wealth through brute strength. This is not God's way. Eventually others will see what has been done. This path only leads to danger.

## MOVING LINE IN THE FIFTH POSITION
A moving line in the fifth position describes one who has achieved an influential position but has remained gentle and true to God's way. At such times, one may reproach oneself for lack of initiative, but this is not worth worrying about. Gains and losses are not important. What is important is that one has gained influence.

## MOVING LINE IN THE SIXTH POSITION
A moving line in the top position suggests that one may go on the offensive now only to deal with the mistakes of one's own people, and even then one must do so carefully. Seek Wisdom's guidance. Be especially careful to avoid exuberance in relating to those who are not closely connected.

## NOTES
Wilhelm/Baynes describes this archetype as *Progress*. Pearson and Barrett both call it *Advancing*. Barrett says, "It is not enough just to be strong and stand firm. You will want to make the most of the strength you have."

# Archetype 36: Darkening

Then the soldiers of the governor took Jesus into the governor's headquarters, and they gathered the whole cohort around him. They stripped him and put a scarlet robe on him, and after twisting some thorns into a crown, they put it on his head. They put a reed in his right hand and knelt before him and mocked him, saying, "Hail, King of the Jews!" They spat on him, and took the reed and struck him on the head. After mocking him, they stripped him of the robe and put his own clothes on him. Then they led him away to crucify him.

—Matthew 27:26–31

## THE READING
Jesus has been beaten, mocked, and humiliated. He has been deserted by his followers. He is alone and facing a terrifying death. The light that he has brought seems about to be snuffed by the darkness and oppression of the Roman Empire.

## THE HEXAGRAM

|       | Trigram | Name   | Image | Attribute | Family          |
|-------|---------|--------|-------|-----------|-----------------|
| Upper |         | Wisdom | Earth | Devotion  | Mother          |
| Lower |         | Christ | Fire  | Light     | Second Daughter |

The image of the lower trigram is Fire. The image of the upper trigram is Earth. The light of the fire has been buried under the earth. Darkness reigns.

## THE ARCHETYPE
There is a time…

- To recognize that evil has taken power.
- To accept that it is the nature of evil to do harm to those who follow Wisdom.
- To not be swept away by evil but remain inwardly committed to the truth.
- To be flexible on the outside while holding to the light on the inside.

- To be willing to hide one's light in the short term to achieve one's goals in the long term.
- To avoid provoking hostility through careless behavior.
- To embrace humility in social interactions.

Now is that time.

## THE LINES

### MOVING LINE IN THE FIRST POSITION
A moving line in the bottom position describes a difficult time. The hero has attempted to soar and has encountered a hostile fate. The hero tries to retreat and hide from the issue, but hiding is not an option. The hero is in turmoil and has no resting place. Ego will not allow compromises, and deprivation is the result. The hero remains true to principle, though with little support from others.

### MOVING LINE IN THE SECOND POSITION
A moving line in the second position describes the situation when the light bearer is temporarily wounded by the Evil One. The injury is not serious and the time is not hopeless. The light bearer thinks only of others and does everything possible to save those who are also in danger. This is acting according to God's laws.

### MOVING LINE IN THE THIRD POSITION
A moving line in the third position describes the situation where a good, strong, and loyal person is trying to create something worthwhile. In doing so, the opponent, the creator of disorder, by chance falls into the hands of one who is pursuing good. This chance event seems lucky, but there is danger. The past has brought many abuses. It is tempting to eliminate these abuses once and for all. But such a hasty act is risky because the abuses have become so institutionalized.

### MOVING LINE IN THE FOURTH POSITION
A moving line in the fourth position suggests that the hero has come close to the dark one, so close that the dark one's thoughts are obvious. This confirms there is no hope for improving the situation and the only thing to be done is to leave before things get worse.

MOVING LINE IN THE FIFTH POSITION

A moving line in the fifth position counsels those who, because of responsibility, cannot leave their posts even though the times are dangerous. This line suggests that they show great caution in dealing with the adversaries, even if it means hiding their true sentiments. But the difficulties of the time must not impede the gathering of great internal strength.

MOVING LINE IN THE SIXTH POSITION

A moving line in the top position suggests that the height of darkness has been reached. It is horrible that so many who followed the light were hurt, but we are consoled knowing that the time of darkness has climaxed. In the end, evil always consumes itself.

## NOTES

Wilhelm/Baynes calls this archetype *Darkening of the Light*. Pearson calls it *Wounded Light*. Barrett calls it *Brightness Hidden*. Pearson says, "This hexagram describes the many dark times in history and human lives, when the sources of light seem wounded, struck down as fatally as a bird shot in flight."

# Archetype 37: Family

Children, obey your parents in the Lord, for this is right. "Honor your father and mother"—this is the first commandment with a promise: "so that it may be well with you and you may live long on the earth." And, parents, do not provoke your children to anger, but bring them up in the discipline and instruction of the Lord.

—Ephesians 6:1–3

## THE READING

Honoring one's parents is a core principle of Judeo-Christian tradition. It is the fifth commandment, and the first of the five commandments that govern how we are to live our lives with other people. In this reading, Paul repeats the traditional requirement that children honor their parents and augments it with the requirement that parents be loving guardians of their children. There are natural roles that must be fulfilled if the family is to thrive. The family must have leadership that offers direction and wisdom. The family must have providers who offer food and shelter. The family must have nurturers who supply love and support. The strong protect the weak, and the weak honor the strong.

## THE HEXAGRAM

|       | Trigram | Name   | Image       | Attribute   | Family         |
|-------|---------|--------|-------------|-------------|----------------|
| Upper |         | Spirit | Gentle Wind | Penetrating | First Daughter |
| Lower |         | Christ | Fire        | Light       | Second Daughter |

The family is held together by strength. This is seen in the hexagram by the strong (solid) lines at the bottom and top positions. The remaining four lines are composed of two complementary line pairs. Each pair consists of one open line on the bottom and one closed line on the top. The pairs represent bonds within the family. One pair represents the bond between parents, and one pair represents the bond between parent and child.

# THE ARCHETYPE
There is a time...

- To honor the laws that govern family relationships and to project those laws out into the world.
- To recognize that the family is nurtured by love, faithfulness, and respect.
- To recognize the need for both authority and loyalty in the family.
- To feel the power of one's words, just as a parent's words have power on a child.
- To know that words have the most power when they are clearly related to the specific issue at hand and not based on generalities.
- To realize that words are only meaningful when they are supported by one's own behavior.
- To temper authority with love and compassion.

Now is that time.

# THE LINES

### MOVING LINE IN THE FIRST POSITION
A moving line in the bottom position describes an ordered family in which everybody is treated with loving fairness and in which all members understand their roles. Children must be gently but firmly indoctrinated into the group so that they know the family rules, structure, and etiquette. Pampered children grow into conceited adolescents who can't see beyond their own egocentric perspectives. It is much easier to teach good behavior from the beginning than it is to correct bad behavior once it is established.

### MOVING LINE IN THE SECOND POSITION
A moving line in the second position encourages the nurturer of the family. This nourishment is both literal (food) and metaphorical (spiritual). This person plays a critically important role for the family and provides a social and religious focus for the family. A true nurturer does not cajole others, but influences by providing loving attention to each person's physical, spiritual, and psychological needs.

### MOVING LINE IN THE THIRD POSITION
A moving line in the third position warns us not to err on the side of strictness and force. Although the family needs structure (and this structure should never be neglected), it should be a structure that accommodates and even encourages individual exploration and growth. If one must err, it is better to err on the side of strictness rather than latitude.

### MOVING LINE IN THE FOURTH POSITION

A moving line in the fourth position encourages the steward of the family. The steward is the one who is responsible for ensuring that expenses are balanced with income. The steward ensures that resources are not wasted, but used in a way that truly benefits the family. In the public sphere, a similar function provides for the general welfare.

### MOVING LINE IN THE FIFTH POSITION

A moving line in the fifth position encourages the wisdom bearer of the family. The wisdom bearer is the one in the family who is best able to set aside Ego and be guided by Wisdom. The wisdom bearer must have a character that is honored and respected. The relationship between the wisdom bearer and the rest of the family is never based on fear, but only on love and trust.

### MOVING LINE IN THE SIXTH POSITION

A moving line in the top position encourages the leader of the family. The personality of the leader sets the personality of the family, so it is especially important that the leader be one who is guided by inner truth. The leader must be one who willingly takes on the burden of responsibility and understands the difference between responsibility and power.

## NOTES

Wilhelm/Baynes calls this archetype *The Family (The Clan)*. The Wilhelm description uses gender stereotypes, but it is the roles that are important in this archetype, not the gender identity of those who take on the roles. Pearson also calls this archetype *Family*. Barrett calls it *People in the Home*.

# Archetype 38: Opposition

But when Cephas [better known as Peter] came to Antioch, I [Paul] opposed him to his face, because he stood self-condemned; for until certain people came from James, he used to eat with the Gentiles. But after they came, he drew back and kept himself separate for fear of the circumcision faction. And the other Jews joined him in this hypocrisy, so that even Barnabas was led astray by their hypocrisy. But when I saw that they were not acting consistently with the truth of the gospel, I said to Cephas [Paul] before them all, "If you, though a Jew, live like a Gentile and not like a Jew, how can you compel the Gentiles to live like Jews?"

—Galatians 2:11–14

## THE READING

The year is sometime around 50 CE. Many in the early church believed that Gentiles could not be Christ followers because Jesus was Jewish. Paul believed that Christ called to all people. From Paul's perspective, "There is no longer Jew or Greek, there is no longer slave or free, there is no longer male and female; for all of you are one in Christ Jesus" (Gal. 3:27–28). Paul thought that Peter, the other major pillar of the early church, understood and agreed with his arguments; until recently, Peter was gladly associating with Gentile converts. But suddenly Peter is succumbing to pressure from hard-line Jewish fundamentalists and having nothing to do with non-Jewish Christ followers. Even worse, Peter is convincing others, including Paul's trusted confidant Barnabas, to do likewise. Peter is simply trying to protect the church by not inflaming the widespread anti-Gentile sentiment. But Paul is having none of this. Paul is furious with what he sees as Peter's hypocrisy.

# THE HEXAGRAM

| | Trigram | Name | Image | Attribute | Family |
|---|---|---|---|---|---|
| Upper | ⚎ | Christ | Fire | Light | Second Daughter |
| Lower | ⚌ | Wonder | Lake | Joy | Third Daughter |

This hexagram consists of the images of Fire over Lake. Fire reaches upward, while Lake drains downward. The two forces are thus in opposition.

# THE ARCHETYPE

There is a time...

- To recognize that opposition and disagreements among the community make it difficult to work together to achieve common goals.
- To refrain from acting out of hurt Ego, which only makes matters worse.
- To focus on making only small advances in areas in which agreement is possible.
- To categorize the divergences and thereby create the seeds of future order.
- To hold true to one's own individuality and not be lulled into pointless bickering.

Now is that time.

# THE LINES

### MOVING LINE IN THE FIRST POSITION

A moving line in the bottom position suggests that when opposition has become manifest, unity cannot be achieved by force. When others are in opposition, it is best to wait for them to decide on their own to return. Conflict may encourage those who should not be part of us to try to join us. Don't force them away; endure them knowing they will drift off on their own.

### MOVING LINE IN THE SECOND POSITION

A moving line in the second position warns that misunderstandings make common ground difficult to find. It is best to wait for God to arrange meetings between those who really belong together.

### MOVING LINE IN THE THIRD POSITION

A moving line in the third position portrays one who feels like Job: conspired against by the whole world, lost, dishonored, and friendless. Now is the time to remain faithful to one's companion and have confidence that a favorable outcome will unfold.

### MOVING LINE IN THE FOURTH POSITION

A moving line in the fourth position suggests that although isolated, one may meet another who is simpatico, a companion who can be trusted. These two wills can then unite and work together for a common vision.

### MOVING LINE IN THE FIFTH POSITION

A moving line in the fifth position counsels that one may be failing to recognize another who is simpatico. Such a person may be hidden because of stressful conditions. Over time, the other reveals an inner affinity, and then it is one's duty to reach out.

### MOVING LINE IN THE SIXTH POSITION

A moving line in the top position warns against misjudging one's best friends. The problem is not external opposition; the problem is one's own suspicious nature. One is advised to look more closely at the other. The other's intentions are pure, and the two can achieve unity in purpose. Just when the conflict seems most severe, the resolution becomes evident.

## NOTES

Wilhelm/Baynes describes this archetype as *Opposition*. Pearson calls it *Double Vision*. Barrett calls it *Opposing*. Pearson says, "This is an example of images gone awry, as they do when a person's eyes focus on separate objects instead of providing a clear image of one."

# Archetype 39: Obstruction

When the king of Egypt was told that the people had fled, the minds of Pharaoh and his officials were changed towards the people, and they said, "What have we done, letting Israel leave our service?" So he had his chariot made ready, and took his army with him; he took six hundred picked chariots and all the other chariots of Egypt with officers over all of them. The Lord hardened the heart of Pharaoh king of Egypt and he pursued the Israelites, who were going out boldly. The Egyptians pursued them, all Pharaoh's horses and chariots, his chariot drivers and his army; they overtook them camped by the sea, by Pi-hahiroth, in front of Baal-zephon.

—Exodus 14:5–9

## THE READING
The Israelites have been enslaved in Egypt for four hundred years. Finally a leader has emerged. Moses has been chosen by God to lead the Israelites to freedom. The Israelites have followed Moses into the desert, as the pilgrimage to the Promised Land has begun. But the pharaoh has reneged on his promise to Moses to let the Israelites free. Instead he sends his army to hunt them down. The Israelites desperately try to stay ahead of the army. But now they have run into an insurmountable obstacle: the Red Sea, a vast body of water almost 1,400 miles long, 220 miles wide, and 1,500 feet deep. With the pharaoh's army rapidly closing in, the Israelites have no place to escape.

## THE HEXAGRAM

|       | Trigram | Name      | Image    | Attribute | Family     |
|-------|---------|-----------|----------|-----------|------------|
| Upper |         | Chaos     | Water    | Danger    | Second Son |
| Lower |         | Stillness | Mountain | Resting   | Third Son  |

The hexagram portrays Chaos in front and the Mountain behind. There is no place to go. The obstruction seems complete. However, the hexagram also contains a hint about how to overcome the obstruction. The upper trigram contains the image of Water. And water winds its way around the mountain.

## THE ARCHETYPE
There is a time…

- To recognize that obstructions appear in the course of events and to not take it personally.
- To see obstructions as challenges that can and should be overcome.
- To accept that not all obstructions can be overcome directly.
- To pause, pull back, join forces with others, and look for leadership that can help overcome the obstruction.
- To detour around the obstruction rather than giving up on the destination.
- To avoid the temptation to blame others for the obstruction and instead look inside.
- To use the obstruction as an opportunity for inner growth and building inner strength.

Now is that time.

## THE LINES

### MOVING LINE IN THE FIRST POSITION
A moving line in the bottom position suggests that when encountering an obstruction, one must take time to contemplate the situation. Retreat doesn't always mean surrender. It can be a time to regroup, reflect, and watch for the right time to move forward.

### MOVING LINE IN THE SECOND POSITION
A moving line in the second position encourages you to take on the obstruction head on. Sometimes the obstacle cannot be avoided or circumvented. But it is important that you make sure you are following the call of duty, not Ego. Only then can you move forward.

### MOVING LINE IN THE THIRD POSITION
A moving line in the third position reminds you that you have a duty to your family or clan as well as to your ideals. These are people who will be devastated and left helpless if you are lost. They need you and will welcome you with love if you turn back and return to them.

### MOVING LINE IN THE FOURTH POSITION

A moving line in the fourth position cautions you to draw back in facing your obstruction. You are not strong enough by yourself. You must gather strength and consolidate support. You cannot push past your obstruction without undergoing preparation. Conditions now are not favorable for moving forward, but are favorable for forging bonds with those who will be your trusted partners.

### MOVING LINE IN THE FIFTH POSITION

A moving line in the fifth position is a call to action. In a true emergency, you cannot avoid the obstruction. You must act despite the risk. The danger seems great, but God has called you to this path. Organize your supporters and work together. Wisdom will show you the way to overcome your obstacle. Listen to her counsel.

### MOVING LINE IN THE SIXTH POSITION

A moving line in the top position is a call to return to the world that has been left behind. You have found a refuge from the pettiness and unhappiness of the world. But now obstructions have materialized in the world you have forgotten. You are tempted to say, "This is not my problem." But it is your problem. You are still connected to your old world, and you can't abandon it. But don't lose the wisdom you have found. It is this wisdom that is precisely what is now needed.

## NOTES

Wilhelm/Baynes calls this archetype *Obstruction*. Pearson calls it *Impeded*. Barrett calls it *Limping*. Barrett says, "This is a time to take a step back from the struggle and connect with people more than with ideals."

# Archetype 40: Deliverance

In the six hundred and first year, in the first month, on the first day of the month, the waters were dried up from the earth; and Noah removed the covering of the ark, and looked, and saw that the face of the ground was drying. In the second month, on the twenty-seventh day of the month, the earth was dry.

Then God said to Noah, "Go out of the ark, you and your wife, and your sons and your sons' wives with you. Bring out with you every living thing that is with you of all flesh—birds and animals and every creeping thing that creeps on the earth—so that they may abound on the earth, and be fruitful and multiply on the earth."

So Noah went out with his sons and his wife and his sons' wives. And every animal, every creeping thing, and every bird, everything that moves on the earth, went out of the ark by families.

—Genesis 8:13–19

## THE READING

For forty days and forty nights, the rain fell upon the earth. Noah and his family remain in the ark, wondering what they will find when the waters finally recede. For another one hundred and fifty days, the ark floats through a watery wasteland. Finally the day has arrived. The tensions of the last six months are behind them. Life can once again blossom forth. The return to normalcy can begin.

## THE HEXAGRAM

|       | Trigram | Name  | Image   | Attribute   | Family     |
|-------|---------|-------|---------|-------------|------------|
| Upper | ☳       | Word  | Thunder | Life Giving | First Son  |
| Lower | ☵       | Chaos | Water   | Danger      | Second Son |

The upper trigram is Word. The bottom trigram is Chaos. The Word has emerged out of Chaos. The time of danger is over.

## THE ARCHETYPE
There is a time…

- To appreciate the potential of all that is now possible.
- To relax one's guard, knowing the danger is in the past.
- To transition back to normalcy as quickly as possible.
- To not let your triumph feed Ego.
- To clean up that which has been left to stagnate.
- To let go of mistakes and errors of judgment and focus on a new beginning.

Now is that time.

## THE LINES

### MOVING LINE IN THE FIRST POSITION
A moving line in the bottom position counsels that the time has come to recover in peace and hold close to stillness. The difficulty is now in the past.

### MOVING LINE IN THE SECOND POSITION
A moving line in the second position warns of those who try to gain influence through flattery. These people are bad influences and must be removed. The removal must be done carefully, with great inner strength and clear focus on the goal of deliverance. It is important to be guided by Wisdom.

### MOVING LINE IN THE THIRD POSITION
A moving line in the third position describes one who has acquired wealth and comfort through no particular merit. Flaunting the wealth leads to envy and jealousy, which only makes the situation worse.

### MOVING LINE IN THE FOURTH POSITION
A moving line in the fourth position cautions against small and petty people who attach themselves like barnacles to those of worth. These hangers-on may even seem indispensable in the accomplishing of mundane tasks, but the day of testing will come. When it does, these parasites must be cast off, or true comrades who could provide meaningful support will pull back in mistrust.

MOVING LINE IN THE FIFTH POSITION

A moving line in the fifth position cautions against alliances with small and petty people. It is best not to attempt to dismiss them, but rather to adopt an inner resolve to separate from them. This inner resolve will soon be felt by the riffraff who will eventually withdraw on their own.

MOVING LINE IN THE SIXTH POSITION

A moving line in the top position warns that a petty person has achieved an influential position. This person is a serious obstruction and must be removed forcefully but with great care.

## NOTES

Wilhelm/Baynes calls this archetype *Deliverance*. Pearson calls it *Released (Untied)*. Barrett calls it *Release*. Pearson says, "This hexagram is about the releasing that must be done by people in high places, those who have more than others."

# Archetype 41: Giving from Below

He sat down opposite the treasury, and watched the crowd putting money into the treasury. Many rich people put in large sums. A poor widow came and put in two small copper coins, which are worth a penny. Then he called his disciples and said to them, "Truly I tell you, this poor widow has put in more than all those who are contributing to the treasury. For all of them have contributed out of their abundance; but she out of her poverty has put in everything she had, all she had to live on."

—Mark 12:41–44

## THE READING

This reading is in contrast to the reading for archetype 42. This reading describes people making offerings to God. In the next reading, God makes an offering to people.

This reading is best understood metaphorically. Obviously Jesus is not looking over the shoulder of those who are donating to God's temple. The widow represents every person who lovingly gives everything they have to God. Jesus is telling us to hold nothing back from God because God holds nothing back from us. In surrendering everything, we are given the opportunity to be all that we can be.

## THE HEXAGRAM

|       | Trigram | Name | Image | Attribute | Family |
|-------|---------|------|-------|-----------|--------|
| Upper | ☶ | Stillness | Mountain | Resting | Third Son |
| Lower | ☱ | Wonder | Lake | Joy | Third Daughter |

This hexagram consists of the trigrams Stillness on top and Wonder on the bottom. These two trigrams have upper lines that seem out of place. The lower trigram is missing a strong solid line to complete its set, and the upper trigram is missing a weak broken line to complete its set. It seems that the missing strong line in the bottom trigram has been given to the upper trigram, which has exchanged it for a weak line.

## THE ARCHETYPE

There is a time…

- For the lower to sacrifice to the higher.
- To simplify and remove what is unnecessary from the facade.
- To find truth in simplicity.
- To control anger with stillness.
- To temper impulses with self-restraint.
- To accept poverty without shame.
- To sacrifice ornamentation for simplicity.
- To present oneself in truth and simplicity before God.

Now is that time.

## THE LINES

### MOVING LINE IN THE FIRST POSITION

A moving line in the bottom position suggests that it is good to help others once one's own responsibilities have been fulfilled. But the one helped is also responsible for not devouring so many resources that the helper is left weak and vulnerable.

### MOVING LINE IN THE SECOND POSITION

A moving line in the second position warns the helper to maintain self-awareness, to remain composed, and to stay dignified. Sacrificing self to serve others is like stealing from the foundation to strengthen the facade.

### MOVING LINE IN THE THIRD POSITION

A moving line in the third position warns that three is an unstable number of people. Two will form a bond, and the third will be jealous. One is also unstable. A single person needs companionship. Thus this moving line suggests two is the ideal number for the team, and that this will soon happen.

### MOVING LINE IN THE FOURTH POSITION

A moving line in the fourth position suggests that the reason people are not helping is because of faults. This is not the time to question others as to why they are unwilling to help. This is the time to look inward and ask yourself what you are doing to make others not want to help. Such introspection is not easy, but it is necessary.

### MOVING LINE IN THE FIFTH POSITION

A moving line in the fifth position brings good news. The signs are favorable. Your path is blessed by God.

### MOVING LINE IN THE SIXTH POSITION

A moving line in the top position describes one who brings blessings to the whole world. Any power this person attracts is immediately used for the benefit of all. In this situation, power is not a zero-sum game. One can gain without others losing. This is a path to success that is blessed.

## NOTES

Wilhelm/Baynes and Pearson call this archetype *Decrease*. Barrett calls it *Decreasing*. Barrett says, "A noble one, when he gives things up, is not without anger and desires: he just keeps them under control."

# Archetype 42: Giving from Above

For God so loved the world that he gave his only Son, so that everyone who believes in him may not perish but may have eternal life.

—John 3:16

## THE READING

This reading is in contrast to the reading for archetype 41. This reading describes God making an offering to people. In the previous reading, people were making offerings to God.

This reading is best understood metaphorically. Obviously God does not have a physical son, and God is not any kind of physical father. God is love (1 John 4:8). This reading describes the essence of God reaching out to us in the most intimate possible way, by incarnation into a human who will model for us the way to live in relationship with the love that is the ground of our being.

## THE HEXAGRAM

|  | Trigram | Name | Image | Attribute | Family |
|---|---|---|---|---|---|
| Upper | | Spirit | Gentle Wind | Penetrating | First Daughter |
| Lower | | Word | Thunder | Life Giving | First Son |

This hexagram consists of the trigrams Spirit on top and Word on the bottom. These two trigrams have bottom lines that seem out of place. The upper trigram is missing a strong solid line to complete its set. It seems that that line has dropped down into the lower trigram, which has exchanged it for a weak line.

# THE ARCHETYPE

There is a time...

- To know that to rule well is to serve.
- For the powerful to make joyful sacrifices for the weak.
- To understand that when the powerful sacrifice for the needy, the needy are given hope and respond with gratitude.
- To realize that grateful people will support even the most difficult and dangerous undertakings.
- To make good use of an auspicious time by cultivating creativity and giving birth to new forms.
- To notice the good in others and emulate it.
- To notice the bad in oneself and correct it.

Now is that time.

# THE LINES

### MOVING LINE IN THE FIRST POSITION

A moving line in the bottom position is advice on how to use help that comes from someone with power. This help is to be used to achieve something great that would have been impossible without the offered help. Thus the energy offered is not to be hoarded, but shared generously.

### MOVING LINE IN THE SECOND POSITION

A moving line in the second position suggests how to attract energy. One attracts energy not by trying to capture the energy, but by creating receptivity to that energy. Like attracts like, and positive energy will be attracted to one with a positive attitude and positive intention. With such energy, one can produce works blessed by God.

### MOVING LINE IN THE THIRD POSITION

A moving line in the third position predicts that a time of blessing has come, and that even seemingly negative events will turn out to be positive. Tough times can lead to our spiritual purification and the burning away of Ego. With Ego out of the way, we are free to act in harmony with Wisdom.

## MOVING LINE IN THE FOURTH POSITION

A moving line in the fourth position points to the need of an intermediary between those who lead and those who follow. These intermediaries must not allow their own Egos to impede the flow from the leaders to the people. It is their job to see to it that what is given arrives where it is most needed and to be a positive influence on the leaders. The importance of this for great undertakings cannot be over-emphasized; this will prove decisive.

## MOVING LINE IN THE FIFTH POSITION

A moving line in the fifth position suggests the need for kindness. True kindness does not look for gratitude; it acts through Wisdom and is satisfied with seeing the positive results achieved.

## MOVING LINE IN THE SIXTH POSITION

A moving line in the top position warns that those in power must not neglect to give to those who are not in power. Failing to give leaves them alone and vulnerable to attack. One must rest before moving, think before speaking, and build relationships before requesting. People do not cooperate with one who is brusque. They don't resonate with one who is angry. They don't give to one who has not developed relationships.

## NOTES

Wilhelm/Baynes and Pearson call this archetype *Increase*. Barrett calls it *Increasing*. Pearson says, "This is a very positive hexagram, encouraging making a major change."

# Archetype 43: Resolution

Meanwhile Saul, still breathing threats and murder against the disciples of the Lord, went to the high priest and asked him for letters to the synagogues at Damascus, so that if he found any who belonged to the Way, men or women, he might bring them bound to Jerusalem.

Now as he was going along and approaching Damascus, suddenly a light from heaven flashed around him. He fell to the ground and heard a voice saying to him, "Saul, Saul, why do you persecute me?" He asked, "Who are you, Lord?"

The reply came, "I am Jesus, whom you are persecuting. But get up and enter the city, and you will be told what you are to do."

—Acts 9:1–6

## THE READING

This reading describes the conversion of Saul, who would later be known as Saint Paul. This reading occurs at the greatest point of tension. Saul had been a fundamentalist Pharisee who persecuted the early Christians without mercy. The fledgling Christian community had been under terrible stress. But then there is a breakthrough, and Saul has the most celebrated conversion experience in history.

## THE HEXAGRAM

|  | Trigram | Name | Image | Attribute | Family |
|---|---|---|---|---|---|
| Upper |  | Wonder | Lake | Joy | Third Daughter |
| Lower |  | God | Heaven | Strength | Father |

This hexagram consists of the lower trigram God and the upper trigram Wonder. The God trigram consists of three strong lines. The Wonder trigram consists of two strong lower lines and a weak upper line. The net result is five strong lines pushing upward against a single weak line. The weak line cannot hold long against this force, and a breakthrough is inevitable.

## THE ARCHETYPE

There is a time…

- To celebrate the turning of the tide against the forces of darkness.
- To be grateful that ignorance is now on the wane.
- To realize that darkness cannot coexist with light; if light is to win, darkness must be completely vanquished.
- To know that darkness can only be overcome by adhering to God's laws, the first of which is that love is the only way.
- To banish all signs of darkness in oneself before looking for the darkness in others.
- To be sure that all accumulation is accompanied by distribution.
- To be guided by Wisdom as one develops one's character.

Now is that time.

## THE LINES

### MOVING LINE IN THE FIRST POSITION

A moving line in the bottom position reminds us that in times of breaking through, it is the beginning that is the most difficult. We want to move forward, but resistance seems insurmountable. This is the time to measure our own strength and move forward only as far as that strength allows. If we start prematurely without the necessary strength, our journey can end disastrously.

### MOVING LINE IN THE SECOND POSITION

A moving line in the second position warns that caution is called for. This is not the time for giving in to excitement and rushing forward. It is the time for seeking Wisdom, being watchful, and preparing to meet the danger even before the danger is manifest. One who is well prepared for danger need have no fear. Be on guard against that which cannot yet be seen and on the alert for that which cannot yet be perceived. Focus on developing strength of character, and people will submit voluntarily. Reason will triumph over passion.

## MOVING LINE IN THE THIRD POSITION

A moving line in the third position describes one caught in a conflict of interest. All others are fighting against the forces of darkness, yet we have a relationship with a member of the darkness. If we confront this person before the time is ready, the person will draw on the forces of darkness. The association with the dark one is beneficial, but one must be careful not to be drawn into the darkness. The association will result in isolation, because others will not understand it. But we must hold firm and remain true. Eventually the right time will come.

## MOVING LINE IN THE FOURTH POSITION

A moving line in the fourth position describes one who is suffering from great restlessness. We cannot stay still; we want to push forward regardless of the power that resists us. Our problem is that we are being led by Ego. If we could let go of Ego and follow Wisdom, all would go well. But the hold of Ego is very strong and not easily ignored.

## MOVING LINE IN THE FIFTH POSITION

A moving line in the fifth position points to a struggle against a follower of the darkness who holds a high position. Due to our relationship with this person, we are tempted to abandon the struggle as hopeless. We are warned not to do this, but to continue moving forward with resolve.

## MOVING LINE IN THE SIXTH POSITION

A moving line in the top position warns against complacency. It seems to us that our goal has been achieved, but some darkness remains. It isn't much, only a tiny residue, but if we don't address it, over time it will grow into a new adversity. Darkness does not go away on its own. It spreads and multiplies until we are once again faced with a new evil.

## NOTES

Wilhelm/Baynes calls this archetype *Break-through (Resoluteness)*. Pearson calls it *Resolute*. Barrett calls it *Deciding*. Barrett says, "The noble one's generosity is like this: a pure, inspired expression of her character, without ulterior motive."

# Archetype 44: Seduction

After this he fell in love with a woman in the valley of Sorek, whose name was Delilah. The lords of the Philistines came to her and said to her, "Coax him, and find out what makes his strength so great, and how we may overpower him, so that we may bind him in order to subdue him; and we will each give you eleven hundred pieces of silver."

So Delilah said to Samson, "Please tell me what makes your strength so great, and how you could be bound, so that one could subdue you"…So he told her his whole secret, and said to her, "A razor has never come upon my head; for I have been a nazirite to God from my mother's womb. If my head were shaved, then my strength would leave me; I would become weak, and be like anyone else."

When Delilah realized that he had told her his whole secret, she sent and called the lords of the Philistines, saying, "This time come up, for he has told his whole secret to me." Then the lords of the Philistines came up to her, and brought the money in their hands.

She let him fall asleep on her lap; and she called a man, and had him shave off the seven locks of his head. He began to weaken, and his strength left him. Then she said, "The Philistines are upon you, Samson!" When he awoke from his sleep, he thought, "I will go out as at other times, and shake myself free." But he did not know that the Lord had left him. So the Philistines seized him and gouged out his eyes. They brought him down to Gaza and bound him with bronze shackles; and he ground at the mill in the prison.

—Judges 16:4–21

## THE READING

Samson and the Philistines are sworn enemies. Many times the Philistines have tried to kill Samson and failed. It would seem that Samson's power is complete. But just when all seems lost to the Philistines, they find an opportunity. They find Delilah. Nobody can defeat Samson, but Delilah has the power to seduce Samson and convince him to defeat himself.

# THE HEXAGRAM

| | Trigram | Name | Image | Attribute | Family |
|---|---|---|---|---|---|
| Upper | ☰ | God | Heaven | Strength | Father |
| Lower | ☴ | Spirit | Gentle Wind | Penetrating | First Daughter |

This hexagram consists of the lower trigram Spirit and the upper trigram God. Together they have five strong lines that would seem insurmountable. And so they might be, except for the weak yielding line in the foundational position. In this position, the otherwise weak line has the power to undermine and seduce the strength above. Contrast this hexagram to the hexagram representing archetype 43, in which the weak line is in the top position and is supported by strength instead of undermining strength.

# THE ARCHETYPE

There is a time…

- To be wary of those who seem weak and innocent but use this innocence to beguile and seduce.
- To be especially wary when one is in a position of power or has something that the seducer wants.
- To realize that a seducer is dangerous precisely because the seducer appears not to be dangerous.
- To realize that the seducer only has power that is willingly surrendered.
- To understand that it is Ego that seeks the gratification of seduction.
- To know that some unions of strong with weak are blessed; for example, the union between the divine and the secular.
- To use Wisdom as a guide in differentiating between positive and negative unions of strong and weak.

Now is that time.

# THE LINES

## MOVING LINE IN THE FIRST POSITION

A moving line in the bottom position warns that when the agent of seduction has found an entry crack, it must be addressed immediately before its influence can take over. There is a temptation to ignore the agent of seduction because it seems so weak and helpless. But if ignored, its power will quickly grow. Then it will be much more dangerous and more difficult to neutralize.

### MOVING LINE IN THE SECOND POSITION

A moving line in the second position suggests how to control the agent of seduction: not through violence, but by keeping it under gentle control. The agent of seduction must also be kept separated from those will feed its evil potential.

### MOVING LINE IN THE THIRD POSITION

A moving line in the third position explains the impasse that exists. The agent of seduction has made a successful appeal to Ego, and this is a dangerous situation. Ego wants to be seduced, but something is preventing this, and Ego is frustrated. Movement seems impossible. But if we can quiet Ego and listen to Wisdom, further damage can be avoided.

### MOVING LINE IN THE FOURTH POSITION

A moving line in the fourth position suggests that sometimes it is best to placate those who are weaker. They may be useful. If we alienate them, they become our enemies. Of what value can they then be?

### MOVING LINE IN THE FIFTH POSITION

A moving line in the fifth position describes a situation in which the person of strength and light is protecting those of weakness and darkness. The strong is guided by Wisdom and is therefore able to control gently but firmly. When the weak are guided like this, they turn around, see the light, and become allies.

### MOVING LINE IN THE SIXTH POSITION

A moving line in the top position describes one who has found the world's problems unbearable and has withdrawn. People who could contribute positively but instead withdraw and rebuff those who seek help are certainly not acting according to God's will. But while they aren't doing any good, at least they aren't doing any harm.

## NOTES

Wilhelm/Baynes calls this archetype *Coming to Meet*. Pearson calls it *The Royal Bride*. Barrett calls it *Coupling*. Barrett says, "The oracle warns you not to take the woman—not to try to seize control of her, and not to marry her."

# Archetype 45: Uniting

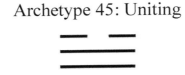

When the hour came, he took his place at the table, and the apostles with him…Then he took a cup, and after giving thanks he said, "Take this and divide it among yourselves; for I tell you that from now on I will not drink of the fruit of the vine until the kingdom of God comes." Then he took a loaf of bread, and when he had given thanks, he broke it and gave it to them, saying, "This is my body, which is given for you. Do this in remembrance of me." And he did the same with the cup after supper, saying, "This cup that is poured out for you is the new covenant in my blood."

—Luke 22:14–20

## THE READING

Jesus is spending his last hours with his disciples. In the morning he will be arrested and, soon after, crucified. Jesus needs to leave his disciples with something that will unify them after he has left. Indeed, something that will unify all his followers for all time. He leaves them with the first Eucharist, that symbolic act in which the participant partakes of the essence of Jesus as spiritual nourishment and that would serve as the core of many Christian worship services for the following two thousand years.

The Book of Common Prayer celebrates the Eucharist and remembers this final act of Jesus with these words: "Sanctify this bread and this wine by your Holy Spirit to be for your people the Body and Blood of your Son, the holy food and drink of new and unending life in him. Sanctify us also that we may faithfully receive this holy Sacrament, and serve you in unity, constancy, and peace."

# THE HEXAGRAM

| | Trigram | Name | Image | Attribute | Family |
|---|---|---|---|---|---|
| Upper | ☱ | Wonder | Lake | Joy | Third Daughter |
| Lower | ☷ | Wisdom | Earth | Devotion | Mother |

The hexagram contains the image of Lake above Earth. Water unites in a lake, and a lake is most naturally found above the earth. The hexagram also consists of two strong lines in the fourth and fifth positions, uniting the weak lines below. There is only one more weak line to unite, that in the top position, so the unification is still in progress but almost complete.

This hexagram is in contrast to the hexagram for archetype 8 (*Holding Together*). In that hexagram, there is only a single strong line uniting the weak lines. Now there are two, so the unity is stronger.

# THE ARCHETYPE

There is a time...

- To unite people into a single group, such as a family, a community, or a state.
- To nurture spiritual traditions that bind the group together over time.
- To identify the central figure of the group.
- To be sure the central figure of the group is one who is grounded in Wisdom.
- To leverage the unity to create great things.
- To take steps to ward off the internal strife that develops in even the closest groups.
- To prepare for the unexpected.

Now is that time.

# THE LINES

### MOVING LINE IN THE FIRST POSITION

A moving line in the bottom position describes the indecision that can accompany the choosing of a group leader. A large group is easily influenced and thus wavers in its decision. But without a leadership decision being made, there is no central core to stabilize the group. The solution is found in discernment and in group prayer. The leader will emerge naturally, and it will be clear to all that the right one has been found. Once this happens, all should support the newly called leader.

### MOVING LINE IN THE SECOND POSITION

A moving line in the second position warns that this is not the time for arbitrary choices. Wisdom is quietly at work, bringing the appropriate people together and creating the necessary relationships. We must give her time to work and follow her lead.

### MOVING LINE IN THE THIRD POSITION

A moving line in the third position describes the predicament of one wanting to be part of the group but not able to break in from the outside. The group is already united, and the outsider feels isolated. The best thing for the outsider to do is to find an ally who is closer to the center of the group. This ally can help the outsider gain acceptance. No one likes being an outsider, but the outsider can take heart knowing there is a way in.

### MOVING LINE IN THE FOURTH POSITION

A moving line in the fourth position describes one who unites in the name of one who is even greater. The uniter is not seeking personal advantage, but is working unselfishly for the greater good. This bodes well for success.

### MOVING LINE IN THE FIFTH POSITION

A moving line in the fifth position reminds us that not everybody who gathers around the center of the group does so for the right reasons. Some do so because they want to be close to the center of power. How do we deal with such people? This line recommends not confronting these people, but gaining their confidence. The way to gain their confidence is for the leader to be absolutely and unswervingly devoted to the goals of the group. Eventually these people will see the Wisdom the leader embodies, and their hearts will be won over.

### MOVING LINE IN THE SIXTH POSITION

A moving line in the top position describes one who wants to be united, but whose intentions are misunderstood. This causes great sadness and misery. But this sadness may be a blessing in disguise, because it can catch the attention of those who have been dismissive. They now see the pain they have caused and reach out to the rejected one. Thus the pain becomes a catalyst for greater unity.

## NOTES

Wilhelm/Baynes calls this archetype *Gathering Together*. Pearson calls it *Gathered Together*. Barrett calls it *Gathering*. Pearson says, "Great changes are possible only when a leader has assembled masses of supporters."

# Archetype 46: Perseverance

Jesus left that place and went away to the district of Tyre and Sidon. Just then a Canaanite woman from that region came out and started shouting, "Have mercy on me, Lord, Son of David; my daughter is tormented by a demon." But he did not answer her at all. And his disciples came and urged him, saying, "Send her away, for she keeps shouting after us." He answered, "I was sent only to the lost sheep of the house of Israel." But she came and knelt before him, saying, "Lord, help me." He answered, "It is not fair to take the children's food and throw it to the dogs." She said, "Yes, Lord, yet even the dogs eat the crumbs that fall from their masters' table." Then Jesus answered her, "Woman, great is your faith! Let it be done for you as you wish." And her daughter was healed instantly.

—Matthew 15:21–28

## THE READING

The Canaanites were the traditional enemies of Israel. In this reading, we have a Canaanite woman asking Jesus, a Jew, to heal her Gentile daughter. She is met with disdain. Jesus won't even answer. His disciples want to send her away. She will not be put off. She comes and kneels before Jesus. Again Jesus rebuffs her, this time even more harshly. He calls her and her people "dogs." But she persists, and then Jesus sees her no longer as a Canaanite, but as a mother. Even Jesus can learn something about love from a mother.

## THE HEXAGRAM

| | Trigram | Name | Image | Attribute | Family |
|---|---|---|---|---|---|
| Upper | ☷ | Wisdom | Earth | Devotion | Mother |
| Lower | ☴ | Spirit | Gentle Wind | Penetrating | First Daughter |

This hexagram consists of two trigrams: Wisdom and Spirit. The hexagram has two strong lines in the lower trigram pushing upward into the upper trigram. These lines are strong. They will get there, but they still have a ways to go.

## THE ARCHETYPE
There is a time…

- To remember that success sometimes takes perseverance and will.
- To not be intimidated by a power imbalance.
- To take advantage of a favorable alignment.
- To gather one's strength and push forward.
- To not resort to violence and force, but engage with modesty and love.
- To adapt one's approach to the needs of the situation.
- To directly approach those with influence.
- To understand that only with persistent effort can a breakthrough occur.

Now is that time.

## THE LINES

### MOVING LINE IN THE FIRST POSITION
A moving line in the bottom position describes the relationship between the lowest and highest places of power. The strength for the perseverance comes from the lowly. But there is a spiritual connection between the low and the high. This synergy gives the lowly the confidence to move forward. As long as humility is shown, success is likely.

### MOVING LINE IN THE SECOND POSITION
A moving line in the second position describes one who is strong but a bit of an oddball. This oddball pays little attention to social niceties and calls it like it is. Still, this oddball has a good character, and people respond positively.

### MOVING LINE IN THE THIRD POSITION
A moving line in the third position describes a time when obstructions are falling away and things are moving forward with little apparent effort. It is wise to move forward and build on recent successes. There is no guarantee that progress will continue, but one should take advantage of the momentum while it lasts.

### MOVING LINE IN THE FOURTH POSITION
A moving line in the fourth position brings good news. The advocate that has persisted is finally successful and wins well-deserved honor. The advocate is elevated to the level of a spiritual leader, thereby achieving a form of immortality.

## MOVING LINE IN THE FIFTH POSITION

A moving line in the fifth position warns the successful advocate not to get anxious and skip necessary steps. Each step is important and must be taken slowly and deliberately. Such deliberation will lead to success.

## MOVING LINE IN THE SIXTH POSITION

A moving line in the top position warns the advocate not to continue pushing blindly. Unless persistence is balanced with rest and perhaps even retreat, exhaustion results. One must take the time to cultivate Wisdom, the only antidote to blind impulse.

## NOTES

Wilhelm/Baynes and Barrett call this archetype *Pushing Upward*. Pearson calls it *Pushing Upwards*. Barrett says, "The noble one has the qualities of both the earth and the seedling—flexible, feeling her way upward, small, and resilient."

# Archetype 47: Oppression

Therefore they set taskmasters over them to oppress them with forced labor. They built supply cities, Pithom and Rameses, for Pharaoh. But the more they were oppressed, the more they multiplied and spread, so that the Egyptians came to dread the Israelites. The Egyptians became ruthless in imposing tasks on the Israelites, and made their lives bitter with hard service in mortar and brick and in every kind of field labor. They were ruthless in all the tasks that they imposed on them.

—Exodus 1:11–14

## THE READING
The Israelites had once been honored guests of Egypt, rightly so because Joseph had saved Egypt from starvation. The Israelites prospered. But now there is a new pharaoh and gratitude has been replaced by fear, envy, and prejudice. The Israelites are now held in slavery and brutally oppressed.

## THE HEXAGRAM

|       | Trigram | Name | Image | Attribute | Family |
|-------|---------|------|-------|-----------|--------|
| Upper |         | Wonder | Lake | Joy | Third Daughter |
| Lower |         | Chaos | Water | Danger | Second Son |

The hexagram consists of two trigrams, Wonder and Chaos, in which weakness is oppressing strength. In the upper trigram, the two strong lines are being held down by a single weak line. In the lower trigram, the single strong line is surrounded and suffocated by weak lines. Thus we see two aspects of oppression, holding down and suffocating.

# THE ARCHETYPE
There is a time...

- To recognize when the lesser oppress the greater.
- To know that the strength and wisdom gained in the struggle with the oppressor can prepare the liberator for ultimate success.
- To meet adversity with the good nature that eventually leads to success.
- To protect our spirits, because if the oppressor breaks our spirits, we have lost.
- To follow the example of a tree in the wind, bending so as not to break, and then springing back when the time is right.
- To remember that Ego is a poor guide in responding to oppression.
- To understand that in times of oppression, even the wise have little influence.
- To use this time to cultivate the deepest inner strength.

Now is that time.

# THE LINES

### MOVING LINE IN THE FIRST POSITION
A moving line in the bottom position reminds the oppressed how important it is to remain inwardly strong. If the oppressed allow weakness to take over, then oppression will quickly overwhelm. This is the beginning of a downward spiral in which the oppressed fall ever deeper into despair. It is the spiral of despair that now must be overcome even more than the oppression itself.

### MOVING LINE IN THE SECOND POSITION
A moving line in the second position points to a different kind of oppression, an inner oppression. Life seems great; everything one might want is in abundance. But the abundance of stuff is superficial and provides no lasting peace. Then a teacher comes and shows a new way. The teacher is calling for disciples. There are still obstacles that must be addressed before this call can be answered. These obstacles cannot be overcome with physical strength; they must be overcome with spiritual strength. One must take the time to gather that spiritual strength through prayer and meditation if one is to be successful.

### MOVING LINE IN THE THIRD POSITION

A moving line in the third position warns against indecision. Indecision results in reckless behavior that aggravates the oppression. Grasping at straws that provide no support makes the situation even worse. Butting your head against the wall does nothing to move the wall. Such behaviors drive away even the most loving partner.

### MOVING LINE IN THE FOURTH POSITION

A moving line in the fourth position describes a generous soul who wants to help those in need. But rather than moving decisively, the benefactor hesitates and meets obstacles. The benefactor is then drawn back into the spheres of the upper class, where concern for the needy is ridiculed. Now the would-be benefactor is compromised. But this is a temporary situation. The benefactor's natural goodness will lead back to Wisdom's way.

### MOVING LINE IN THE FIFTH POSITION

A moving line in the fifth position describes one who wants to help, but is isolated. Those who have responsibility to provide support are unwilling. Those who need the help turn away. Fortunately the situation is temporary. The best use of this time is to meditate and pray for those in need.

### MOVING LINE IN THE SIXTH POSITION

A moving line in the top position describes one whose oppression can be easily overcome. The chains of oppression are fragile. The real problem now is mental attitude. The oppressed are afraid to move and feel powerless. But this is a conditioned response. It is time to stop thinking of oneself as a victim and claim the power that one has. There is no oppression greater than the belief that one is oppressed.

## NOTES

Wilhelm/Baynes calls this archetype *Oppression (Exhaustion)*. Pearson calls it *Exhaustion*. Barrett calls it *Confined*. Pearson says, "Going on beyond what is sustainable should only be done for the noblest of goals."

# Archetype 48: The Well

But he had to go through Samaria. So he came to a Samaritan city called Sychar, near the plot of ground that Jacob had given to his son Joseph. Jacob's well was there, and Jesus, tired out by his journey, was sitting by the well. It was about noon.

A Samaritan woman came to draw water, and Jesus said to her, "Give me a drink." (His disciples had gone to the city to buy food.) The Samaritan woman said to him, "How is it that you, a Jew, ask a drink of me, a woman of Samaria?" (Jews do not share things in common with Samaritans.) Jesus answered her, "If you knew the gift of God, and who it is that is saying to you, 'Give me a drink,' you would have asked him, and he would have given you living water."

The woman said to him, "Sir, you have no bucket, and the well is deep. Where do you get that living water? Are you greater than our ancestor Jacob, who gave us the well, and with his sons and his flocks drank from it?"

Jesus said to her, "Everyone who drinks of this water will be thirsty again, but those who drink of the water that I will give them will never be thirsty. The water that I will give will become in them a spring of water gushing up to eternal life."

—John 4:4–14

## THE READING

In the ancient regions of Israel, water was a precious resource. The idea that there could be an eternal well of water was a powerful metaphor for the nourishment that can only come from God.

## THE HEXAGRAM

|        | Trigram | Name  | Image       | Attribute   | Family         |
|--------|---------|-------|-------------|-------------|----------------|
| Upper  | ☵       | Chaos | Water       | Danger      | Second Son     |
| Lower  | ☴       | Spirit | Gentle Wind | Penetrating | First Daughter |

This hexagram consists of the trigram Spirit guiding Chaos. The image for Spirit is Gentle Wind, and for Chaos, Water. Thus we have a gentle wind pushing the water up to the earth, where it provides an ever flowing source of nourishment.

## THE ARCHETYPE
There is a time…

- To see the well as a symbol for what remains constant in life.
- To realize that even the greatest accomplishments are worth nothing if they do not satisfy our deepest needs.
- To strengthen the foundations for religious institutions, social structures, and individual character for the good of all.
- To see that the well is freely provided by God, and that God wants all to drink deeply.
- To understand that knowledge without Wisdom is as dangerous as ignorance.

Now is that time.

## THE LINES

### MOVING LINE IN THE FIRST POSITION
A moving line in the bottom position describes one who is wallowing in Ego. Such a person offers nothing of value and is ultimately forgotten.

### MOVING LINE IN THE SECOND POSITION
A moving line in the second position describes one who has some Wisdom but does not bother to cultivate it. The quest for Wisdom's way is never ending and requires dedication and commitment. Without dedication and commitment, what Wisdom one has accumulated becomes cloudy. Over time, the Wisdom becomes overshadowed by Ego. Those who are Ego driven associate with others who are Ego driven. Folks like these have nothing to contribute to the Kingdom of God.

### MOVING LINE IN THE THIRD POSITION
A moving line in the third position describes one who is wise and able to help but ignored by those in power. Those who understand are sorry, and wish those who need help could recognize the Wisdom that is available. All would benefit from this.

### MOVING LINE IN THE FOURTH POSITION
A moving line in the fourth position describes a time when Wisdom is being accumulated and a wise one is still in preparation. The wise one is not ready to offer help, but this time is important because it allows time for prayer, meditation, and inner development. This leaves the wise one in a better position to accomplish what is needed.

### MOVING LINE IN THE FIFTH POSITION
A moving line in the fifth position describes a natural leader and savior who offers the gift of living water. But living water can only be offered; one cannot force others to drink. It is up to each individual to choose to accept this gift and use it to facilitate the Kingdom of God.

### MOVING LINE IN THE SIXTH POSITION
A moving line in the top position describes the source of the living water. It is inexhaustible. It is available for all. It is a blessing for all. A fully actualized wise one is like this; the more people take, the more is available.

## NOTES
Wilhelm/Baynes, Pearson, and Barrett all call this archetype *The Well*. Pearson says, "An enlightened leader avoids calamities by making sure all these components are kept in good working order, and sees that access to the well is shared."

# Archetype 49: Revolution

"Do not think that I have come to bring peace to the earth; I have not
come to bring peace, but a sword.
For I have come to set a man against his father,
and a daughter against her mother,
and a daughter-in-law against her mother-in-law;
and one's foes will be members of one's own household.
Whoever loves father or mother more than me is not worthy of me;
and whoever loves son or daughter more than me is not worthy of me;
and whoever does not take up the cross and follow me is not worthy
of me. Those who find their life will lose it, and those who lose their
life for my sake will find it."

—Matthew 10:34–39

## THE READING

One might think Jesus wants an armed revolution. But this is not the case.
On the contrary, Jesus is calling for an overturning of Pax Romana, the peace
through force that is the calling card of the Roman Empire. Jesus brings
instead Pax Christi, the peace of Christ, a peace based on love, compassion,
and equality. Jesus knows that the Roman Empire is not going to give up
power willingly. They will respond as the powerful always respond: with
coercion, intimidation, and violence.

Jesus is telling his followers that this is not an easy path he has laid before
them. His prophecy comes true. In short order, Jesus is crucified, Stephen is
stoned to death, and James is murdered by King Herod Agrippa's sword.
Before long, most of Jesus's original apostles will meet violent deaths. The
persecution of the early Christians will continue for another three hundred
years. But Jesus promises us that the Kingdom of God will eventually
overcome, and, in fact, that it is already present within us. But we must
understand that those who choose to follow the path of light will be
ostracized by those who follow the path of darkness. Darkness can only
survive by attacking light.

# THE HEXAGRAM

| | Trigram | Name | Image | Attribute | Family |
|---|---|---|---|---|---|
| Upper | ☱ | Wonder | Lake | Joy | Third Daughter |
| Lower | ☲ | Christ | Fire | Light | Second Daughter |

This hexagram consists of the lower trigram Christ under the upper trigram Wonder. The image of Christ is Fire, and the image of Wonder is Lake. Thus we have the lake over the fire. This is an unstable situation. Fire cannot long survive like this. Soon the fire will be extinguished, and a new order will emerge.

# THE ARCHETYPE

There is a time...

- To bring about social revolutions, but only as a last resort; revolutions have a high cost and result in much sorrow.
- To know that not all are able to bring about a successful revolution. It requires the support of the people and precise timing.
- To be clear that the leader of the revolution must be free from Ego and closely follow Wisdom's way.
- To lead the people wisely, by uplifting them and teaching them how to move forward in accordance with God's will.
- To carefully observe the internal patterns of that which seems chaotic, and to thus bring clarity and order to the chaos.

Now is that time.

# THE LINES

## MOVING LINE IN THE FIRST POSITION
A moving line in the bottom position warns changes should not be undertaken lightly. Restraint is called for. Now is the time for cultivating Wisdom, not for rushing into action.

## MOVING LINE IN THE SECOND POSITION
A moving line in the second position suggests that the time for revolution has come. But preparations must first be made. The right leader must be found, one who is wise and is trusted by the people. And great Wisdom is called for. But there is no other alternative. Revolution is no longer avoidable.

## MOVING LINE IN THE THIRD POSITION

A moving line in the third position warns of two mistakes that can be made. One is to move too quickly and too aggressively. The other is to move too slowly and too conservatively. Either of these is dangerous. Not every demand for change is to be heeded. On the other hand, valid issues must be addressed. How can one tell the difference between the frivolous and the substantial? One test is simple: where there is smoke, there's fire. When the demands are heard again and again, it becomes clear that action is called for.

## MOVING LINE IN THE FOURTH POSITION

A moving line in the fourth position suggests that the more radical the change, the more important the character of the leader. For radical change to be successful, the leader must have adequate authority, influence, and great inner strength. Even this is not enough; the leader must have access to great Wisdom and thus have successfully vanquished Ego. Any revolution that is not built on such a foundation will fail.

## MOVING LINE IN THE FIFTH POSITION

A moving line in the fifth position describes a revolution led by a great leader. Such a revolution has clearly defined guiding principles that are easily understood and attract widespread support.

## MOVING LINE IN THE SIXTH POSITION

A moving line in the top position describes the aftermath of the revolution. This is the time to undertake additional minor reforms and solidify the gains that have been achieved. People need to adjust to the new times. This is not a time to expect major changes, but to be satisfied with relatively small adjustments. These adjustments will give long-term stability to the great changes that have been achieved.

## NOTES

Wilhelm/Baynes calls this archetype *Revolution (Molting)*. Pearson calls it *Molting (Shedding)*. Barrett calls it *Radical Change*. Barrett says, "It is time for transformation."

# Archetype 50: The Breadbasket

Give us this day our daily bread.

—Matthew 6:11

## THE READING

In the original Greek, the word that became the English *daily* was ἐπιούσιος, or *epiousios*. Surprisingly, this word appears nowhere else in the entire Bible. Even more surprisingly, it appears nowhere else in all of Greek literature up to that date. The reality is we don't know what the word means. It is not likely that the word means *daily*, since there were other words used in the Bible for that.

We can only assume that the adjective that modifies the word *bread* had a very special meaning to the writers of Matthew and Mark, who both used that highly unusual word in their recommended prayer form. We will probably never know what the word meant to them. What does the word mean to you?

## THE HEXAGRAM

|       | Trigram | Name   | Image       | Attribute   | Family          |
|-------|---------|--------|-------------|-------------|-----------------|
| Upper |         | Christ | Fire        | Light       | Second Daughter |
| Lower |         | Spirit | Gentle Wind | Penetrating | First Daughter  |

This hexagram consists of the lower trigram Spirit and the upper trigram Christ. The image of Spirit is Gentle Wind. The image of Christ is Fire. Thus we have a gentle wind fanning the fire. This provides the heat to transform the raw ingredients into nourishment.

## THE ARCHETYPE

There is a time…

- To see God in those who hold true to Wisdom's way.
- To accept the will of God as revealed by the wise.
- To nourish society through its weakest members.
- To help others grow into their divine potential.
- To understand that both spiritual and physical nourishment are needed.
- To be sure that the need for nourishment has been met.
- To offer sacrifices that will hasten God's Kingdom.
- To find the harmony in God's will and one's own interest.
- To remember that nourishment is necessary for both physical and spiritual growth.
- To find the harmony in fate and life.

Now is that time.

## THE LINES

### MOVING LINE IN THE FIRST POSITION

A moving line in the bottom position describes a breadbasket turned upside down. This is not bad. It is how the crumbs are removed. Everything has importance, even the lowliest. It is not one's position in life that determines one's value; it is one's willingness to be consecrated to the will of God.

### MOVING LINE IN THE SECOND POSITION

A moving line in the second position describes a breadbasket that is filled with bread. This suggests the importance of achieving something of significance. Each person is tasked by God with a purpose. If we are able to discern our calling and focus our energy on what God wants from us, we can accomplish great things. But this line also warns us not to claim undue credit, which only provokes the jealousy of others.

### MOVING LINE IN THE THIRD POSITION

A moving line in the third position describes a bread basket with a broken handle. When the handle is broken, the basket cannot be lifted, and it is no longer useful. It still contains food, but the food cannot be eaten. This also describes one who goes unrecognized. Without recognition, it is difficult to be effective. What a waste. The unrecognized one is counseled to focus on developing spiritual strengths and biding one's time. If one does this, the current tension will be resolved.

## MOVING LINE IN THE FOURTH POSITION

A moving line in the fourth position describes a breadbasket with broken legs. When the legs are broken, the contents spill out. This also describes one who has a difficult task and is not equal to it. Part of the problem is that one has not devoted all of one's strength to the task. Even worse, one is affiliated with inferior people. When one is not dedicated to what must be done and hangs with others who are similarly uninterested, little of value can be accomplished.

## MOVING LINE IN THE FIFTH POSITION

A moving line in the fifth position describes a breadbasket with gold handles. Gold signifies strength. This also describes one who is modest and approachable. Such a person will easily attract able helpers. But it is important to be ever diligent against the corrosive effects of Ego.

## MOVING LINE IN THE SIXTH POSITION

A moving line in the top position describes a breadbasket with jade handles. Jade represents something that is hard but with a soft luster. This line therefore suggests that hardness must be combined with softness. One is to give strong counsel, but that counsel is to be delivered delicately and softly.

## NOTES

Wilhelm/Baynes and Pearson call this archetype *The Cauldron*. Barrett calls it *The Vessel*. Barrett says, "This marks a new beginning."

# Archetype 51: Thunder

On the morning of the third day there was thunder and lightning, as well as a thick cloud on the mountain, and a blast of a trumpet so loud that all the people who were in the camp trembled. Moses brought the people out of the camp to meet God. They took their stand at the foot of the mountain. Now Mount Sinai was wrapped in smoke, because the Lord had descended upon it in fire; the smoke went up like the smoke of a kiln, while the whole mountain shook violently. As the blast of the trumpet grew louder and louder, Moses would speak and God would answer him in thunder.

When the Lord descended upon Mount Sinai, to the top of the mountain, the Lord summoned Moses to the top of the mountain, and Moses went up...When all the people witnessed the thunder and lightning, the sound of the trumpet, and the mountain smoking, they were afraid and trembled and stood at a distance, and said to Moses, "You speak to us, and we will listen; but do not let God speak to us, or we will die."

—Exodus 19:16–20; 20:18–19

## THE READING
It is now the first day of the seventh week since the Israelites fled Egypt. Seven is one of the mystical numbers of the Hebrew scripture. It is the number of divine fulfillment. On this day, the Israelites are to meet God. They hear the voice of God in the fearsome thunder, lightning, and smoking mountain. The people are terrified. Perhaps God takes pity on the Israelites. God does not meet them physically. God meets them in God's words, yhe Ten Commandments.

# THE HEXAGRAM

| | Trigram | Name | Image | Attribute | Family |
|---|---|---|---|---|---|
| Upper | ☳ | Word | Thunder | Life Giving | First Son |
| Lower | ☳ | Word | Thunder | Life Giving | First Son |

This hexagram consists of a doubled Word trigram. The image of the Word is Thunder. Thunder is shown as the strong lower line breaking through the two upper weak lines. In this hexagram, Thunder is doubled, giving it that much more power. When the strong breaks through the weak, the weak can never be the same. Shock, fear, and even nervous laughter are the immediate results, but long-term changes will also set in as the weak readjusts itself to the awesome presence of the strong.

# THE ARCHETYPE
There is a time…

- To expect a great manifestation of God.
- To understand that this manifestation will cause shock and fear.
- To be reassured that the shock will be followed by rejoicing.
- To look within for the Wisdom to guide one in addressing the terror of the Thunder.
- To recognize the thunder for what it is, a visible manifestation of a great change.
- To welcome the Thunder with calmness and acceptance.
- To continue honoring the religious traditions.

Now is that time.

# THE LINES

### MOVING LINE IN THE FIRST POSITION
A moving line in the bottom position portrays the shocked one as one who is at a disadvantage relative to others. It may seem that others are ridiculing the shocked one. But this will soon be over. Eventually relief comes, and the initial terror gives way to a positive outcome.

### MOVING LINE IN THE SECOND POSITION
A moving line in the second position describes a situation in which the shocked one is in danger and has suffered great loss. This is not the time to resist shock. Now is the time to retreat to where one can be safe. One must simply endure one's losses, knowing that they will eventually be repaid.

## MOVING LINE IN THE THIRD POSITION

A moving line in the third position describes a particular kind of shock: the shock of fate. It seems that fate has dealt a cruel blow, and it is easy to give way to despair. God does not promise us a life without hardship, and now it seems hardship has overwhelmed all hope. However, God also promises that any hardship can be turned into a wonderful thing, even a miracle. It is a matter of following Wisdom's way, which will show the path to transformation.

## MOVING LINE IN THE FOURTH POSITION

A moving line in the fourth position describes a situation in which movement seems impossible. All seems caught in a quagmire. There is no energy for moving either forward or backward.

## MOVING LINE IN THE FIFTH POSITION

A moving line in the fifth position describes not a single shock, but multiple shocks, with little time for recovery in between. But one can withstand the repeated buffeting of the waves if one can just remain centered and grounded.

## MOVING LINE IN THE SIXTH POSITION

A moving line in the top position describes a situation when the shock seems at its height. At such a time, it is difficult to remain centered and grounded. It is hard to hear Wisdom's counsel. This is a time to stay focused and wait for clarity to be restored, a time to withdraw from the tumult that is all around and to look inside oneself. Others will be caught up in the strife and express their unhappiness at the withdrawal. This is their problem. One can only control one's own responses.

## NOTES

Wilhelm/Baynes calls this archetype *The Arousing (Shock, Thunder)*. Pearson calls it *Thunder*. Barrett calls it *Shock*. Pearson says, "Even in times as terrifying as this, it is important to keep steady hands and heart."

# Archetype 52: Holding Still

And when Jesus got into the boat, his disciples followed him. A gale arose on the lake, so great that the boat was being swamped by the waves; but he was asleep. And they went and woke him up, saying, "Lord, save us! We are perishing!" And he said to them, "Why are you afraid, you of little faith?" Then he got up and rebuked the winds and the sea; and there was a dead calm. They were amazed, saying, "What sort of man is this, that even the winds and the sea obey him?"

—Matthew 8:23–27

## THE READING

In this reading, we are given a wonderful metaphor. Through faith, meditation, and prayer, we can transform the storms of life into "a great calm."

## THE HEXAGRAM

|       | Trigram | Name | Image | Attribute | Family |
|-------|---------|------|-------|-----------|--------|
| Upper | ☶ | Stillness | Mountain | Resting | Third Son |
| Lower | ☶ | Stillness | Mountain | Resting | Third Son |

This hexagram is the opposite of the last hexagram, that for *Thunder* (archetype 51). Both of these hexagrams consist of a doubled trigram, and both trigrams consist of a single strong line and two weak lines. In *Thunder*, the solid line is at the bottom of the two broken lines. Now the solid line is above the broken lines, where it can rest peacefully in its natural position. The image of Stillness is Mountain, which conveys an eternal picture of stillness. In this hexagram, we have Stillness doubled, which conveys the great calm Jesus spoke of.

# THE ARCHETYPE
There is a time...

- To understand that the nature of calmness is being still when stillness is called for and moving when movement is called for.
- To take the time to quiet and center the mind.
- To persevere in the quest for stillness despite the difficulties.
- To let go of the struggles and tumult of daily life.
- To turn to the world only when a state of calmness has been achieved.
- To see past the storms and tribulations of Ego and cultivate the faith and wisdom that lead to inner peace.
- To acutely focus the thoughts on the immediate problem.

Now is that time.

# THE LINES

### MOVING LINE IN THE FIRST POSITION
A moving line in the bottom position counsels on the importance of holding still, especially in the beginning. This is a time when mistakes have not yet been made, and there is a natural harmony with Wisdom's way. Ego has not yet run amok, and one can more easily see the truth of things as they are. It takes effort and resolve to hold to stillness at the beginning, but the effort is worthwhile.

### MOVING LINE IN THE SECOND POSITION
A moving line in the second position warns of being carried along by the motion of one's superior. Even if one is striving to build a centered calm, there is little one can do to mitigate the anxious thoughts of those in power.

### MOVING LINE IN THE THIRD POSITION
A moving line in the third position describes a calm that is brought about through force. True calmness comes about naturally and cannot be forced. If one is trying to force calmness through meditation and/or other approaches, the result is a phony calmness that is really a mask for Ego. This creates the potential for considerable harm.

### MOVING LINE IN THE FOURTH POSITION
A moving line in the fourth position tells us that the highest stage of rest is one in which the Ego has been completely silenced. At this time, this goal has not been achieved. Still, one is making important progress and is encouraged to continue.

## MOVING LINE IN THE FIFTH POSITION

A moving line in the fifth position warns that one is in a dangerous situation and feels out of control, and that one is inclined to be careless in speech. This exacerbates the situation. On the other hand, if one is careful with words, these words gain power.

## MOVING LINE IN THE SIXTH POSITION

A moving line in the top position describes one who has achieved great inner tranquility. Everything in life can now be approached from a position of calmness. A person like this is a source of peace and calm that has a universal impact.

## NOTES

Wilhelm/Baynes calls this archetype *Keeping Still, Mountain*. Pearson calls it *Stillness*. Barrett calls it *Stilling*. Barrett says, "To still yourself is to come to rest in your own right place."

# Archetype 53: Gradual Progress

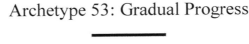

And not only that, but we also boast in our sufferings, knowing that suffering produces endurance, and endurance produces character, and character produces hope, and hope does not disappoint us, because God's love has been poured into our hearts through the Holy Spirit that has been given to us.

—Romans 5:2–5

## THE READING

The reading is from Paul's letters to the Romans. This is not an easy time for Christians. Paul wants to ensure the Christians in Rome understand that the road ahead will be one of slow but consistent progress. They must persevere and not lose hope. The future of the world depends on this.

## THE HEXAGRAM

|       | Trigram | Name | Image | Attribute | Family |
|-------|---------|------|-------|-----------|--------|
| Upper |         | Spirit | Gentle Wind | Penetrating | First Daughter |
| Lower |         | Stillness | Mountain | Resting | Third Son |

The hexagram consists of the lower trigram Stillness and the upper trigram Spirit. This conveys the picture of slow movement of Spirit. Further, the attribute of Spirit is Penetrating, and that of Stillness is Resting. Again we see a slow progress, a gentle penetrating of Spirit grounded in Stillness.

## THE ARCHETYPE

There is a time…

- To move forward slowly, deliberately, step by step.
- To seek safe resting places for rejuvenation.
- To cultivate internal tranquility.
- To accept that progress will occur, but that it will happen gradually.
- To influence others by the gentle determination of one's character.

Now is that time.

# THE LINES

### MOVING LINE IN THE FIRST POSITION
A moving line in the bottom position describes a lonely young person who is just starting life. Without help, progress is slow and hesitant. Danger is all around, and criticism is frequent. The net result of this is a natural impediment to rapid progress. The only way forward is slow and deliberate, but ultimately, this is more likely to lead to success.

### MOVING LINE IN THE SECOND POSITION
A moving line in the second position is the next stage from a moving line in the first position. Now a position of safety has been found, and one's basic needs are being met. The first signs of success bring great relief, and one's path is now more certain. It is a good time to share one's fortune with others.

### MOVING LINE IN THE THIRD POSITION
A moving line in the third position warns against moving too quickly. Things need to progress slowly. Rushing results in strife, and this can threaten not only one's goals but even one's life. The important point is to follow not Ego, which wants to confront opposition, but Wisdom's way, which tells us to remain centered and resolute. This is not a time for passivity; if one is attacked, these attacks must be repelled. But it is not a time for aggressive expansion. Let things happen in their own time.

### MOVING LINE IN THE FOURTH POSITION
A moving line in the fourth position describes one who is in an inappropriate situation. It is a time in which maintaining one's position is difficult. The best recourse is to be realistic and yield to the opposing strength. This is not a time for making progress. It is a time for finding a new safe place from whence one can better withstand the dangers.

### MOVING LINE IN THE FIFTH POSITION
A moving line in the fifth position warns that we have become isolated from those whose support is critical. Misunderstandings are getting in the way of relationships. These relationships are foundational, and now that these relationships have been poisoned, everything is moribund. The problem is not in the relationships; the problem is that others with their own agendas have manipulated the situation. This is not a serious situation. Misunderstandings will soon be cleared up, and the relationships will be returned to their natural wholeness.

## Moving Line in the Sixth Position

A moving line in the top position describes a goal that has been achieved, a work that has been completed, a life that has achieved its purpose. Now a new phase begins in which this life serves as an example to others.

## NOTES

Wilhelm/Baynes calls this archetype *Development (Gradual Progress)*. Pearson and Barrett call it *Gradual Progress*. Pearson says, "We need to come to earth and refuel."

# Archetype 54: Affection

"This is my commandment, that you love one another as I have loved you. No one has greater love than this, to lay down one's life for one's friends. You are my friends if you do what I command you. I do not call you servants any longer, because the servant does not know what the master is doing; but I have called you friends, because I have made known to you everything that I have heard from my Father."

—John 15:12–15

## THE READING

This reading describes a transition in the relationship between Jesus and his disciples. Until now, their relationship has been a student/master relationship. Now Jesus has accepted his disciples as his most intimate friends. Still, they are not equals. Jesus will continue to provide them (and us) guidance, even after his looming death on the cross.

## THE HEXAGRAM

| | Trigram | Name | Image | Attribute | Family |
|---|---|---|---|---|---|
| Upper | | Word | Thunder | Life Giving | First Son |
| Lower | | Wonder | Lake | Joy | Third Daughter |

The hexagram consists of the trigram Word over the trigram Wonder. These two concepts describe the kind of love captured in this archetype: a younger lover who follows a beloved. Wonder characterizes the younger lover, and the Word characterizes the older, wiser consort.

## THE ARCHETYPE

There is a time...

- To be taken into the family, but to be careful not to upset existing relationships.
- To assimilate into the relationship with discretion.
- To be mindful of the risk of miscommunication, which can lead to misunderstandings and hurt feelings.
- To remember that even the best relationships require ongoing work and commitment.

Now is that time.

## THE LINES

### MOVING LINE IN THE FIRST POSITION

A moving line in the bottom position describes one whose status is due to a special relationship with another who is higher. This is a time not to gloat, but to work quietly and try to fit in to existing patterns. This does not imply passivity, but rather a softer and subtler way of achieving things.

### MOVING LINE IN THE SECOND POSITION

A moving line in the second position describes a lover who has been disillusioned with a partner and is now in a state of loneliness. Perhaps the disappointing partner has been unfaithful or has left the relationship. But still, the disappointed lover remains loyal and true.

### MOVING LINE IN THE THIRD POSITION

A moving line in the third position describes one who dreams for what is not likely to be granted. The dreamer is not being realistic. But if the dreamer can compromise, some of what the dreamer wants may be obtainable.

### MOVING LINE IN THE FOURTH POSITION

A moving line in the fourth position counsels patience. It seems that it is too late to achieve one's dreams. But the line tells the dreamer to remain committed to Wisdom's way and to resist the temptation to give in to sorrow. What one truly needs is going to be granted.

### MOVING LINE IN THE FIFTH POSITION

A moving line in the fifth position describes a lover who has been taken into a relationship of modest needs. Success depends on the lover adapting with grace, modesty, and humility to this situation.

MOVING LINE IN THE SIXTH POSITION

A moving line in the top position describes a relationship in which the partners are simply acting their parts without feeling, involvement, or commitment. They look on the relationship with disdain and disrespect. If this doesn't change, the relationship has little hope.

## NOTES

Wilhelm/Baynes and Barrett call this archetype *The Marrying Maiden*. Pearson calls it *Coming Home*. Pearson says, "This hexagram describes the moment when a newly married bride reaches the home where she will belong for the rest of her life."

# Archetype 55: Abundance

Now King Hiram of Tyre sent his servants to Solomon, when he heard that they had anointed him king in place of his father; for Hiram had always been a friend to David. Solomon sent word to Hiram, saying, "You know that my father David could not build a house for the name of the Lord his God because of the warfare with which his enemies surrounded him, until the Lord put them under the soles of his feet. But now the Lord my God has given me rest on every side; there is neither adversary nor misfortune. So I intend to build a house for the name of the Lord my God, as the Lord said to my father David, 'Your son, whom I will set on your throne in your place, shall build the house for my name.' Therefore command that cedars from the Lebanon be cut for me. My servants will join your servants, and I will give you whatever wages you set for your servants; for you know that there is no one among us who knows how to cut timber like the Sidonians."

When Hiram heard the words of Solomon, he rejoiced greatly, and said, "Blessed be the Lord today, who has given to David a wise son to be over this great people."

—1 Kings 5:1–7

## THE READING

The reading describes a time when the Jewish civilization was at its most advanced and powerful. Solomon is now king. He is going to use this time of peace, prosperity, and abundance to fulfill a promise that his father had made. He would build a great temple for God. The temple will stand for more than four hundred years, but not even Solomon's temple can last forever.

# THE HEXAGRAM

| | Trigram | Name | Image | Attribute | Family |
|---|---|---|---|---|---|
| Upper | ☳ | Word | Thunder | Life Giving | First Son |
| Lower | ☲ | Christ | Fire | Light | Second Daughter |

This hexagram consists of the lower trigram Christ and the upper trigram Word. The Word and Christ are two aspects of the same manifestation. The Word is the creative outpouring of God power. Christ is God power made manifest as human. Christ is the God child who shows us the way to also become God children. We are then no longer aligned with the finite and limited but with the infinite and unlimited, and we have within our grasp the inexhaustible abundance the Word promises.

# THE ARCHETYPE

There is a time...

- To appreciate the great abundance that God has provided, knowing that all worldly wealth is fleeting.
- To recognize that not all are equally able to bring about a time of abundance; it takes a great leader.
- To understand that not all are equally able to lead in a time of abundance; it takes wisdom to understand how to make use of the abundance God has given.
- To carefully investigate the facts, enforce the laws, and apply discipline swiftly and fairly.

Now is that time.

# THE LINES

### MOVING LINE IN THE FIRST POSITION
A moving line in the bottom position gives advice on how to bring about desired abundance. It takes the union of clarity and energy. These two attributes may be found in two people who form a close partnership and commit to that partnership for the long term.

## MOVING LINE IN THE SECOND POSITION

A moving line in the second position suggests that politics and conspiracies have come between a leader who has a plan to bring about abundance and a helper who is critical to that plan. The line warns against moving forward at this time. Doing so will only result in obstructions. Instead, the line suggests remaining outwardly still while inwardly gathering wisdom. In time, truth will win out.

## MOVING LINE IN THE THIRD POSITION

A moving line in the third position warns that the inauspicious conditions warned about in the previous (second) moving line have become even more pronounced. The intrigue is now so intense that the leader has little allure. Now, even the pettiest and most insignificant riffraff are able to distract from what needs to be accomplished. There is nothing the leader can do at this time.

## MOVING LINE IN THE FOURTH POSITION

A moving line in the fourth position suggests that the darkness that has been described in the last two moving lines is beginning to ebb. It is now time to bring Wisdom and Action together into one joyful whole.

## MOVING LINE IN THE FIFTH POSITION

A moving line in the fifth position advises the ruler to be open to the wisdom of others. Fortunately, there are many wise and able people who can offer wise counsel. This brings success to all.

## MOVING LINE IN THE SIXTH POSITION

A moving line in the top position describes one who is arrogant and seeks abundance only for Ego satisfaction. This person's thirst for power quickly alienates everybody and leaves the arrogant one isolated.

## NOTES

Wilhelm/Baynes calls this archetype *Abundance (Fullness)*. Pearson and Barrett call it *Abundance*. Pearson says, "This is a time to enjoy the present and the illustrious colleagues abundance brings, and to spread one's own light widely."

# Archetype 56: The Wanderer

A scribe then approached and said, "Teacher, I will follow you wherever you go." And Jesus said to him, "Foxes have holes, and birds of the air have nests; but the Son of Man has nowhere to lay his head."

—Matthew 8:19–20

## THE READING

Jesus has chosen the precarious and lonely life of a wanderer.

## THE HEXAGRAM

| | Trigram | Name | Image | Attribute | Family |
|---|---|---|---|---|---|
| Upper | | Christ | Fire | Light | Second Daughter |
| Lower | | Stillness | Mountain | Resting | Third Son |

This hexagram consists of the lower trigram Stillness, whose image is Mountain, and the upper trigram Christ, whose image is Fire. Fire on the mountain cannot remain in a fixed position. It must move forward, seeking new fuel.

## THE ARCHETYPE
There is a time...

- To not remain rigidly in place, but to wander through new, strange lands far from home.
- To accept the insecurity of having few resources to draw upon, few friends nearby, and little protection.
- To understand that the way to win allies in the distant lands is to be accommodating, considerate, and courteous to those you encounter.
- To be cautious in the places one tarries and in the people with whom one associates.
- To treat imprisonment as a temporary state of affairs and not to allow it to become a way of life.
- To deal with lawsuits and penalties quickly and then move on.

Now is that time.

## THE LINES

### MOVING LINE IN THE FIRST POSITION
A moving line in the bottom position tells the wanderer not to get distracted with things encountered that are of little value. These things are demeaning. This is also not the time to try to make friends by demeaning oneself. This can only result in contempt and degradation. Now is not the time for the wanderer to appear soft spoken and defenseless, but to cultivate the inner dignity that will see one through.

### MOVING LINE IN THE SECOND POSITION
A moving line in the second position reassures the wanderer that modesty and humility are proving helpful. The wanderer is in touch with Wisdom. Interiorly, the wanderer is grounded. Exteriorily, people are supportive and goals can be accomplished. The time is also right to gain the allegiance of a new supporter, one who will prove valuable in future wanderings.

### MOVING LINE IN THE THIRD POSITION
A moving line in the third position describes a wanderer who is in trouble. The wanderer has nobody to blame but Ego. The wanderer has treated followers with contempt and has lost their loyalty. The wanderer is minding other people's business, behaving poorly, and acting arrogantly. No wonder the people have turned the wanderer out. A stranger in a strange land is particularly vulnerable, and the wanderer would best remember this.

## MOVING LINE IN THE FOURTH POSITION

A moving line in the fourth position describes a wanderer who has learned to control Ego and stay true to Wisdom's way. Shelter has been found, property has been acquired, and the wanderer has a respite. Still the danger persists, and the wanderer must remain on guard, ready to defend possessions. Despite the respite, the wanderer is not truly safe and remains a stranger in a strange land.

## MOVING LINE IN THE FIFTH POSITION

A moving line in the fifth position describes a wanderer who knows how to greet circumstances and make introductions. Doing so, the wanderer may find supporters and make progress in reaching goals.

## MOVING LINE IN THE SIXTH POSITION

A moving line in the top position describes a wanderer who has forgotten the rules of wandering. The wanderer has begun to laugh at others' expense. Needless to say, others are not amused by this, and the wanderer will be forced away. The wanderer is warned to not forget the importance of humility and versatility.

## NOTES

Wilhelm/Baynes and Pearson call this archetype *The Wanderer*. Barrett calls it *Traveling*. Pearson says, "We are more vulnerable when on the road, away from our homes and families, and among people who may misunderstand our motives or mistrust us simply because we are strangers."

# Archetype 57: The Gentle

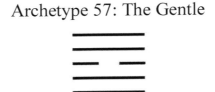

He said therefore, "What is the kingdom of God like? And to what should I compare it? It is like a mustard seed that someone took and sowed in the garden; it grew and became a tree, and the birds of the air made nests in its branches."

And again he said, "To what should I compare the kingdom of God? It is like yeast that a woman took and mixed in with three measures of flour until all of it was leavened."

—Luke 13:18–21

## THE READING

The listeners of Jesus must have been shocked. They are looking for a messiah to lead them out of Roman oppression. The only language Rome understands is violence. So what will God's response to Rome look like? Perhaps a raging storm that destroys all evil. Perhaps a thundering army that vanquishes the evildoers. But Jesus chooses the gentlest metaphors to describe God's kingdom. A tiny seed that grows into a place of shelter. A speck of yeast that converts barrels of flour into bread. The Kingdom of God, Jesus tells us, starts with something small and seemingly insignificant that works its magical transformation over time, until the utterly profane is transformed into the gloriously sacred.

# THE HEXAGRAM

| | Trigram | Name | Image | Attribute | Family |
|---|---|---|---|---|---|
| Upper | ☴ | Spirit | Gentle Wind | Penetrating | First Daughter |
| Lower | ☴ | Spirit | Gentle Wind | Penetrating | First Daughter |

This hexagram consists of a doubling of the Spirit trigram. The image of Spirit is Gentle Wind, and its attribute is Penetrating. Thus we have a doubling of the gentleness that, over time, penetrates even the hardest substance and transforms it.

# THE ARCHETYPE

There is a time…

- To meet rigid darkness with gentle light.
- To meet dark, sinister motives with the penetrating light of judgment.
- To understand that meeting force with force results in hardening, while meeting force with gentleness results in softening.
- To understand that the gains one makes through gentleness are more complete and enduring than the gains one makes through force.
- To remember that the positive changes brought about by gentleness do not take place overnight, and that time is the natural ally of gentleness.
- To understand that the force of gentleness must be focused and continuous, so that the hard will eventually give way to the gentle.
- To find a leader who understands how to marshal gentleness to change people's souls.

Now is that time.

# THE LINES

### MOVING LINE IN THE FIRST POSITION

A moving line in the bottom position reminds us that there is a difference between gentleness and indecisiveness. One who is indecisive wavers between pushing forward and pulling back. Such an approach can never be successful. Even resolute discipline is better than this. The positive force of gentleness works differently. It maintains its focus and effort, never faltering and never wavering, and in this way it gradually wears away the resistance.

### MOVING LINE IN THE SECOND POSITION

A moving line in the second position suggests that there are hidden enemies and influences that are corroding the work of the gentle. It is now necessary to focus on these forces, painstakingly tracing them back to their covert and obscure origins. Once found, the sources of this negativity must be revealed for what they are. They will wither when exposed to the light.

### MOVING LINE IN THE THIRD POSITION

A moving line in the third position warns that there is such a thing as too much reflection. Reflection can eventually deteriorate into ineffectual indecisiveness. Once all sides of an issue have been studied, bring the discussion to an end, decide on a course of action, act decisively, and follow through.

### MOVING LINE IN THE FOURTH POSITION

A moving line in the fourth position points to the synergistic relationship between genuine modesty and energetic action. When these two come together, great success is assured. The line also suggests the situation requires equal attention to three related areas: spirituality, hospitality, and sustainability.

### MOVING LINE IN THE FIFTH POSITION

A moving line in the fifth position describes how to deal with a situation that is not going well. It is not time to abandon the effort, but only to take a new direction. It is a time for refining the approach, improving where possible and changing where necessary. The line warns that such adaptations should be made only after careful thought. Once the adaptations are put into effect, the line tells us to once again pause and reflect on whether the changes have had their intended effect.

### MOVING LINE IN THE SIXTH POSITION

A moving line in the top position describes one who understands what needs to be done and has chased negativity into its hidden corners. But the effort has been draining, and the gentle no longer has the strength to continue the struggle. Further efforts at this time can therefore only bring defeat.

## NOTES

Wilhelm/Baynes calls this archetype *The Gentle (The Penetrating, Wind)*. Pearson calls it *Calculation, Choosing*. Barrett calls it *Subtly Penetrating*. Barrett says, "You penetrate subtly by feeling your way into things, yielding gently to their nature."

# Archetype 58: Wonder

When the angels had left them and gone into heaven, the shepherds said to one another, "Let us go now to Bethlehem and see this thing that has taken place, which the Lord has made known to us." So they went with haste and found Mary and Joseph, and the child lying in the manger. When they saw this, they made known what had been told them about this child; and all who heard it were amazed at what the shepherds told them. But Mary treasured all these words and pondered them in her heart. The shepherds returned, glorifying and praising God for all they had heard and seen, as it had been told them.

—Luke 2:15–20

## THE READING

The shepherds were the country bumpkins of the ancient world. They had no education and little understanding of religious niceties. Perhaps that is why God chose them to reveal this "good news of great joy," the birth of the Messiah. They weren't about to start endless debates about whether or not this accorded with Jewish prophesy. They did what any ordinary person would do upon hearing about something wonderful: they went to see it. And, after seeing the baby, they shared their wonder and joy with any who would listen.

## THE HEXAGRAM

| Trigram | | Name | Image | Attribute | Family |
|---|---|---|---|---|---|
| Upper | | Wonder | Lake | Joy | Third Daughter |
| Lower | | Wonder | Lake | Joy | Third Daughter |

This hexagram is a doubling of the Wonder trigram. With Wonder above and Wonder below, Wonder reinforces itself.

# THE ARCHETYPE
There is a time...

- To understand that wonder is different from frivolity; frivolity is superficial and fleeting, whereas wonder has strength and depth and leaves the wonderer a changed person.
- To know that wonder cannot be forced on anybody through intimidation; it must be an inner response.
- To experience wonder through faith, because without faith, wonder is experienced as bewilderment or confusion.
- To resist Ego's attempts to transform wonder into something self-serving and ugly.
- To transmit wonder from person to person, and by doing so, grow wonder into a gentle force that can drive change.
- To find Wisdom's way in discussions and interactions with close friends.

Now is that time.

# THE LINES

### MOVING LINE IN THE FIRST POSITION
A moving line in the bottom position describes a quiet, self-contained wonder that desires nothing and is content to simply be. This kind of wonder drives a special kind of joy: joy in the complete trust of God's love.

### MOVING LINE IN THE SECOND POSITION
A moving line in the second position warns that wonder can be tarnished by consorting with those who seek trivial frivolity. This is the time to stay true to course and not be distracted by disreputable characters and inappropriate pleasures.

### MOVING LINE IN THE THIRD POSITION
A moving line in the third position warns that spiritual emptiness attracts only that which has no value. No wonder will be found in a spiritual desert. Wonder springs from inside; it cannot be sought.

### MOVING LINE IN THE FOURTH POSITION
A moving line in the fourth position describes one who is torn between worldly pleasures. This can only cause suffering. The cure for this is to know that desire eventually turns to disappointment. Only spiritual joy brings ultimate satisfaction.

## MOVING LINE IN THE FIFTH POSITION
A moving line in the fifth position warns that dangerous elements threaten even the best of people. These elements act slowly but surely to degrade those who do not take steps to guard themselves. The best protection is understanding the nature of the danger.

## MOVING LINE IN THE SIXTH POSITION
A moving line in the top position brings a strong warning that one who is controlled by Ego is easily diverted by frivolous pleasures, and these pleasures can quickly become addictive. Once this happens, there is little hope of salvation.

## NOTES
Wilhelm/Baynes calls this archetype *The Joyous, Lake*. Pearson calls it *Joy*. Barrett calls it *Opening*. Pearson says, "The qualities which nourish friendship also nurture true joys: sincerity and receptivity."

# Archetype 59: Dispersion

Then Jesus called the twelve together and gave them power and authority over all demons and to cure diseases, and he sent them out to proclaim the kingdom of God and to heal. He said to them, "Take nothing for your journey, no staff, nor bag, nor bread, nor money—not even an extra tunic. Whatever house you enter, stay there, and leave from there. Wherever they do not welcome you, as you are leaving that town shake the dust off your feet as a testimony against them." They departed and went through the villages, bringing the good news and curing diseases everywhere.

—Luke 9:1–6

## THE READING

This must have been a dramatic moment for Jesus and his disciples. In the previous chapter of Luke, Jesus's disciples are portrayed as not understanding his teachings (Luke 8:9–10) and of not having faith (Luke 8:22–25). Jesus is clearly frustrated with their immaturity. Now with little evidence that anything has changed, Jesus is sending them out on their own.

Why would Jesus do this? He needed to break the bonds of dependency. As long as they stayed together as a codependent clump, they had little chance of maturing. By forcing them to disband, Jesus also forces them to grow.

# THE HEXAGRAM

| | Trigram | Name | Image | Attribute | Family |
|---|---|---|---|---|---|
| Upper | ☴ | Spirit | Gentle Wind | Penetrating | First Daughter |
| Lower | ☵ | Chaos | Water | Danger | Second Son |

The lower trigram of this hexagram is Chaos, whose image is Water. Water often represents a destructive force in the Bible, as when God tells Noah, "I am going to bring a flood of waters on the earth, to destroy from under heaven all flesh in which is the breath of life; everything that is on the earth shall die" (Gen. 6:17–18).

But the danger inherent in the lower trigram is dissipated by the upper trigram, Spirit, whose image is Gentle Wind. Again we hear an echo from Genesis. It is the wind that finally dissipates the destructive flood God has unleashed: "And God made a wind blow over the earth, and the waters subsided; the fountains of the deep and the windows of the heavens were closed, the rain from the heavens was restrained, and the waters gradually receded from the earth" (Gen. 8:1–3).

# THE ARCHETYPE

There is a time...

- To gently disperse the internal energy that has been stored up and is creating a blockage.
- To allow dispersal to occur so that unification becomes possible.
- To let go of the Ego that has proven so divisive.
- To use religious rituals and devotion to overcome Ego and unite the people.
- To use common goals to overcome individual Ego.
- To realize that through hardness and selfishness the heart grows rigid.
- To understand that rigidity in the heart leads to separation.
- To see in the divine presence the unity of all.

Now is that time.

# THE LINES

### MOVING LINE IN THE FIRST POSITION

A moving line in the bottom position warns that the time for dispersal is at the beginning, before that which needs to be dispersed has had time to solidify. Misunderstandings and mistrust must be dispersed quickly and decisively.

## MOVING LINE IN THE SECOND POSITION

A moving line in the second position recommends a dispersal of a blockage within an individual. The blockage could be anger, distrust, or disgust. Whatever it is, it is causing alienation. This is a time to seek moderation, Wisdom, and the support of others.

## MOVING LINE IN THE THIRD POSITION

A moving line in the third position describes a time when work has become so difficult that rational thought is no longer possible. This is the time to set aside personal desires and the barriers that have been created against others. This dispersal is necessary to achieve a goal that requires great self-sacrifice and strength.

## MOVING LINE IN THE FOURTH POSITION

A moving line in the fourth position recommends a dispersal of short-sighted interests and private alliances. The task that must be accomplished is one that affects everybody. To accomplish such a task, one must have great Wisdom and the ability to see beyond self-interest. Short-term interests must be sacrificed for long-term goals. Not many can achieve this. One must truly be able to see the unity of all life.

## MOVING LINE IN THE FIFTH POSITION

A moving line in the fifth position describes the recovery that follows dispersal. The line suggests that a great idea championed by a person in power is the rallying point for recovery. This same person is the one who can disperse misunderstandings that block unification.

## MOVING LINE IN THE SIXTH POSITION

A moving line in the top position describes the need to disperse a dangerous situation. The danger is not directed at an individual, but at a group. The dispersal may be in the form of getting away before danger comes, keeping danger at a distance, or escaping from a danger that is already present.

## NOTES

Wilhelm/Baynes calls this archetype *Dispersion (Dissolution)*. Pearson calls it *Dispersion (Spreading Waters)*. Barrett calls it *Dispersing*. Barrett says, "All that holds things together now is the constancy of the flow itself."

# Archetype 60: Limitations

But now more than ever the word about Jesus spread abroad; many crowds would gather to hear him and to be cured of their diseases. But he would withdraw to deserted places and pray.

—Luke 5:15–16

## THE READING

The demands on Jesus are enormous. Everywhere he goes, people need healing, feeding, comforting, loving, caring, and forgiving. But Jesus understands that he must put limitations on what he can do. He frequently goes off alone to meditate, pray, and renew his relationship with God. These are the times when Jesus turns away from ministering to others and toward ministering to his own soul. Without these times of renewal, Jesus would quickly burn out. Ultimately, it is the limitations Jesus places on his public ministry that make his public ministry possible.

## THE HEXAGRAM

|        | Trigram | Name   | Image | Attribute | Family         |
|--------|---------|--------|-------|-----------|----------------|
| Upper  |         | Chaos  | Water | Danger    | Second Son     |
| Lower  |         | Wonder | Lake  | Joy       | Third Daughter |

This hexagram consists of the lower trigram Wonder, whose image is Lake, and the upper trigram Chaos, whose image is Water. Water is above the lake. If the lake cannot contain the water, the water overflows and causes destruction. If the lake can set boundaries around the water, then the water is contained and supports life. The difference between destruction and supporting life is determined by the ability of the lake to provide limitations to the water.

# THE ARCHETYPE

There is a time…

- To recognize that sometimes limitations must be placed on things.
- To be thriftier in the use of resources.
- To understand that limitations are necessary to preserve resources for the future.
- To know that even limitations need limitations to prevent limitations from becoming unnecessary burdens.
- To recognize the limitations one places on oneself by the choices one makes.
- To appreciate the sometimes paradoxical relationship between limitations and freedom.

Now is that time.

# THE LINES

### MOVING LINE IN THE FIRST POSITION
A moving line in the bottom position describes one who is confronted by insurmountable limitations. Ego tells us that the limitations need to be destroyed. Wisdom tells us that the limitations are giving us time to rest, reflect, and gather strength.

### MOVING LINE IN THE SECOND POSITION
A moving line in the second position describes the time when action should be taken. Hesitation is good only up until a point; it gives time for removing obstacles. However, once those obstacles have been removed, further hesitation reduces the possibility of success.

### MOVING LINE IN THE THIRD POSITION
A moving line in the third position warns that one can get lost in the search for gratification. The need for limitations can be lost, and the need to be grounded in God can be forgotten. When this happens, the line tells us to accept responsibility for our lapses.

### MOVING LINE IN THE FOURTH POSITION
A moving line in the fourth position tells us to differentiate between those limitations that help us conserve strength from those that drain strength. We will have more success if we go with the flow of natural limitations than if we fight them. It is easier to swim with the current than against it.

MOVING LINE IN THE FIFTH POSITION

A moving line in the fifth position describes the correct way to impose limitations on others: by first imposing the limitations on ourselves. When a respected person takes on limitations and thereby sets an example, others follow suit. No force is necessary.

MOVING LINE IN THE SIXTH POSITION

A moving line in the top position reminds us that limitations themselves should have limitations. If we are overly strict in demanding limitations, people will rebel. Generally, in imposing limitations a middle ground must be sought, not too lenient and not too strict. In those situations in which strictness is required, we are reminded of the advice of the previous line, that the best way to get others to accept limitations is to apply them first of all to oneself. This line also recognizes that sometimes a ruthless severity in applying limitations to oneself is the only way to prevent guilt and remorse and to save one's soul.

## NOTES

Wilhelm/Baynes and Pearson call this archetype *Limitation*. Barrett calls it *Measuring*. Pearson says, "While destructive restraints should be avoided or discarded, the appropriate limits are actually supportive."

# Archetype 61: Inner Truth

You desire truth in the inward being;
therefore teach me wisdom in my secret heart.
Purge me with hyssop, and I shall be clean;
wash me, and I shall be whiter than snow.
Let me hear joy and gladness;
let the bones that you have crushed rejoice.
Hide your face from my sins,
and blot out all my iniquities.
Create in me a clean heart, O God,
and put a new and right spirit within me.

—Psalm 51:6–10

## THE READING

These words were written by King David. Although David had a reputation as a great warrior, his ability to access inner truth at first left much to be desired. While his army was off fighting and dying in distant wars, he spent his nights skulking on the palace rooftop, where he could spy on women undressing and bathing.

One in particular caught his fancy: Bathsheba. David had Bathsheba taken to his bedroom, where he raped her. When she became pregnant, David panicked. Bathsheba's husband, Uriah, was a soldier in David's army, away at battle. David knew that raping a soldier's wife would not look good, especially one who at that time was off fighting in one of David's wars. So David tried to arrange things so that it would appear that Uriah had gotten Bathsheba pregnant. When Uriah wouldn't cooperate, David had Uriah murdered. He then took Bathsheba as one of his many wives.

God was not amused by David's shenanigans, and so he sent the prophet Nathan to read David the riot act. When Bathsheba's baby was born, it was sickly and soon died. Nathan told David that this was God's punishment for his sins. David then went through a period of intense introspection, which led to his deep repentance and acquisition of great inner wisdom. It was the much wiser David who wrote these words in Psalm 51.

# THE HEXAGRAM

|       | Trigram | Name | Image | Attribute | Family |
|-------|---------|------|-------|-----------|--------|
| Upper |  | Spirit | Gentle Wind | Penetrating | First Daughter |
| Lower |  | Wonder | Lake | Joy | Third Daughter |

This hexagram consists of the upper trigram Spirit and the lower trigram Wonder. Placed together, we see two strong lines at the top and bottom and two open lines in the center. The openness at the center of the hexagram signifies the openness of a heart to inner truth.

# THE ARCHETYPE

There is a time…

- To cultivate a heart free of prejudice and malice and to find one's inner truth.
- To be open and adaptable in how one works with others, allowing one's inner truth to reach out to the others and draw them in.
- To understand that inner truth is not intimacy; inner truth is substantial, whereas intimacy is temporary.
- To recognize that a life grounded in divinely inspired inner truth has great power to make change.
- To call on the clarity that comes from Wisdom when judging the mistakes of others.
- To recognize that sometimes a pardon is the highest form of justice.

Now is that time.

# THE LINES

### MOVING LINE IN THE FIRST POSITION
A moving line in the bottom position tells us of the need to cultivate the inner stability and alertness that lead to inner truth. The line warns not to cultivate secret alliances that will result in dependencies. These dependencies will not stand up over time and will rob one of clarity.

### MOVING LINE IN THE SECOND POSITION
A moving line in the second position describes how inner truth is able to impact others in a mysterious way. Inner truth gives one's voice a special clarity and one's deeds a charisma that others find irresistible. The sphere of influence starts small, reaching those in near proximity. But it gradually grows in influence until even those at a great distance are drawn in.

## MOVING LINE IN THE THIRD POSITION
A moving line in the third position describes one whose strength does not come from inside, but from one's relationship to others. In such a situation, one has little control over one's own happiness.

## MOVING LINE IN THE FOURTH POSITION
A moving line in the fourth position recommends that the seeker turn to a wiser one for help in cultivating inner truth. The line also reminds the seeker that such a relationship requires humility and dedication.

## MOVING LINE IN THE FIFTH POSITION
A moving line in the fifth position describes the need for a unifying presence of strength and leadership. The strength described here is inner strength, not outer, and of character, not power. Such a ruler can unite the many into a cohesive whole. Without this unifying force, the line warns us that the cohesion will fail at the critical moment.

## MOVING LINE IN THE SIXTH POSITION
A moving line in the top position warns us not to depend on mere words to influence people. Although words alone may occasionally suffice, they can't be counted upon when times are critical.

## NOTES
Wilhelm/Baynes and Barrett call this archetype *Inner Truth*. Pearson calls it *Sincere to the Core*. Barrett says, "The very present truth vibrates through you like a drumbeat; you apprehend it directly as an inner resonance."

# Archetype 62: Strength in Weakness

When Jesus saw the crowds, he went up the mountain; and after he sat down, his disciples came to him. Then he began to speak, and taught them, saying:

"Blessed are the poor in spirit, for theirs is the kingdom of heaven."

"Blessed are those who mourn, for they will be comforted."

"Blessed are the meek, for they will inherit the earth."

"Blessed are those who hunger and thirst for righteousness, for they will be filled."

"Blessed are the merciful, for they will receive mercy."

"Blessed are the pure in heart, for they will see God."

"Blessed are the peacemakers, for they will be called children of God."

"Blessed are those who are persecuted for righteousness's sake, for theirs is the kingdom of heaven."

"Blessed are you when people revile you and persecute you and utter all kinds of evil against you falsely on my account. Rejoice and be glad, for your reward is great in heaven, for in the same way they persecuted the prophets who were before you."

—Matthew 5:1–12

## THE READING

This reading is known as the Beatitudes. It is the prelude to the famous Sermon on the Mount, which continues for three chapters of Matthew. This reading sets the revolutionary tone of Jesus's message. In a world in which stature is defined by strength, we are told to be meek. In a world that craves wealth, we are told to crave righteousness. In a world that idolizes warriors, we are told to be peacemakers. In a world that promotes jingoism, we are told to be children of God.

## THE HEXAGRAM

| | Trigram | Name | Image | Attribute | Family |
|---|---|---|---|---|---|
| Upper | ☳ | Word | Thunder | Life Giving | First Son |
| Lower | ☶ | Stillness | Mountain | Resting | Third Son |

This hexagram consists of the lower trigram Stillness and the upper trigram Word. These two trigrams are mirror images of each other. Stillness (lower) has two weak lines in the first and second positions and a strong line in the third position. Word (upper) has its two weak lines in the second and third positions and its strong line in the first position.

When these two trigrams are stacked, we end up with two weak lines in the bottom two and the top two positions. Sandwiched in between are the two strong lines. Looking at the hexagram from the outside world, we see only weak lines. But at the core of the hexagram is strength.

This gives a sense of the archetype: strength held interiorly and weakness presented exteriorly.

## THE ARCHETYPE
There is a time...

- To be wary about holding authority when not ready.
- To cultivate humility, modesty, and conscientiousness combined with dignified personal behavior.
- To let go of grandiose goals that are driven by Ego and focus on small, meaningful achievements.
- To favor emotion over ceremony, simplicity over pretentiousness, and thrift over ostentatiousness.
- To remember that the smallest deeds of love can have a long-term impact.
- To maintain dignity in one's behavior, even when doing so seems petty to others.
- To be in solidarity with those who are considered the lowly.

Now is that time.

## THE LINES

### MOVING LINE IN THE FIRST POSITION
A moving line in the bottom position warns that one should not run before one can walk. We should try simple solutions before we resort to complex solutions, lest we exhaust ourselves and accomplish nothing.

## MOVING LINE IN THE SECOND POSITION

A moving line in the second position offers guidance in dealing with unusual situations. The line suggests another approach to family relationships, one based on natural attractions rather than hierarchical expectations. The line also suggests that if one is faced with a decision that requires approval from a superior, one should seek that superior's approval. If the approval is not forthcoming, then this is not the time to force one's own will but rather to show restraint and fulfill one's obligations.

## MOVING LINE IN THE THIRD POSITION

A moving line in the third position warns us that we need to be cautious. Ego may tell us that because we are right, we don't need to be careful. But Ego is deluding us. The line tells us that there are dangers for which we are not yet prepared. This is the time to pay close attention to the smallest and seemingly least significant issues.

## MOVING LINE IN THE FOURTH POSITION

A moving line in the fourth position warns that there is a great danger of making mistakes. The line suggests that we yield and make no attempt to reach our goals. Instead, the line suggests using this time to build interior strength and character.

## MOVING LINE IN THE FIFTH POSITION

A moving line in the fifth position advises how to accomplish an important task. The line suggests that there is a leader who is well qualified to achieve the task but is unable to do so because of a lack of support. Helpers are needed who have proven their ability but have since retired. These helpers will need to be coaxed out of retirement. With these helpers, the line tells us the task will be completed.

## MOVING LINE IN THE SIXTH POSITION

A moving line in the top position warns that there is danger of overstepping our bounds. This is not the time for big accomplishment, but for accomplishing seemingly small things. Thus, pushing on relentlessly to big goals will lead to failure.

## NOTES

Wilhelm/Baynes calls this archetype *Preponderance of the Small*. Pearson calls it *Minor Surplus*. Barrett calls it *Small Exceeding*. Pearson says, "Your strength is still only slightly superior, and thus you are too vulnerable to do much at this time."

# Archetype 63: After Completion

Now the eleven disciples went to Galilee, to the mountain to which Jesus had directed them. When they saw him, they worshipped him; but some doubted. And Jesus came and said to them, "All authority in heaven and on earth has been given to me. Go therefore and make disciples of all nations, baptizing them in the name of the Father and of the Son and of the Holy Spirit, and teaching them to obey everything that I have commanded you. And remember, I am with you always, to the end of the age."

—Matthew 28:16–20

## THE READING

The human incarnation of the word eternal has come to an end. Jesus has delivered his message of love. He has proven that love cannot be killed, even by the feared Roman Empire. If love can survive the cruelty of Rome, it can survive anything. We hope.

The Jesus who appears in this reading is the word resurrected. This is the word that lives on in the hearts of all who turn away from the darkness and commit themselves to being children of love. It would seem that we have reached the end of the story. Jesus has preached. Jesus has been murdered. Christ has been resurrected. Love has triumphed.

However, as we all know, the battle between love and darkness continues. Even today, the outcome is uncertain. At any moment, the world could slip into an abyss of hatred that even God's love cannot penetrate.

Before us lies a divergence in the road. In one direction lies destruction and darkness, the way of Ego. In the other direction lies love and light, the way of Wisdom. Jesus died making a desperate plea to us to choose Wisdom's way. The future of the human race depends on whether we listen.

# THE HEXAGRAM

| | Trigram | Name | Image | Attribute | Family |
|---|---|---|---|---|---|
| Upper | ☵ | Chaos | Water | Danger | Second Son |
| Lower | ☲ | Christ | Fire | Light | Second Daughter |

This hexagram consists of the lower trigram Christ and the upper trigram Chaos. In hexagram numerology, the first, third, and fifth positions are considered strong. The second, fourth, and sixth positions are considered weak. This is the only hexagram in which every weak position is taken by a weak line and every strong position is taken by a strong line. This is the perfect equilibrium. However, it is also fragile. Just a single line change destabilizes the hexagram.

# THE ARCHETYPE

There is a time...

- To celebrate the climax, when everything seems aligned just so.
- To know that the climax is a delicate time, when even a small miscalculation can result in unraveling.
- To pay the most careful attention to details so that we can avoid disintegration.
- To understand that the only path to maintaining what has been accomplished is Wisdom's way.

Now is that time.

# THE LINES

### MOVING LINE IN THE FIRST POSITION

A moving line in the bottom position describes a transition after which there is great jubilation over the progress that has been made. The momentum is pressing forward, but this is not the time to be carried forward by that momentum. Doing so will cause us to move too fast and miss our goal. The line advises that time must be taken to fully understand the forces at play and move with caution, lest we be forced to retrace our steps.

## MOVING LINE IN THE SECOND POSITION

A moving line in the second position warns that there is a danger that those in power will use this completion as a time to regress into Ego. When that happens, they fail to support those who are needed to move forward. We may feel we no longer enjoy their trust. We are tempted to respond with a power grab. But the line advises this is ill advised. This is a time to wait and cultivate Wisdom. Our time is coming.

## MOVING LINE IN THE THIRD POSITION

A moving line in the third position describes the period of rapid expansion that inevitably follows times of completion. The line tells us it is critical to take the best possible care of the newly acquired territories and dedicate only the wisest administrators to overseeing them. The expansion being discussed can be literal or metaphorical.

## MOVING LINE IN THE FOURTH POSITION

A moving line in the fourth position describes the inevitable scandals that accompany any great intellectual movement. Sometimes a hidden problem is uncovered, and this can cause great consternation. There is a temptation to ignore the issue and sweep it under the rug. While this may result in apparent concord, this line tells us to pay careful attention to these issues, lest they fester and flare up in the future.

## MOVING LINE IN THE FIFTH POSITION

A moving line in the fifth position describes the ceremonies that follow a great completion. The old ceremonies are replaced by new ceremonies that were created to be even more elaborate, even more inspirational. But this is all an appeal to Ego, and it invites idolatry. God is not interested in elaborate shows and ceremonies. God is interested in a pure and contrite heart. This is a good time to meditate on Psalm 51.

## MOVING LINE IN THE SIXTH POSITION

A moving line in the top position warns that this is not the time to sit around admiring our accomplishments. Doing so places us in danger. This is the time to move forward with determination.

## NOTES

Wilhelm/Baynes calls this archetype *After Completion*. Pearson calls it *After the Crossing*. Barrett calls it *Already Across*. Pearson says, "It is never safe to rest on our laurels."

# Archetype 64: Before Completion

It was now about noon, and darkness came over the whole land until three in the afternoon, while the sun's light failed; and the curtain of the temple was torn in two. Then Jesus, crying with a loud voice, said, "Father, into your hands I commend my spirit." Having said this, he breathed his last. When the centurion saw what had taken place, he praised God and said, "Certainly this man was innocent." And when all the crowds who had gathered there for this spectacle saw what had taken place, they returned home, beating their breasts. But all his acquaintances, including the women who had followed him from Galilee, stood at a distance, watching these things.

—Luke 23:44–49

## THE READING

The ministry of Jesus has come to an end. But his mission has not been completed. There are signs. The temple curtain that separated the inner sanctum (God's dwelling place) from the rest of the temple has symbolically been torn in two. The earth has been plunged into darkness for three hours and then restored to light. Even the Roman centurion has recognized something special has just occurred. The mission of Jesus was to establish the Kingdom of God, a new era for the earth grounded in love, justice, and peace for all of God's creation. All the pieces are in place. But Ego still rules. And the earth is still a place that rejects the Kingdom of God. Will Jesus have suffered in vain? That question remains unanswered.

## THE HEXAGRAM

|  | Trigram | Name | Image | Attribute | Family |
|---|---|---|---|---|---|
| Upper |  | Christ | Fire | Light | Second Daughter |
| Lower |  | Chaos | Water | Danger | Second Son |

This hexagram consists of the lower trigram Chaos and the upper trigram Christ. Chaos is the order of the day. Christ carries the message of redemption. Christ hovers over Chaos, but has not yet won.

## THE ARCHETYPE
There is a time…

- To see the task that must be completed as one of cosmic significance, of leading the world out of Chaos and into the Kingdom of God.
- To understand the seriousness and difficulty of the task that must be completed.
- To take heart knowing that God is with us on this path.
- To proceed with the greatest caution.
- To clearly understand the forces that oppose.
- To begin the transformation in our own hearts.

Now is that time.

## THE LINES

### MOVING LINE IN THE FIRST POSITION
A moving line in the bottom position tells us to slow down. We are tempted to move quickly and seize the moment. But if the time for change is not here, we cannot be successful. The line tells us that the time is not right.

### MOVING LINE IN THE SECOND POSITION
A moving line in the second position reiterates the message of the previous line: the time is not right. But this line suggests that we use this time to build up our internal strength. We will need this strength to move forward.

### MOVING LINE IN THE THIRD POSITION
A moving line in the third position suggests that the time for change has come, but we are not ready. We are not strong enough. Pushing forward now will only result in disaster. We must first redefine the situation by building relationships and engaging the energy of others. Once we have done this, change will be possible.

### MOVING LINE IN THE FOURTH POSITION
A moving line in the fourth position proclaims that the time for change has come. We are in a do-or-die situation; we must make the change happen. We must be resolute and put aside all doubts. We must understand the importance of the change that is to be; a failure will mean that darkness has won and Ego has triumphed. What we do now will lay the foundations for the future.

MOVING LINE IN THE FIFTH POSITION

A moving line in the fifth position tells us that we have won. The change has occurred. The forces of darkness have been overcome. The light of a wise one shines forth, and the children of light have come together in support. A new era has begun, an era that replaces darkness by light. The changes are welcomed and energizing and are in marked contrast to the misery of the old era.

MOVING LINE IN THE SIXTH POSITION

A moving line in the top position tells us that we are at the dawning of the new era. We are waiting and watching, drunk with anticipation. However, the line warns us to maintain our dignity and remain centered. Otherwise the forward momentum may be lost.

## NOTES

Wilhelm/Baynes calls this archetype *Before Completion*. Pearson and Barrett call it *Not Yet Across*. Barrett says, "Here at the very end of the Yijing [I Ching] nothing is settled or complete; everything is in flux."

# Appendices

# Appendix 1: Mathematical Probabilities and the I Ching

There is no reason you need to understand the relationship between mathematical probabilities and the I Ching to use the I Ching. Some people are interested in this, and there is a lot of confusion out there about probability and the I Ching, so for those who are interested, I will cover this topic in this appendix. Keep in mind that I am not suggesting that the I Ching is governed by random chance. But it helps to understand how it would be governed by random chance, if for no other reason than to appreciate how nonrandom the I Ching is in actual use.

In this appendix I will show you how to answer questions like the following:

- What are the relative probabilities of getting the different archetypes?
- What are the relative probabilities of getting a yin (open) line versus a yang (closed) line?
- What are the chances of a yin line being moving versus static?
- Given a particular starting archetype, what are the chances of that archetype transforming through moving lines into one particular archetype versus another particular archetype?
- How does your choice of using the coin versus the yarrow protocol affect these probabilities?

First, let's start with some basic probability theory.

## DEFINITION: PERCENTAGE AND ODDS

Say an event is repeated a very large number of times, and it is determined that a specific outcome occurs on average N times out of 100. Then we say that specific outcome has a probability of $N/100$.

For example, if you flip a fair coin 100 times, you will find that on average it comes up heads 50 times. Therefore we say the outcome of heads is $50/100$, or 0.5.

## DEFINITION: MUTUALLY EXCLUSIVE EVENTS

Two events, say A and B, are said to be *mutually exclusive* if either A or B can occur, but not both.

For example, when we flip a single coin, the events of the coin coming up heads or coming up tails are *mutually exclusive*.

## DEFINITION: INDEPENDENT EVENTS

Two events, say A and B, are said to be *independent* (or non-mutually exclusive) if the event A happening has no impact on whether or not the event B will happen, and visa versa.

For example, if we flip two coins, the event of the first coin coming up heads is *independent* of the event of the second coin coming up heads.

## PROBABILITY LAW ONE: PROBABILITY OF INDEPENDENT OUTCOMES OCCURRING

To determine the probability that more than one independent outcome will occur at the same time, you multiply the probabilities of the individual outcomes.

Say you want to know the probability of two coins both coming up heads. You multiply the probability of the first coin coming up heads by the probability of the second coin coming up heads. Since the first coin has a 0.5 probability of coming up heads, and the second coin also has a 0.5 probability of coming up heads, the probability of both coins coming up heads is 0.5 X 0.5, or 0.25. In other words, if you throw two coins 100 times, you would expect both coins to come up heads approximately 25 percent of the time.

## PROBABILITY LAW TWO: PROBABILITY OF MULTIPLE MUTUALLY EXCLUSIVE OUTCOMES OCCURRING

When determining the probability that any one of several mutually exclusive outcomes will occur, you add the probabilities of the individual outcomes.

Say you want to know the probability that a fair six-sided die will come up either 1 or 2. You add the probability of it coming up 1 (0.167) to the probability of it coming up 2 (0.167) to get 0.333 (within rounding error). This tells you that if you throw a fair six-sided die 100 times, it will come up either 1 or 2 about 33 times.

Caution: be careful when using this law. For example, say you want to know the probability of getting at least one head from tossing two coins. You might be tempted to add 0.5 to 0.5, giving 1.0 (which says there is no probability of anything else happening). Yet we know there is at least some chance that both coins will come up tails. What did we do wrong? The problem is that the two coins are not mutually exclusive. *Mutually exclusive* means that only one of the multiple outcomes can occur. However, in this case, both outcomes (both coins coming up heads) can occur. If both can occur, the outcomes are not mutually exclusive (they are independent), and this law does not apply.

## PROBABILITY LAW THREE: OUTCOMES AND PROBABILITIES

Say an event has N outcomes that all have an equal probability of occurring. Then the probability of any one of the N outcomes occurring is 1/N.

Consider spinning a fair roulette wheel with 100 numbered slots, each equally spaced. The probability of any one of the 100 numbered slots being chosen is 1/100, or 0.01. In other words, if you spin this wheel 100 times, you will get a 9 about once.

## PROBABILITY LAW FOUR: COMBINING SIMILAR OUTCOMES

Say an event has N outcomes that all have an equal probability of occurring, but M of the outcomes are effectively the same. Then the probability of one of those equivalent outcomes occurring is M X 1/N.

Consider spinning a fair roulette wheel with 100 numbered slots, but ten of those slots all have the same number, 9. Then the probability of a nine being chosen is 10 X 1/100, or 0.10. In other words, if you spin this wheel 100 times, you will get a 9 about 10 times.

## PROBABILITY LAW FIVE: PROBABILITY OF AT LEAST ONE INDEPENDENT OUTCOME

Say an event has N outcomes that are independent. The chances that at least one of the outcomes will occur is 1 minus the probability that none of the independent events will occur.

Consider the chances of throwing two coins and getting at least one to come up heads. Since these events are independent, we can't use Law Two. But Law Five says the chances that at least one head will occur is equal to 1 minus the chances that no heads will occur, which is the chance that two tails will occur. The chance that two tails will occur is 0.25, or 1/4. Thus the chance that at least one head will occur is 1 minus 0.25, or 0.75. In other words, if you throw two coins 100 times, you will get at least one head about 75 times.

With these basic laws, we can learn a lot about the probabilities of different outcomes of I Ching readings.

## PROBABILITY AND THE COIN PROTOCOL

The probabilities of the coin protocol are so simple that they are almost not worth calculating. However, doing so illustrates the main concepts of probability and the I Ching in an easy-to-understand mathematical model. Understanding how the coin protocol drives probability will make it easier to understand how the more complex yarrow protocol drives probability. So let's start with this "simple" system of coins.

First, make sure you understand the coin protocol as described in Chapter 6. Recall that the tails were assigned 2 and heads were assigned 3. If three heads come up, the sum is 9, and the result is a moving yang line. If three tails come up, the sum is 6, and the result is a moving yin line. If two tails and one head come up, the sum is 7, and the result is a static yang line. If one tail and two heads come up, the sum is 8, and the result is a static yin line.

So what are the chances of getting each of these four possibilities?

One way to determine this is to construct an outcome possibility graph. Let's consider a potential coin toss of the three coins.

Start with the first coin, which I will call C1. It can come up either heads (H) or tails (T). This is represented by the following outcome possibility graph:

C1=H

C1=T

Now suppose C1 came up H. What about C2? It can also come up either H or T. Thus we extend the outcome possibility graph:

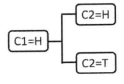

Now suppose C1 came up T. C2 still has the same possibilities. So we again extend the outcome possibility graph:

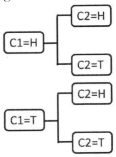

Regardless of how C1 and C2 turned out, C3 can still be either H or T. So we extend the outcome possibility graph:

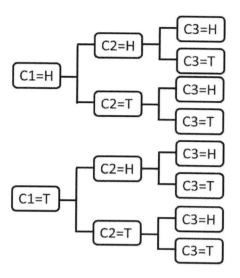

Thus we have eight possible outcomes:

- C1=H; C2=H; C3=H
- C1=H; C2=H; C3=T
- C1=H; C2=T; C3=H
- C1=H; C2=T; C3=T
- C1=T; C2=H; C3=H
- C1=T; C2=H; C3=T
- C1=T; C2=T; C3=H
- C1=T; C2=T; C3=T

Any of these eight possible outcomes is equally likely. Thus by Law Three, any of these outcomes has a 1/8 chance of occurring, or 0.125.

What are the chances of getting two Hs and one T, or a static yin? Of the eight possible outcomes, three give us two Hs and one T, shown in bold:

- C1=H; C2=H; C3=H
- **C1=H; C2=H; C3=T**
- **C1=H; C2=T; C3=H**
- C1=H; C2=T; C3=T
- **C1=T; C2=H; C3=H**
- C1=T; C2=H; C3=T
- C1=T; C2=T; C3=H

- C1=T; C2=T; C3=T

These three outcomes are equivalent in that they produce a static yin line. So by Law Four the chances that one of these will occur is 3 X 1/8, or 3 X 0.125 or 0.375. In other words, if you throw three coins 100 times, you expect to get a static yin line about 37 times.

By similar logic, three of the eight outcomes are equivalent in that they produce a static yang line, namely these (in bold):

- C1=H; C2=H; C3=H
- C1=H; C2=H; C3=T
- C1=H; C2=T; C3=H
- **C1=H; C2=T; C3=T**
- C1=T; C2=H; C3=H
- **C1=T; C2=H; C3=T**
- **C1=T; C2=T; C3=H**
- C1=T; C2=T; C3=T

So we also have a 0.375 chance of getting a static yang line.

What about a moving yin line? Only one path gives us a moving yin line:

- C1=H; C2=H; C3=H
- C1=H; C2=H; C3=T
- C1=H; C2=T; C3=H
- C1=H; C2=T; C3=T
- C1=T; C2=H; C3=H
- C1=T; C2=H; C3=T
- C1=T; C2=T; C3=H
- **C1=T; C2=T; C3=T**

Thus the chances of getting a moving yin line are 1/8, or 0.125.

Similarly, only one path gives a moving yang line:

- **C1=H; C2=H; C3=H**
- C1=H; C2=H; C3=T
- C1=H; C2=T; C3=H
- C1=H; C2=T; C3=T
- C1=T; C2=H; C3=H
- C1=T; C2=H; C3=T
- C1=T; C2=T; C3=H
- C1=T; C2=T; C3=T

Thus the chances of getting a moving yang line are 1/8, or 0.125.

What about the chances of getting any yang line, either moving or static? Since these are two mutually exclusive events, Law Two tells us to add the two probabilities together. So we add the chances of getting a static yang line (0.375) to the chances of getting a moving yang line (0.125). The result is 0.5. So we have a 0.5 chance of getting a yang line, either static or moving. Similar logic will lead us to conclude that we have a 0.5 chance of getting a yin line, either static or moving.

Since we have a 0.5 chance of getting a yin line and a 0.5 chance of getting a yang line, we have equal chances of getting a yin or a yang line. Since any line is equally likely to be yin as yang, for a given reading any of the sixty-four archetypes are just as likely to result.

What about the chances of getting a static line? There are two outcomes that produce this: a static yang line and a static yin line. Each has a 0.375 chance of occurring. These events are mutually exclusive (we can get either a static yin line or a static yang line, but never both), so Law Two applies. The chance that either a static yang line or a static yin line will occur is 0.375 + 0.375, or 0.750.

We can also calculate the probability that we will have a static archetype, that is, one with no moving lines. We have already determined that the probability that a given line will be static (either yin or yang) is 0.750. So by Law One, the chance that all six lines will be static is 0.750 X 0.750 X 0.750 X 0.750 X 0.750 X 0.750, or $0.750^6$. This is 0.178. And by Law Five, the chance that at least one of the lines will be moving is 1 minus 0.178, or 0.82. In other words, if you use the coin protocol to randomly throw 100 archetypes, about 18 will be static with no resultant archetype, and 82 will be changing with some resultant archetype.

Suppose I tell you we have a yin line but I don't tell you whether it is static or moving. What are the chances of either? If we go back to the outcome table, we see that there are four that give us some yin line:

- **C1=H; C2=H; C3=H**
- **C1=H; C2=H; C3=T**
- **C1=H; C2=T; C3=H**
- C1=H; C2=T; C3=T
- C1=T; C2=H; C3=H
- C1=T; C2=H; C3=T
- C1=T; C2=T; C3=H
- **C1=T; C2=T; C3=T**

Of these four, 1 gives us a moving yin line, the last possibility. So once you know a line is yin, you also know it has a 0.75 probability of being static and a 0.25 probability of being moving. The same is true for the yang lines.

And finally, we can calculate the probability that a specific archetype, say A, will transform into another specific archetype, say B. To do this, figure out how many lines would need to be static. Say this number is N. Then figure out how many lines would need to be moving. Say this number is M. Then the probability that A will transform into B is given by $0.750^N \times 0.250^M$. The 0.750 comes from the chances that the given line is static, and the 0.250 comes from the chances that the given line is moving.

For example, let's say you received archetype 14, which has this hexagram:

Now you want to know the chances that it will turn into archetype 1. Archetype 1 has this hexagram:

To get this particular transformation, you would need five static lines (1, 2, 3, 4, and 6) and one moving line (5). So the chances this will occur are $0.750^5 \times 0.250^1$. Since $0.750^5$ is 0.24 and $0.250^1$ is 0.250, the number of times you get an archetype 14 that transforms into archetype 1 is 0.24 X 0.25 = 0.06. In other words, for every 100 times you draw archetype 14, about 6 times you will get the resultant archetype 1.

What about the chances that archetype 14 will transform into archetype 11? Archetype 11 has this hexagram:

Now we need four static lines (1, 2, 3, 5) and two moving lines (4, 6). The chances of this are $0.750^4 \times 0.250^2$, or $0.32 \times 0.06 = 0.02$. In other words, for every 100 times you draw archetype 14, about 2 times you will get the resultant archetype 11.

So given that we have drawn archetype 14, we have three times the probability of getting the resultant archetype 1 as getting the resultant archetype 11.

This gives us an interesting result. The chances of drawing any one of the sixty-four archetypes are about the same, 1/64. However, once you know the initial archetype, the chances of getting a specific resultant archetype are not equal. It seems from a probability perspective that each archetype has some resultants archetypes with a higher affinity than others.

We can go further and construct affinity subsets for each archetype. We can say affinity subset 0 is the set of all resultant archetypes that can be generated with no moving lines. This subset always contains exactly one archetype, the archetype we started with. Affinity subset 1 is the set of all resultant archetypes that can be generated with exactly one moving line. There are six archetypes in this subset. Affinity subset 2 is the subset of all resultant archetypes that can be generated with exactly two moving lines. And so on. Each one of these subsets will contain archetypes that have the same probability of being generated. And since each of the sixty-four archetypes will live in one and only one of the affinity subsets, mathematically we can say that the set of affinity subsets is a *partition* of the archetypes.

So much for the coin protocol. Next we will look at the yarrow protocol. The principles are the same. The probability laws are the same. The only difference is the probabilities of various things happening.

## PROBABILITY AND THE YARROW PROTOCOL

The first thing you should do is review the yarrow protocol described in Chapter 5. This discussion assumes you are familiar with this protocol. And remember that I use stones rather than yarrow stalks. However, the probabilities are dependent only on the protocol, not on the material being manipulated.

The yarrow protocol is very repetitious. We follow a specific sequence over and over. We start with a pile of stones. We divide them into left-hand and right-hand piles. We take one stone from the left-hand pile and put it at the top. We count off the left-hand pile by fours and put the remainder under the first stone. We count off the right-hand pile by fours and put the remainder under the remainder from the left-hand pile. And then, depending on where we are in the protocol, we either combine the two remaining left-hand and right-hand piles or we count the remaining piles of four.

First, let me define some terminology for this discussion. I will call the pile of stones that has not yet been separated the *starting pile*, which I will abbreviate as SP. Once the starting pile has been separated into two piles, I will call these two piles the *left-hand pile* (LHP) and the *right-hand pile* (RHP).

I will call the three piles at the top of the work area the *result piles*, which I will abbreviate as RP. So we have RP1, RP2, and RP3. Once we have completed RP3, we can determine the type of the line. Each result pile has three groups of stones. The top stone I will call the *seed*. The second group I will call the *left-hand contribution*, or LHC. The third group I will call the *right-hand contribution*, or RHC.

When we have finished each cycle of the sequence, we are left with a bunch of stones in the LHP and the RHP. I will refer to the combined pile of these stones as the *remainder pile* (RP). Notice that the RP that is left at the end of one sequence becomes the SP for the beginning of the next cycle of the sequence.

Now let's start from the beginning. We start with an SP of 49. We separate into LHP and RHP. We take one stone from the LHP and make it a seed. At this point we have some number of stones in the LHP and RHP, and the total of these stones must equal 48. Here are some possibilities:

- Case 1: LHP has 24 and RHP has 24
- Case 2: LHP has 25 and RHP has 23
- Case 3: LHP has 26 and RHP has 22
- Case 4: LHP has 27 and RHP has 21
- Case 5: LHP has 28 and RHP has 20
- Case 6: LHP has 29 and RHP has 19
- ...

We also have the mirror-image cases where the RHP has the larger number.

Let's consider Case 1. Our LHP has 24 and our RHP has 24. We count out the LHP into fours and get a remainder of 4, which becomes the LHC, leaving 20. We count out the RHP into fours and get a remainder of 4, which becomes the RHC. RP1 now has 1 (seed) + 4 (LHC) + 4 (RHC). And we have 40 left in the RP: 20 in the LHP and 20 in the RHP. These two piles get combined to become the new SP, which has 40. To summarize this, Case 1 has an SP of 49 and a new SP of 40.

Now let's consider Case 2. Our LHP has 25 and our RHP has 23. We count out the LHP into fours and get a remainder of 1, which becomes the LHC, leaving 24. We count out the RHP into fours and get a remainder of 3, which becomes the RHC, leaving 20. And we have 44 left at the bottom: 24 in the LHP and 20 in the RHP. These two piles get combined to become the new SP, which has 44. To summarize this, Case 2 has an SP of 49 and a new SP of 44.

If you continue this logic with Cases 3, 4, 5, and 6, you will get the following outcomes:

- Case 1: SP = 49, new SP = 40
- Case 2: SP = 49, new SP = 44
- Case 3: SP = 49, new SP = 44
- Case 4: SP = 49, new SP = 44
- Case 5: SP = 49, new SP = 40
- Case 6: SP = 49, new SP = 44

At this point, we notice a pattern. We continue getting new SPs of 40, 44, 44, and 44. In other words, there are only two possible outcomes: a new SP of 40 and a new SP of 44. Further, for every outcome with a new SP of 40, there are three outcomes with a new SP of 44. We will see this same pattern emerge if we consider the mirror-image cases, when the right-hand piles have the larger amounts.

Since the outcomes are mutually exclusive, we can use Law Four to combine like outcomes. This gives us two outcomes: one with a new SP of 44 and a probability of 0.75, and one with a new SP of 40 and a probability of 0.25. This can be summarized by the following outcome possibility chart:

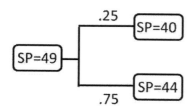

We now have completed the first of our result piles, RP1. Now let's start RP2. As we start RP2, we can be in one of two situations: SP = 40 or SP = 44. We need to analyze each case just like we did SP = 49.

If we follow this same logic with an SP of 40 instead of an SP of 49, you will see that there are only two possible outcomes: a new SP of 36 and a new SP of 32. These two possibilities occur in a 0.50/0.50 split (rather than the 0.25/0.75 split we observed with an SP of 49). This gives us the following outcome possibility chart:

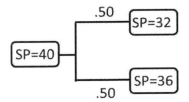

We can now combine the two outcome charts, giving this:

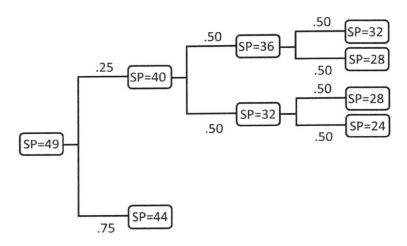

If we continue filling in the outcome chart for all possible outcomes of the three iterations (the number of iterations it takes to determine the three remainder piles at the top), we get the following:

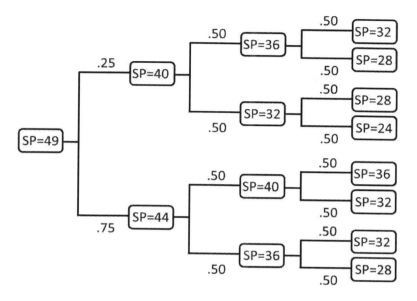

This gives us the eight possible outcomes. We can also determine the final line number by dividing the final stack size by 4, giving this:

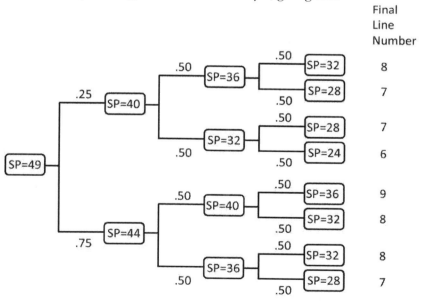

Since the outcomes are independent as we move from left to right, we use Law One to determine the probability (P) of each path being followed. From this we get:

- P of path 1 resulting in line 8 is 0.25 X 0.50 X 0.50 = 0.06250
- P of path 2 resulting in line 7 is 0.25 X 0.50 X 0.50 = 0.06250
- P of path 3 resulting in line 7 is 0.25 X 0.50 X 0.50 = 0.06250
- P of path 4 resulting in line 6 is 0.25 X 0.50 X 0.50 = 0.06250
- P of path 5 resulting in line 9 is 0.75 X 0.50 X 0.50 = 0.1875
- P of path 6 resulting in line 8 is 0.75 X 0.50 X 0.50 = 0.1875
- P of path 7 resulting in line 8 is 0.75 X 0.50 X 0.50 = 0.1875
- P of path 8 resulting in line 7 is 0.75 X 0.50 X 0.50 = 0.1875

Notice one path ends with a line 6, three paths end with a line 7, three paths end with a line 8, and one path ends with a line 9. Since these outcomes are similar and mutually exclusive, they can be combined using Law Four. This tells us that we have the following probabilities:

- P of line 6 = 0.0625
- P of line 7 = 0.0625 + 0.0625 + 0.1875 = 0.3125
- P of line 8 = 0.0625 + 0.1875 + 0.1875 = 0.4375
- P of line 9 = 0.1875

Since lines 6, 7, 8, and 9 are moving yin, static yang, static yin, and moving yang, respectively, we now know the probability of receiving any of these lines.

- P of moving yin = 0.0625
- P of static yang = 0.3125
- P of static yin = 0.4375
- P of moving yang = 0.1875

We can make a few observations. First, the chances of getting a yin line and a yang line in the yarrow protocol are the same: 0.5. This means that the chance of drawing any of the sixty-four archetypes is the same, 1/64. However, the chance of a yang line being a moving line is three times greater than the chance of a yin line being a moving line. This means that resulting archetypes that come from moving yang lines are more likely to materialize than are archetypes that result from moving yin lines.

What about the chances of getting a static line? There are two outcomes that produce this: a static yang line (P = 0.3125) and a static yin line (P = 0.4375). These events are mutually exclusive (we can get either a static yin line or a static yang line, but never both), so Law Two applies. The chance that either a static yang line or a static yin line will occur is 0.3125 + 0.4375, or 0.750. This is the same result as we observed in the coin protocol.

We can also calculate the probability that we will have a static archetype, that is, one with no moving lines. We have already determined that the probability that a given line will be static (either yin or yang) is 0.750. So by Law One, the chance that all six lines will be static is 0.750 X 0.750 X 0.750 X 0.750 X 0.750 X 0.750, or $0.750^6$. This is 0.178. And by Law Five, the chance that at least one of the lines will be moving is 1 minus 0.178, or 0.82. In other words, if you use the yarrow protocol to randomly derive 100 archetypes, about 18 will be static with no resultant archetype, and 82 will be changing with some resultant archetype.

This last result is the same result we obtained with the coin method. So regardless of whether you use the coin or the yarrow method, the probability of obtaining any given starting archetype is the same (0.015625, or 1/64). And the chance of getting *some* resultant archetype is the same (0.82).

So what is the difference between the two protocols? It has to do with the probabilities of the specific resultant archetypes you might get. Let's say you want to know the probability that starting archetype A will be paired with resultant archetype B. In other words, how often when you get starting archetype A will you also get resultant archetype B? Here is how you calculate this.

First, figure out how many static yin lines, static yang lines, moving yin lines, and moving yang lines you would need. Let's call these numbers SF, SM, MF, and MM, respectively.

Second, you need to know the probability that a yin line will be static. In other words, given that you have a yin line, what is the probability that that yin line is static? I'll call this P(SF). Similarly, you need to know the probability that a yin line is moving (P(MF)), that a yang line is static (P(SM)), and that a yang line is moving (P(MM)).

Given that a line is yin, the probability that the line is also moving is given by this formula:

(Probability of moving yin)/(probability of moving yin + probability of static yin).

You can calculate these numbers, but I'll save you the trouble:

|        | Coin  | Yarrow |
|--------|-------|--------|
| P(SF)  | 0.750 | 0.8724 |
| P(MF)  | 0.250 | 0.1275 |
| P(SM)  | 0.750 | 0.6250 |
| P(MM)  | 0.250 | 0.3750 |

With either method, the chance of pairing starting archetype A and resultant archetype B is given by this formula:

$$P(SF)^{SF} \times P(SM)^{SM} \times P(MF)^{MF} \times P(MM)^{MM}$$

Let's see how this works in practice. Let's say you are studying archetype 14 (*Wealth*), and you want to know how often it will result in archetype 13 (*Fellowship*). Pictorially, this is represented as

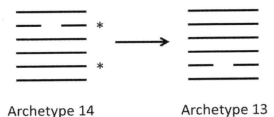

**Archetype 14**          **Archetype 13**

This would require that the first, third, fourth, and sixth lines be static (counting from the bottom, as always), and that the second and fifth line be moving. To be even more precise, it means that we need the first yang line to be static, the second yang line to be moving, the third yang line to be static, the fourth yang line to be static, the fifth yin line to be moving, and the sixth yang line to be static. In total, we will need one moving yin line, one moving yang line, and four static yang lines.

How often do we get this? With the coin protocol, the probability of this happening is

$$0.250^1 \text{ X } 0.250^1 \text{ X } 0.750^4 = 0.0200$$

With the yarrow protocol, the probability of this happening is

$$0.1275^1 \text{ X } 0.3750^1 \text{ X } 0.6250^4 = 0.0073$$

The likelihood of archetype 14 resulting in archetype 13 is thus about three times greater with the coin protocol than with the yarrow protocol. Why is this? There are two reasons. First, we need a moving yin line, which is harder to get in the yarrow protocol. Second, we need four static yang lines, which are also harder to get in the yarrow protocol.

You can loosely predict which protocol will do better for different transformations by thinking about the number of line types you need to produce the transformation. Static yang lines and moving yin lines are easier to get in the coin protocol. Moving yang lines and static yin lines are easier to get in the yarrow protocol.

Is any of the information in this appendix useful? Probably not, but it is interesting.

# Appendix 2: The Readings by Biblical Order

| Bible Location | Reading | Arch # |
|---|---|---|
| Mark 10:17–22 | Rich young man | 4 |
| Mark 12:41–44 | The widow's penny | 41 |
| Luke 1:46–49 | Mary's magnificat | 25 |
| Luke 2:15–20 | Shepherds visiting baby Jesus | 58 |
| Luke 5:15–16 | Jesus withdraws to pray | 60 |
| Luke 4:1–2 | Jesus in the wilderness | 3 |
| Luke 9:1–6 | Sending out the disciples | 59 |
| Luke 10:38–42 | Martha | 31 |
| Luke 13:18–21 | Kingdom of God like leaven | 57 |
| Luke 15:11–24 | Prodigal son | 24 |
| Luke 22:14–20 | First communion | 45 |
| Luke 23:44–49 | Jesus breathes his last | 64 |
| John 1:9–13 | The true light was coming | 30 |
| John 2:1–4 | Wedding at Cana | 5 |
| John 3:16 | God gave his only son | 42 |
| John 4:4–14 | The woman at the well | 48 |
| John 13:1–5 | Jesus washes the feet | 17 |
| John 15:12–15 | Love one another | 54 |
| Philippians 1:9–14 | The slave Onesimus | 6 |
| Acts 2:43–47 | Breaking bread together | 13 |
| Acts 9:1–9 | Conversion of Paul | 43 |
| Acts 9:23–25 | Saul escaping through the wall | 33 |
| Romans 5:1–5 | Rejoice in our sufferings | 53 |
| Galatians 2:11–14 | Paul in conflict with Peter | 38 |
| Ephesians 6:1–3 | Obey your parents | 37 |

# Appendix 3: Summary of Dialogue Steps

This appendix is a crib sheet for a Christian I Ching dialogue.

- **Step 1.** Prepare and write down your question as described in Chapter 4.
- **Step 2.** Prepare your space as described in Chapter 4.
- **Step 3.** Prepare yourself by a short meditation as described in Chapter 4.
- **Step 4.** Decide on one of the protocols described in Chapter 5.
- **Step 5.** Using the chosen protocol, determine the six lines of the hexagram starting from the bottom and working up. Your protocol will deliver a number between 6 and 8. The following table shows how the numbers are interpreted.

| Number | Line Type | Energy | Drawn as |
|--------|-----------|--------|----------|
| 6 | Yin | In flux | —— —— * |
| 7 | Yang | Stable | ———— |
| 8 | Yin | Stable | —— —— |
| 9 | Yang | In flux | ———— * |

- **Step 6.** Determine the resultant hexagram by keeping each stable line the same and changing each line that is in flux (if any) into its opposite.
- **Step 7.** Divide your hexagram into a lower and upper trigram. Find the lower trigram in the first column of the hexagram index (Appendix 5). Find the upper trigram in the first row of the hexagram index. Find the intersection of that row and column to determine the hexagram index number.
- **Step 8.** Repeat Step 7 for the resultant hexagram (if there is one).
- **Step 9.** Find the index of the hexagram in *The Christian I Ching*.
- **Step 10.** Read the general sections (not the line sections) for the hexagram.
- **Step 11.** Read the line sections for the lines that are in flux.
- **Step 12.** Find the index of the resultant hexagram in *The Christian I Ching*.
- **Step 13.** Read the general sections (not the line sections) for the resultant hexagram.

## INTERPRETATIONS

- The *original hexagram* is describing the starting situation.
- The *resultant hexagram* is describing the situation that will unfold.
- The *lines* describe the energy patterns of the hexagram. If the lines seem in conflict with the hexagram reading, the lines get priority. If the lines seem in conflict with each other, that is because there is conflicting energy in the situation.

# Appendix 4: Yarrow Protocol at a Glance

This is a summary of the yarrow protocol described in Chapter 5.

Create a work space and think of it as divided as follows:

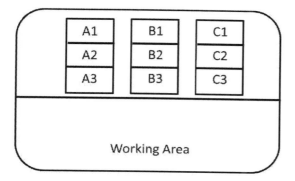

- Place a pile of 49 stones in the working area.
- While meditating on the question, divide the pile into a left-hand pile and a right-hand pile, both in the working area.
- Take one stone from the left-hand pile and place in A1.
- Count off groups of four from the left-hand pile and place the remainder in A2.
- Count off groups of four from the right-hand pile and place the remainder in A3.
- Consolidate the remaining left-hand and right-hand piles into one pile, still in the working area.
- While meditating on the question, divide the pile into a left-hand pile and a right-hand pile, still in the working area.
- Take one stone from the left-hand pile and place in B1.
- Count off groups of four from the left-hand pile and place the remainder in B2.
- Count off groups of four from the right-hand pile and place the remainder in B3.
- Consolidate the remaining left-hand and right-hand piles into one pile, still in the working area.
- While meditating on the question, divide the pile into a left-hand pile and a right-hand pile, still in the working area.
- Take one stone from the left-hand pile and place in C1.

- Count off groups of four from the left-hand pile and place the remainder in C2.
- Count off groups of four from the right-hand pile and place the remainder in C3.
- Count the piles of four in the working area. If you have done everything correctly, you will have 6, 7, 8, or 9 piles. The number of piles of four you have is the number for this line.
- Repeat this process five more times, building your hexagram from the bottom up.

The numbers for the lines are interpreted as follows:

- 6: yin line in flux.
- 7: yang line stable.
- 8: yin line stable.
- 9: yang line in flux.

# Appendix 5: The Hexagram Index

Upper Trigram

Lower Trigram

| | ☰ | ☳ | ☵ | ☶ | ☷ | ☴ | ☲ | ☱ |
|---|---|---|---|---|---|---|---|---|
| ☰ | 1 | 34 | 5 | 26 | 11 | 9 | 14 | 43 |
| ☳ | 25 | 51 | 3 | 27 | 24 | 42 | 21 | 17 |
| ☵ | 6 | 40 | 29 | 4 | 7 | 59 | 64 | 47 |
| ☶ | 33 | 62 | 39 | 52 | 15 | 53 | 56 | 31 |
| ☷ | 12 | 16 | 8 | 23 | 2 | 20 | 35 | 45 |
| ☴ | 44 | 32 | 48 | 18 | 46 | 57 | 50 | 28 |
| ☲ | 13 | 55 | 63 | 22 | 36 | 37 | 30 | 49 |
| ☱ | 10 | 54 | 60 | 41 | 19 | 61 | 38 | 58 |

I ask for a responce that will help
me deeern Gods will with in the
Context of this specific Situation

Made in the USA
Columbia, SC
21 May 2019